The Rise and Fall of the Byzantine Empire

by Stephen B. Plaster, Ph.D.

The Rise and Fall of the Byzantine Empire

Copyright © 2013, by Stephen B. Plaster, Ph.D.

First Printing

ISBN: 978-1-937064-45-7

All rights reserved. No part of this book may be reproduced or transmitted in any form, or by any method, electronic or mechanical, without written permission of the author.

TRINITY PRESS PUBLISHING
Author's Society

Printed in the USA by Trinity Press Publishing, LLC
Newburgh, Indiana 47630

TABLE OF CONTENTS

CHAPTER ONE: INTRODUCTION — 1

CHAPTER TWO: ORIGIN AND BASIS FOR THE
MONOPHYSITE BELIEF — 14

    Theology of the Monophysite Belief 15
    A Description of the Monophysite Belief of Apollinaris 16
    Detailed Explanation of the Belief of Apollinaris 18
    The Monophysite Belief and Nestorius 19
    Detailed Explanation of the Belief of Nestorius 20
    The Monophysite Belief of Eutyches 23
    Detailed Explanation of the Belief of Eutyches 24
    Analysis of the History of the Monophysite Belief 26
    How the Monophysite Belief Originated 28
    Detailed Explanation of the Alexandrian School 30
    Detailed Explanation of the Antiochene School 31
    The Monophysite Belief of Cyril 32
    Detailed Explanation of the Belief of Cyril 34
    The Dyophysite Belief of Athanasius 35
    Detailed Explanation of the Belief of Athanasius 36

CHAPTER THREE: AN ANALYSIS OF THE DEBATE REGARDING THE NATURE(S) OF CHRIST   **40**

    Doctrinal Analysis of the Meaning and Importance of the One Nature of Christ 40

    Description of the One Nature Belief Deemed Heretical 42

    Doctrinal Analysis of the Meaning and Importance of the Two Natures of Christ.. 44

    Two Nature Belief of Church Leaders Deemed Orthodox........... 51

CHAPTER FOUR: HISTORICAL TIMELINE OF THE MONOPHYSITE CONTROVERSY   **55**

    Description of the Events During the Monophysite Controversy 60

    Brief Explanation of the Events 73

    Description of the Relevant Persons During the Monophysite Controversy 80

    Biographical Description of Relevant Persons............................. 82

    Brief Explanation of Relevant Persons... 84

CHAPTER FIVE: ANALYSIS OF THE CANONS, CREEDS, AND COUNCILS DURING THE MONOPHYSITE CONTROVERSY   **88**

    Analysis of Church Canons 91

    Analysis of the Church Creeds 101

    Description of Church Creeds 103

    Detailed Description of Church Creeds....................................... 112

Analysis of the Church Councils 122

Description of the Relevant Church Councils 124

CHAPTER SIX: IMPACT OF THE MONOPHYSITE CONTROVERSY ON THE BYZANTINE EMPIRE AND THE SPREAD OF ISLAM   131

Division and Weakening of the Byzantine Empire 132

Segmentation of the Byzantine Empire 140

Local Monophysite Churches 141

Causes of the Spread of Islam Between 610-700 CE 143

Overthrow of Christian Lands by the Muslims 146

Analysis of Islamic Theology Concerning Christ 149

Life of Muhammad and Contacts with Christians 152

Influences of People on Beliefs of Muhammad 158

Theology of the Koran Pertaining to Jesus Christ 160

CONCLUSIONS   166

CHAPTER REFERENCES 169

BIBLIOGRAPHY 204

CHAPTER 1

INTRODUCTION

The Monophysite Controversy was an important event in the history of Christianity. Following the apostolic age, the church spread geographically from Jerusalem to all parts of the Roman Empire. Bishops were appointed in cities across the empire. An age of persecution threatened Christianity until the emperor Constantine in 313 CE legalized and embraced Christianity. The church began to interpret the meaning of New Testament Scripture within the universal Christian community. The focus of interest was primarily on the person of Christ. During the period beginning around 313 CE until a final resolution around 638 CE, the controversy over the nature of Christ was debated between church and secular leaders within Christianity. The outcome of the debate determined the orthodox position on the nature of Christ. The non-orthodox position was labeled heretical. The Monophysite position was condemned as heretical. Some church leaders and their followers chose to continue in their support of the Monophysite belief causing a division in the Christian church. This division weakened the testimony of the church and the loyalty of Monophysite Christians to the Byzantine Empire. This led to two problems. First, the missionary outreach of the orthodox faith was hindered from spreading south and east by the dominance of Monophysitism in these areas of the empire. Second, the Byzantine Empire was weakened politically because the Monophysite Christians were not loyal to its spiritual and political leaders. As a result, the rise and spread of Islam, beginning in 610 C.E. came in contact with Monophysite Christianity. The lands which were dominated by Monophysites were the first to fall to Islam by 700 CE.

From a theological perspective, Muhammad claimed to receive the revelation from the angel Gabriel from 610 C.E. until 632 CE. His travels before this as a caravan trader were limited to the north-south route between Mecca, Arabia and Damascus, Syria. During his travels to Syria, he came in contact with both Jews and Christians. When reciting the message of the Koran, the explanation of the nature of Jesus is similar to the Monophysite belief. The Monophysites were prevalent in Syria at this time. Therefore, Mohammed and the Koran both formulated a non-orthodox and heretical view of Jesus Christ.

The purpose of this study is to determine the impact of the Monophysite Controversy on the growth and spread of Christianity during the critical period when the orthodox position was being formulated and as Christianity came in contact with the new religion of Islam. The first step in this process will be to understand the origin and basis for Monophysite belief. This includes: (1) defining Monophysitism, (2) determining the time, place, and persons who supported this concept, (3) interpreting the theology underlying Monophysitism; and (4) examining the history of the controversy based on early writings and subsequent commentaries on the subject. The second step will be to explore the theological debate concerning the one nature of Christ, versus the two natures of Christ. Arguments in support and in condemnation of both positions were debated during the controversy. These will be presented during the research. It should also be understood that there were differing explanations of the one nature position between Monophysite apologists. Equally, there were differing explanations of the two nature position between Dyophysites. These various explanations will also be explored to determine which one became the orthodox position within Christianity and which one became the dominant position within Monophysite Christianity. The third step will be to examine the people, places, and events that undertook to propagate, condemn, or reconcile the Monophysite Controversy. The period of activity extended from the beginning of the fourth century CE to the middle of the seventh century CE. The geographic context resided in the decline of the Western Roman Empire and in the highpoint of the Byzantine Empire focusing on Asia-Minor, Syria, Palestine, Egypt, north and northeastern Africa, and Rome. An historical timeline of the people, places, and events will be developed to provide space-time context to the controversy. The fourth step will be to analyze the writings of the canons, creeds, and councils of the period of the controversy. The councils recorded the debates and the conclusion of the majority attending the councils. The creeds were often the summarized synopsis of the orthodox position. The canons were manuscripts of church leaders arguing for their understanding of a doctrinal issue. The writings of the church leaders, bishops, patriarchs, popes, monks, and emperors who addressed the Monophysite controversy will be explored to determine each person's relevant position and contribution to the debate. One result of this will be to determine if the person's contribution had an historical, theological, or political impact on Christianity. The fifth step will be to research early Islamic belief regarding the nature of Christ. The Islamic belief regarding Christ is recorded in the Koran, which was received between 610 CE and 632 CE. Islam came in contact with Monophysite Christianity during the entire period of the seventh century CE. The study will focus on how Monophysite teaching regarding the nature of Christ impacted Islamic belief in the formative years. In addition, the study will explore how the Monophysite Controversy weakened the Byzantine Empire, making the Monophysite controlled lands more susceptible to the spread of Islam.

The research objectives are to investigate the history and theology of the Monophysite Controversy in order to help the reader understand the impact on the development of Christianity and of Islam. This will involve answering many questions. First, the research will investigate the origin and basis of the historical setting and theological arguments for the Monophysite Controversy. The key question to answer is why is it important to establish whether Christ has one nature or two natures? Second, the research will investigate the process regarding the debate. The key question to answer is how a majority position becomes orthodox and a minority position is condemned as heretical. Third, the research will investigate the chronology of the events. The key question is when each doctrine was debated, what was the timeline for debate and resolution. Fourth, the research will investigate the persons who entered into the debate. The key question is who led the debate either for or against the Monophysite position. Fifth, the research will investigate the impact of the controversy on Christianity and Islam. The key questions will be: (1) how were Christianity and the Byzantine Empire weakened; and (2) how was early Islamic theology affected.

The research will add to the body of historical and theological knowledge of Christianity. The majority of research on early church history focuses on issues that resulted in the orthodox position. Controversies are given limited research time because the non-orthodox position is dismissed as an error which should be forgotten. In the example of the Monophysite Controversy, the Monophysite segment of Christianity survived intact. These churches were the remaining testimony in lands on the eastern and southern borders of the Christian world. This placed Monophysite Christians in the important position of spreading Christianity beyond these borders to pagan lands. In addition, with the advent of Islam in Arabia, a competition for believers occurred which shaped the culture of the Middle East. The history of this contact between Monophysite Christians and Muslims has not been the focus of significant research.

The theoretical implications of this study are significant. If the Monophysite Christians had won the argument regarding the nature of Christ, orthodox Christianity would be constantly defending a savior, who is not a completely human nor completely divine person in his nature. This would be an endless and defenseless apologetic. If the Monophysite Christians had been absorbed within Christianity, the Byzantine Empire would have been strengthened rather than weakened by the lack of support for the Byzantine spiritual and political leaders. If the orthodox view of the nature of Christ had influenced Muhammad, the theology concerning Christ in the Koran might have been closer to orthodox Christianity such that a new religion separate from Christianity might not have emerged. If the Christians in the entire expanse of the Byzantine Empire were united in their beliefs regarding the nature of Christ, the spread of Islam might have been halted and limited to Arabia, while the spread of Christianity might have been more effective and permanent in the Middle East.

The literature which is available provides an introduction into the research concerning the history and theology of the Monophysite Controversy. For example, several Bible dictionaries provide complete and concise definitions. Texts are available on dogmatic and systematic theology which describe the various interpretations of the nature of Christ in terms of theology. A number of texts provide a survey of church history. Bible commentaries provide some insight to the people, places, and events. The value of many of these resources is limited because the dictionaries are too brief, the texts on dogmatic and systematic theology do not always explain the context, surveys of church history may be biased from a given theological perspective, and the Bible commentaries may be segmented in their approach and produced much later than when the events took place. The original writings from the persons involved are more informative. These are produced in the Ante-Nicene, Nicene, and Post-Nicene Series. The creeds and council's publications in the original are helpful in analyzing the positions debated. The Koran is the source for

Islamic theology. The early history of Islam needs to be presented by both Western and Islamic scholars such that both sides of this history are explored. The history of the Monophysites is usually presented by orthodox Christians; therefore, this bias must be weighed in one's conclusions. The research proposed is focused on exploring and determining how the controversy weakened the Byzantine Empire, divided the Christian community, influenced Islamic theology, and facilitated the spread of Islam.

Statement of the problem

The major research question is to determine if the Byzantine Empire was weakened by the lack of support for the spiritual and political leaders from the Monophysite Christians. As a result, the orthodox form of Christianity was hindered from spreading to adjacent pagan lands and the spread of Islam was rendered more successful. Finally, the theology of Islam was affected in regard to Muhammad's understanding of the nature of Christ due to the influence of Monophysite teaching.

The areas of inquiry which are in the nature of minor research questions will be identified. The following questions relate to Monophysite Christianity. First, what is the Monophysite belief? Second, who was the first church leader to teach the one nature of Christ? Third, who resolved the controversy? Fourth, when did the controversy first begin? Fifth, when was the controversy resolved? Sixth, what variations were supported for the interpretation of the one nature position? The following questions relate to the theology of the nature of Christ. First, what are the arguments in support of the one nature position? Second, what are the arguments in support of the two natures position? Third, what factors determined the orthodox position? Fourth, what became of the one nature position after being condemned as heretical? Fifth, did the controversy contribute to the progressive schism between the Western and Eastern branches of orthodox Christianity? Sixth, in what way did the one nature interpretation weaken Christianity theologically?

The following questions relate to the historical understanding of the Monophysite Controversy. First, what was the chronological progression of people, places, and events in support or in condemnation of the controversy? Second, what position on the nature of Christ was held by the schools at Jerusalem, Antioch, Rome, Alexandria, and Constantinople? Third, what position did the emperors Constantine, Zeno, Justinian, Justin II, Heraclius, Pulcheria (empress), Theodosius II, and Marcian hold during the period of the controversy? Fourth, what position did the patriarchs Severus, Peter Mongo, Timothy, Timothy Aelurus, Anatolius, and Flavian hold? Fifth, what position did the popes Vigilius, Leo the Great, Simplicius, Gelasius I, Gregory, and Honorius support? Sixth, what position did the bishops Cyril of Alexandria, Julian of Halicarnassus, Facundus of Hermiane, and Athanasius of Antioch maintain? Seventh, what position did other key persons in the dispute hold including Eutyches, Jacobobus Baradaeus, Theodora I, John the Grammarian, and Theodoret? The following questions relate to the canons, creeds, and councils of the period between 300-700 CE. First, what was resolved in the Henoticon, Tome of Leo the Great, Canon LXXXI, Epistle L, Three Chapters, Syriac canon, Epistle LXVI I, Monophysite canon, and the New Testament canon? Second, what was resolved in the Nicene Creed, the Chalcedonian Creed, the Athanasian Creed, the anathemas of the second Council of Constantinople, and the Creed from the third Council of Constantinople? Third, what was resolved at the following councils: Nicene 325 CE, Constantinople 381 CE, Ephesus 431 CE, Chalcedon 451 CE, and Constantinople 553 CE? The following questions relate to the hindrance or spread of Christianity and Islam. First, what factors promoted the spread of Monophysite Christianity? Second, what factors hindered the spread of orthodox Christianity? Third, what factors promoted the spread of Islam. Fourth, why did Islam largely replace Monophysite Christianity in the Middle East? Fifth, how did Mohammed develop his understanding of the nature of Christ?

  The thesis is that the missionary outreach of the orthodox Christian faith was hindered from spreading south and east due to the dominance of the Monophysite Christian faith in these areas. As a result, the Byzantine Empire was weakened resulting in the rapid spread of Islam into these geographic areas. Further, Muhammad may have been influenced by the Monophysite teaching regarding the one nature of Christ, which became the theology incorporated within the Koran.

  The study will be limited in several important ways. First, the study will be delimited to Christology as it pertains to theology. Within the area of Christology, the study will be limited to the Monophysite

Controversy. The theological concern will be delimited to the debate over the person of Christ having one nature or two natures. This will entail analyzing both the orthodox and the heretical arguments. Some other earlier heresies, if they had been accepted as orthodox such as Gnosticism or Arianism, would have been fatal to Christianity. Once these heresies were rejected, later heresies were contentious but not fatal to Christianity. Controversies such as that of the Monophysite position tended to divide and weaken Christianity. The following heresies will not be extensively included in the study: Gnosticism, Docetism, Marcionism, Montanism, Patripassianism, Monarchianism, Sabellianism, Arianism, and Pelagianism. Second, the study will be delimited to a specific timeframe during the early church age. The study will exclude the apostolic age (33-100 CE) and the age of persecution (100-313 C.E.). By 313 CE, Christianity as a religion had become both legal and the official religion of the empire. The Monophysite Controversy occurred between Christians rather than between Christians and pagans. Other heresies such as Gnosticism and Arianism passed into history leaving no functioning church. Monophysite Christianity, while a minority church in Christianity, still exists as a functioning church today. The study will incorporate the theologies and history of Apollinaris, Nestorius, and Eutyches because they influenced the doctrine concerning the nature of Christ. The Council of Chalcedon (451 CE) was the high point for the declaration of the orthodox position of the Dyophysites. This position was argued and debated with the Monophysites until the orthodox position was reaffirmed in 680 CE. Thereafter, the issues moved on to the use of icons and the political survival from the threats of Islam to Christian lands. Third, the study will be limited to those church leaders, bishops, patriarchs, popes, monks, and the emperors of the Roman and Byzantine empires of the period. The study will not include writings of the apostles nor the early church fathers. The study will focus on the Eastern theologians rather than the Latin writers. However, the contributions on this subject of Hillary of Poitier, Ambrose of Milan, and Augustine of Hippo will be included. The study will not include Greek or Persian writers of the period. Fourth, the study will be limited to the period of Muhammad's life and the first succeeding Muslim caliphs up to the completion of the Koran and the overthrow of the Christian Middle Eastern lands by the Muslims by the date of 700 CE. The theology of the Koran will be limited to the writings concerning the person of Jesus Christ. The scope of the history of the spread of Islam during this period will be limited to only those Christian occupied lands where the Monophysites were dominant. The histories will include both Christian and Muslim writers in the English language only. Fifth, the geographic area to be studied will include the Near East, Asia-Minor, North Africa, and Rome. The study will not include Greece, Persia, the balance of Europe, or the Far East. The schools of Christianity which will be the focus of the study will include Alexandria, Antioch, and Constantinople with a lesser focus on Rome and Carthage.

A number of key terms will be used repeatedly in the study:

Canon: The orthodox interpretation of the scriptural doctrine expressed in writing and sanctioned by an official church council;

Council: An official meeting of authorized church leaders held at a specific place and time to debate and decide on a church issue;

Creed: The summarized orthodox position on a doctrinal issue produced in writing and meant to be taught in all the churches;

Coptic: The Monophysite church in Egypt which utilizes the Coptic language;

Heresy: Any teaching which has been judged by the majority of a church council to be in error and was forbidden to be taught;

Monophysite: The belief and teaching that Christ has only one nature;

Nature (s): The view of a person (Christ) that identifies one, two, or three essences of the person such as divine, human, or merged;

Orthodox: Any teaching which has been judged by the majority of a church council to be acceptable and taught by the churches;

Syriac: The Monophysite church in Syria which utilizes the Syriac language.

A number of concepts will be presented in the study. First, there is a progression from the Trinity, to the nature, to the will of Christ; which is central to the doctrine of Christology. The progression moves from the concept of divinity to the concept of humanity. The debate centers on an understanding of the God-man that had never existed before or after the earthly ministry of Jesus Christ. The natural question arises as to two parallel claims. Jesus is the eternal, pre-existent Son, and at the same time He is also an obedient individual, a historic human being. The orthodox position asserts the unity of deity and humanity in one person. The heretical position maintains that the deity or the humanity dominates the person such that one or the other is absorbed into the other or into a third person. This was important because it suggests limits to the power of Christ to fulfill the plan of redemption. If he is not fully and completely divine, then he may not as less than God be able to save humans from their sins. In like manner, then how can his suffering and death be put to the account of human beings? Apollinaris argued that Christ had two natures before the incarnation, one divine and one human, but afterward he had only one nature. His explanation is based on the Logos (Spirit of God) indwelling a human body with a Spirit intellect rather than a human intellect. This understanding placed Apollinaris into the position of a Monophysite where the Word made flesh results in the one nature of God. Apollinaris began to teach this doctrine in 352 CE. He was labeled a heretic by 362 CE by Athanasius because he believed if Christ was not fully human then his followers were not his brethren as human beings as he claimed believers to be. For Christ to be the substitute for the salvation of mankind, He must be a man subject to suffering and death. Further, Christ must be a man with a human intellect and will if he is to be obedient to God where Adam had failed and thereby become mankind's Redeemer. He was exiled in 388 C.E. by Emperor Theodosius I. Second, the Antiochene School supported the Dyophysite concept of the two natures of Christ as distinct but united in one person. The objective of the Antiochene School was to preserve the unity of Christ in one person while supporting the fullness of Christ in two natures. The Dyophysite teaching of this concept is adamant about not mixing, blending, or absorbing the two natures into one. The resolution of this position was that Jesus Christ was not a deified man nor a humanized deity but rather the God-man. The Alexandrian school supported the Monophysite concept of the one nature of Christ. The leading proponent of the Alexandrian school was Cyril who supported the idea of the unity of the unchanged, unmixed divine and human natures in one person. The one incarnate nature of Christ became the settled position of the Alexandrian school. Third, the study will explore the methodology to resolve theological disputes. Attempts were made by various means such as the Tome of Leo the Great, the hastily called Robber Council in 449 CE, the Henoticon writing, the Three Chapters writings, the official Chalcedonian Council in 451 CE, and the Chalcedonian Creed. Each of these methods represented a concept of the way to resolve a doctrinal dispute. Which methods failed to resolve the dispute of the Monophysite Controversy and which method succeeded resulted in a proven methodology to resolve future controversies in the church. Fourth, the Monophysite position is not a single doctrine but rather encompasses a variety of interpretations. For example, some Monophysites by definition are labeled as such only because they opposed the findings of the Council of Chalcedon. This would include Eutyches. Severus was a Monophysite because he taught that a synthesis of Christ's two natures occurred in the incarnation. Julian of Halicarnassus was a Monophysite who taught that Jesus possessed a glorified nature after the incarnation such that his humanity was indestructible. Leontius of Byzantium was a Monophysite who taught that the two natures are united according to their essence, while preserving the distinctiveness of each where Christ's human nature received its distinctiveness only after it had united with the Logos. Each of these concepts which interpreted the nature of Christ is different, but each is called Monophysite. Two actions led to the separation of the Monophysites from the orthodox church. The actual words and meaning of their writings separated church leaders due to their differing beliefs within the church. Also, the animosities and political power struggles separated church leaders in regard to their fellowship with each other within the church. Fifth, Muhammad claims to have received visions from the angel Gabriel, wherein he was instructed to recite the words of God. As with all biblical authors, the human factors of language, custom, location, education, and experience are incorporated in the biblical writings. Muhammad had the same tendencies which are evident in the text of the Koran and from the history of Muhammad's life as recorded by some of his followers. He knew Christians and commented on his understanding of who Christ was. The concept he expressed is a partly divine, but mostly human understanding of the nature of Christ. The study will explore how Muhammad conceptualized the person and nature of Jesus Christ.

  The study is based upon five theological and philosophical assumptions. First, the development of a consensus of learned men is the method by which a theological belief becomes the orthodox position. The minority consensus becomes heretical because the majority declares it to be so. Despite the heretical status, the minority position may live on and become central to a segment of Christianity. Second, during any controversy, leaders take sides in expressing their opinion. It was inevitable that men exercising power from competing positions and locations would debate the important issue of the nature of Christ. This competition surfaced between: the schools of Alexandria and Antioch, the church leaders from Constantinople and Rome, and Western versus Eastern geographical bishoprics. Third, political events during the period affected the outcome of the controversy. The fall of Rome strengthened the position of the emperors and patriarchs in Constantinople after 476 CE. The theological debates strengthened the orthodox church, but weakened the Byzantine Empire. Fourth, canons, creeds, and councils served as the structure to argue and decide the issues of church doctrine. These meetings and publications served the purpose of deciding what the church would believe and teach. These records also serve as the record for inquiry today of the controversies thereby enabling modern historical research. Fifth, Islam originated in the Arabian Desert during the period 610 CE and 632 CE. Islam claims Jesus as a prophet with a human nature. The Koran incorporates an understanding of Jesus which seems to have been learned from Monophysite Christians. The contact between the Arab Muslims and Christian Monophysites weakened the Byzantine Empire rendering it susceptible to the spread of Islam.

The following focus statements will be used to explore the research thesis in detail:

(1) To determine the origin and basis for the Monophysite belief regarding the nature of Christ.
(2) To research the arguments supporting and condemning the one nature versus the two natures of Christ debate.
(3) To develop an historical timeline of the Monophysite Controversy which includes people, persons, and events.
(4) To research the writings, canons, and creeds which document the positions of persons engaged in the controversy and the findings of church councils of the period in order to determine the impact on Christianity.
(5) To investigate the impact on Muhammad's teaching as reflected in the Koran and the impact on the spread of Islam.

Procedural Overview

The content chapters will be outlined as follows:
   Chapter 2: Origin and Basis for Monophysite Belief
The origin of the belief that Christ has only one nature will be explored. Monophysite belief will be defined and discussed as to how this interpretation originated. The theology and history of this position will be reviewed.
   Chapter 3: Christ: One Nature or Two Natures
The debate regarding the nature of Christ will be explored. The arguments supporting and condemning each position will be discussed. The two nature position became orthodox Christology while the one nature position became the teaching of the Oriental churches.
   Chapter 4: Historical Timeline of the Monophysite Controversy
The period of the controversy extended from 300 CE until 700 CE. A timeline of people, places, and events will be presented to provide a chronological history of the controversy. The setting of the Byzantine and Roman empires will provide geographic and political context to the research.
   Chapter 5: Canons, Creeds, and Councils
The writings of church leaders, bishops, patriarchs, popes, monks, and emperors will be explored to discover the contributions of each relevant person addressing the Monophysite Controversy. These positions were either accepted or rejected by the church councils of the period. The official findings of the church councils will be presented.
   Chapter 6: Impact of Monophysite Christianity and the Spread of Islam.
Muhammad received the recitation of the Koran between 610 CE and 632 CE. The research will explore the teachings of early Islamic belief regarding the person of Jesus of Christ. The Monophysite teaching impacted this belief and the controversy weakened the Byzantine Empire at a time when Islam began to spread.
   Conclusions
Implications of Findings
Applications of Findings
Further Study
   The mode of reasoning will research two disciplines. First, the process will be to research and understand the complex nature of the

theology of the Monophysite Controversy. The primary sources of original writings will be reviewed followed by resource material of secondary sources. Second, the process will be to determine the history of the controversy. This will involve researching various dictionaries, commentaries, and church histories. In regard to the church histories, the primary sources will be original publications while secondary sources will be researched from various modern texts discussing church history. Third, the writings of the church canons and creeds and the publications from the church councils will be researched from primary sources. Secondary sources consisting of encyclopedias, systematic theologies, handbooks, and articles will be researched. Fourth, the Islamic history and theology of the person of Christ will be researched. The primary source will be the Koran. Secondary sources will be commentaries and histories on early Islam provided by Western and Islamic authors. The plan for each chapter (2-6) will be to define, describe, compare, analyze, and summarize Monophysite theology and history of the period between 300-700 CE. This process will form the foundation to the next step, which is to determine the impact of the controversy on the Byzantine Empire and on the spread of Islam as the two peoples, religions, and cultures came into contact.

CHAPTER 2

ORIGIN AND BASIS FOR THE MONOPHYSITE BELIEF

Monophysitism comes from the word *monos* (one) and *physis* (nature). It is the belief that the incarnate Christ possessed only one nature. "The Monophysites believed that the incarnation resulted in a single divine-human nature in the person of Christ, rather than, as orthodox Christology asserts, two distinct natures (divine and human) joined hypostatically in a single person."[1] A further definition asserts that "a Monophysite is a person who holds that there is only one inseparable nature (partly divine, partly and subordinately human) in the person of Christ."[2] The latter definition introduces the critical element to the nature of Monophysitism which is the subordinate nature of Christ's humanity. Any antinomy states two truths which appear to be contradictory. The fact that Scripture refers to Christ's divinity and His humanity suggests to the finite mind an apparent contradiction. How can a person be both divine and human at the same time? What has the infinite, eternal, immaterial have in common with the finite, temporal, and material? The acceptance of the one divine nature concerning the incarnate Christ is not disputed between orthodoxy and Monophysite whereby Christ possessed only a divine nature prior to the incarnation.

Literature was written primarily in the Greek language throughout the Roman Empire. This was due to the spread of the Greek language in the Middle East as a result of the conquests of Alexander the Great. However, literature was also written or copied in other languages such as Syriac, Armenian, Coptic, Latin and Arabic. This copying process included Scripture, as well as available Greek literature. Much of the Monophysite literature was copied in the Syriac language, but unfortunately not much of this literature has been preserved. In contrast to the works of the Church Fathers, whether in the Eastern or the Western portion of the Roman Empire, whose works were copied and circulated and of which we have copies available today; the Monophysite writings were not preserved, primarily because they were termed heretical and of no significance. In other words these works were considered not worth preserving, and in fact in some instances were forbidden to be copied and retained. Therefore works of the Monophysites and including those of the Nestorians, both of which were prominent in Syria, were only preserved in these Syriac translations. "From the fourth century, heretical works were destroyed, and their possession was forbidden. Consequently, we know this literature only from quotations in works written against it or from its being handed down under orthodox names. Many works of authors who were declared heretics (e.g., Origenists, Nestorians, Monophysites) have been preserved in Near Eastern translations."[3]

There were five controversies during the period from 300-700 C.E. which will be discussed. The first was the Apollinarian controversy. This controversy concerned the humanity of Christ. The argument was that Christ acquired a human body and a human soul but not a human spirit. The second was the Nestorian controversy. This was resolved at the Council of Ephesus in 431 C.E. by condemning Nestorius. The third was the Eutychian controversy. The argument was over the two natures of Christ becoming one new third nature where the two natures had merged into one nature. This was resolved at the Council of Chalcedon in 451 C.E. The fourth was the Three Chapter controversy. This was resolved at the Council of Constantinople in 553 C.E. The fifth was the Monothelite controversy. The argument was whether Christ had one will or two wills. This was resolved at the Council of Constantinople in 680 C.E.

Theology of the Monophysite Belief

Monophysitism surfaced from the traditions of the School of Alexandria. The theological focus was on the humanity of Christ after the Incarnation. Generally the theologians from Chalcedon, Antioch, and Rome opposed the Monophysite doctrine of the one nature of Christ. These schools regarded the two natures as an acceptable expression of divinity and humanity whereas the School of Alexandria preserved the one nature of the Logos based on the influence of Plato in describing the unity of the human body and soul. The School of Alexandria was more open to allegorical interpretation of the Scripture since the days of Origen. "In such cases he must provide the connection on the level of intelligible reality between a statement impossible in its literal sense and those statements which are not only possible but true according to the historical narrative, allegorizing the latter along with the texts which did not happen according to the letter. For with regard to divine Scripture as a whole we are of the opinion that all of it has a spiritual sense, but not all of it has a bodily sense."[4] Rather than focusing on the meaning and history of Jesus, Alexandrian theologians were more prone to theorizing about the nature of Christ. This was a result of the allegorical tradition of persons like Origen from Alexandria as opposed to the literal tradition of exegetes like Diodore of Tarsus from Antioch. The primary belief of the Monophysite was that the unity of the divine and the human natures in Christ were acted out in the physical life of Christ in one nature. This was based on the understanding that "nature" is synonymous with "person" when John 1:14 says "And the Word was made flesh, and dwelt among us . . ." The divine Logos became flesh resulting in the flesh becoming divine. Any theologian who opposed the two natures finding of the Council of Chalcedon was labeled a Monophysite. Misunderstandings sometimes earned a theologian a heretical label even when he subscribed to the orthodox position. For example, as will be discussed later, Severus acknowledged the two natures of Christ but his explanation confused the terms "person" and "nature" by substituting the former for the latter which was heretical to the orthodox position. The Monophysite view stated that a "nature" is a hypostasis which, in this view, was interpreted as a "person". Therefore Christ would be said to be two persons, a concept which they could not accept. Ironically the orthodox likewise did not claim Christ to be two persons.

A Description of the Monophysite Belief of Apollinaris

Apollinaris was Bishop of Laodicea in Syria. He was an early theologian who emphasized the human nature of Christ, suggesting that Christ had a human soul. "Apollinarius, however, rightly chose to state his theory the other way-that the Divine Word assumed a human body and a human soul, and himself took the place of a human spirit. So far we see no great advance on the Arian theory of the incarnation. If the Lord had no true human spirit, he is no more true man than if he had nothing human but body. We get a better explanation of his sinlessness, but we still get it at the expense of his humanity."[5] Apollinaris was a native of Alexandria, and therefore was influenced by the beliefs of the Alexandrian theology. He was a strong supporter of the developments from the Nicene Council. Since Apollinaris was such a strong supporter of the deity of Christ he subordinated the importance of the humanity of Christ and of His teachings. "He specifically attributed to Christ, a human body and a human soul, but not a human spirit. But in his zeal for the true deity of Christ, and his fear of a double personality, he fell into the error of denying his integral humanity. Adopting the psychological trichotomy, he attributed to Christ a human body, and a human (animal) soul, but not a human spirit or reason; putting the divine Logos in the place of the human spirit."[6]

He therefore substituted the human spirit in Christ with the divine Logos. "Our confession is not that the Logos of God sojourned in a holy man as happened to the prophets; but that the very Logos became flesh, not assuming a human mind, a mind changeable and the prey of filthy thoughts but being Himself divine mind, changeless, heavenly."[7] This was his understanding of the relationship of the divine Logos to the human spirit. Others had seen a connection of the divine Logos with the man Jesus, and sought to unite the two. He based his reasoning on the Scripture passage which indicates that the Word was made flesh, whereas Scripture does not say the Word was made spirit. In this regard, the divine Logos, with its divine attributes were transferred to the human nature of Christ, merging them into a new single nature of Christ. "In this way Apollinaris established so close a connection of the Logos with human flesh, that all the divine attributes were transferred to the human nature, and all the human attributes to the divine, and the two were merged in *one* nature in Christ."[8] Christ then became a mediator between God and man. This belief reduced the percentage of humanity in the human nature of Christ to two thirds rather than a full one hundred percent. In 362 C.E. at a Council convened at Alexandria, the position of Apollinaris was rejected. "So early as 362, a council at Alexandria rejected this doctrine (though without naming the author), and asserted that Christ possessed a reasonable soul. But Apollinaris did not secede from the communion of the Church, and began to form a sect of his own, till 375. He died in 390. His writings, except numerous fragments in the works of his opponents, are lost."[9]

Detailed Explanation of the Belief of Apollinaris

The position of Apollinaris was to teach the full deity of Christ, while denying the fullness of his humanity. This belief held that by replacing the human spirit in Christ with the divine Logos a better explanation of the nature of Christ resulted. He believed that the union of the full divinity and the complete humanity in one person was impossible as he worked out his argument. "He held the union of full divinity with full humanity in one person, therefore, of two wholes in one whole, to be impossible."[10] He proposed that the unity of the person of Christ regarding the attribute of sinlessness could only be maintained if the human spirit in Christ was replaced by the divine. This is because the human spirit was thought to be changeable, and anything changeable therefore would be subject to sin. If the human spirit had been replaced by the divine Logos, it would be unchangeable, and therefore not subject to sin. This reasoning made the sinlessness of Christ, compatible with the Apollinaris' explanation. He further argued that the full humanity of Christ did not fully atone for the sins of mankind. His reasoning was that if Christ was a man then how could the death of a man destroy death for all men. "He also charged the Church doctrine of the full humanity of Christ with limiting the atoning suffering of Christ to the human nature, and so detracting from the atoning virtue of the work of Christ; for the death of a man could not destroy death. The divine nature must participate in the suffering throughout."[11] During this process, he incorporated the idea of suffering as a component of the crucifixion and subsequent resurrection of Christ. However by adding his understanding of suffering this meant that the divine Christ suffered. This was in opposition to the orthodox position that God in His deity did not experience suffering. Therefore he made a distinction between the components of the divine Logos such that the human side of the divine Logos was capable of suffering, but the divine side of the Logos was not capable of suffering. "He made, however, a distinction between two sides of the Logos, the one allied to man and capable of suffering, and the other allied to God and exalted above all suffering. The relation of the divine pneumatic nature in Christ to the human psychical and bodily nature Apollinaris illustrated by the mingling of wine and water, the glowing fire in the iron, and the union of soul and body in man, which, though distinct, interpenetrate and form one thing."[12] "Apollinarius can speak of Christ as 'a mean between God and man, neither wholly man nor wholly God, but a combination of God and man . . ."[13]

This of course defeats the definition of the divine Logos as becoming incarnate. Another component of Apollinaris' theology was his belief that the human nature of Christ was brought with him from heaven and had existed from all eternity. "He alleges from this text, that Christ was the Son of man before He descended from heaven . . . The body and soul formed two parts, as in other men, but there was no intellect, but the Word of God filled the place of intellect."[14] The removal of the human intellect then confused the doctrine because his opponents could claim that deity could not suffer and die. The overall opposition of the orthodox position was based on the confusion that resulted when one struggles to understand the mixing of the human and divine natures of Christ from the beginning into eternity future. The orthodox position held that the Logos became completely man. This requires the belief that the nature of man is undivided, and that sin is an aspect outside of man that enters into the nature of man. This did not resolve the controversy.

The Monophysite Belief and Nestorius

The Monophysite and Nestorian controversies were never resolved to everyone's satisfaction. These two controversies form the basis of churches which are still functioning today. Nestorianism was expelled from the Byzantine Empire in the fifth century. Many of the Nestorian teachers resided in the theological school in Edessa. From there they fled to the safety of Persia. "After Nestorianism was exterminated from the Roman Empire, it found an asylum in the kingdom of Persia, whither several teachers of the theological school of Edessa fled."[15] They rebelled against the ruling of the Council of Ephesus in 431 C.E. where their beliefs were renounced. They supported the Persian kings politically which further separated them from the bonds of unity to both the Orthodox Church and the Byzantine political authority. From Persia, Nestorian belief spread eastward to India, Arabia, and China. The sect of Christianity residing in Malabar India is a branch of the Nestorians who venerate the apostle Thomas, who is supposed to have preached the gospel on the coast of Malabar. "The THOMAS-CHRISTIANS in East India are a branch of the Nestorians, named from the apostle Thomas, who is supposed to have preached the gospel on the coast of Malabar."[16]

Nestorius was Bishop of Constantinople in 430 C.E. His teaching included the belief that Christ exists in two persons according to his detractors because he refused to call the infant Jesus God. He served from 430-431 C.E. in the capacity of bishop. His teaching was condemned at the Council of Ephesus in 431 C.E. and he was deposed from his office in the church. The Monophysites often confused the orthodox supporters of the Council of Chalcedon with the Nestorians. "Owing to their different understandings of the meaning of the term 'nature', the Monophysites rejected the final form of the Definition ('One Person in Two Natures') on the grounds that it obscured the full reality of the Incarnation and appeared to them to verge on Nestorianism."[17] The primary teaching of Nestorius was that his definition of Christ as two persons did not mix Christ's humanity with His divinity and did not result in the confusion of terminology of others who sought to explain the joining of humanity with divinity as two natures which to him caused confusion. "Nestorius thus acquired the reputation among the masses of asserting the blasphemous dogma that the Lord is a mere man . . ."[18] A second teaching of Nestorius regarding the title of the Virgin Mary was rejected at the Council. Nestorius taught that the appropriate title for Mary was "Christotokos" meaning birth giver of Christ. The Council settled on the term "Theotokos" which is translated as birth giver of God. Nestorius sought to restrict Mary's role and title to giving birth only to Christ's humanity. "The NESTORIANS differ from the orthodox Greek church in their repudiation of the council of Ephesus and of the worship of Mary as mother of God . . ."[19]

Detailed Explanation of the Belief of Nestorius

Nestorius served as Bishop of Constantinople for less than two years. He was deposed in 431 C.E. and exiled to Egypt in 435 C.E. In examining the natures of Christ, he attributed only inspiration to Christ the man. ". . . He, separating the divine and the human nature of Christ, saw in our Saviour nothing but an inspired man."[20] The Orthodox Church punished its heretics by deposition, condemnation, exile, and destruction of the heretic's writings. By edict of Emperor Theodosius II in 435 C.E., Nestorius' writings were burned. Five works have survived as Syriac fragments: "Tragedy", "Book of Heraclides", "Letter to Cosmas", "Book of Letters", and "Book of homilies and sermons." "Tragedy" is about his condemnation in 431 C.E. at the Council of Ephesus. The "Book of

Heraclides" denounced the intrigues of Cyril against him. He laments his plight as follows: "This tragedy is composed of five acts: first the undivided affection of his parish was robbed from him, then the sympathies of the Occident, then the favour of the court and his episcopal office; then he was brought into disfavour as a heretic also amongst the majority of his friends, and finally as an exiled and forgotten man he was exposed to common condemnation."[21] Nestorius died in 450 C.E. He did not attend the Council at Chalcedon. He agreed with the Tome of Leo written to Emperor Flavian residing in Constantinople which theoretically placed him within the limits of orthodoxy.

The controversy over the title of Mary occurred in Constantinople in 428 C.E. between those who claimed the appropriate title should be mother of God as opposed to those who favored mother of Christ. Nestorius was asked to write his opinion. "Nestorius...delivered several public discourses on the subject, in which he assumed a controversial attitude, and totally rejected the epithet 'Theotocos.'"[22] Paul of Samosata was the first (430 C.E.) recorded critic of Nestorius claiming he taught Christ was a mere man.

Theologians opposed each other just because their tradition was different where some represented Alexandria and others represented Antioch. "But it is certain that a reason for opposing the doctrine of Nestorius was to be found by Cyril in the party-difference between the Alexandrian and the Antiochian schools and in the rivalry between the sees of Alexandria and Constantinople."[23] Cyril convinced Pope Celestine that Nestorius was a heretic. Celestine of Rome sided with Cyril and excommunicated Nestorius in 430 C.E. Nestorius requested the Emperor to call the Council of Ephesus in 431 C.E. Cyril praised and bribed the Emperor to gain favor for his own views while Nestorius refused gifts and denounced Empress Pulcheria for a lack of moral virtue. ". . . Augusta Pulcheria supported Cyril, because he, Nestorius, offended her by not paying her, on account of doubts about her virtue . . ."[24] The Antiochenes continued to support Nestorius and rejected the twelve Anathemas of Cyril which will be examined later. Maximus became the new Bishop of Constantinople in 433 C.E. with the support of the emperor Theodosius. Nestorius remained in Antioch from 431-435 C.E. John of Antioch, his former friend, succeeded in getting him banished to Egypt. Nestorius was a passionate, critical, and dogmatic personality.

The Antiochene belief at the time of Nestorius had also rejected the position of Apollinaris by maintaining that the two natures after the union maintained their full and complete independence, each perfect. Nestorius was educated theologically at the School of Antioch. Nestorius opposed Apollinaris' views throughout his life. He rejected the Apollinarian view that due to the union the divine Logos suffered with Jesus in the flesh. "Apollinaris saw in Christ but one substance, viz. the substance of the Logos, to which in addition to its own characteristics those of the imperfect human nature were attached. Nestorius was as strong an opponent of this Apollinaristic doctrine as any other Antiochian."[25] Nestorius taught the separateness and retention of normal attributes of each nature in Christ. Cyril taught the suppression of the human attributes of Christ after the incarnation. The Antiochenes and hence Nestorius were criticized for not asserting the Oneness of Christ and for making of Him, two persons. But Nestorius was misunderstood as he accepted the Tome of Leo and he protested against his detractors that he believed Christ to be a single person as recorded in the "Treatise of Heraclides" which he authored.

Nestorius taught that the two natures were in union after the incarnation which did not cause confusion, mixture, or composition by forming a third person. It is not the Logos who has become twofold; it is the one Lord Jesus Christ who is twofold in his natures. In him are seen all the characteristics of the God-Logos, who has a nature eternal and unable to suffer and die, and also those of the manhood, that is a nature mortal, created and able to suffer, and lastly those of the union and the incarnation. To understand this idea of Nestorius all thoughts of a substantial union ought to be dismissed. A substantial union- so Nestorius argues- including a confusion, a mixture, a natural composition, would result in a new being.[26]

That the form co-exists, is a concept recalled in Philippians 2:6 which is not understood as that of one form (servant) succeeding another form (God). Nestorius taught that the Logos was the son of God before the incarnation and only His manhood came into existence at the incarnation resulting in one Son of God, not two. He asserted that Christ in His manhood could have sinned but didn't because His will was in perfect obedience to the Father's will. ". . . the man (Christ) is God not by nature, but only because God reveals Himself in him, and that the Logos is not flesh by nature, but only manifest himself in the flesh."[27] Nestorius was not fairly condemned for his doctrine at the Council of Ephesus in 431 C.E. because only his detractors were present and voted accordingly against him. The Council of Chalcedon accepted both the Tome of Leo and the Twelve Anathemas of Cyril as a compromise which resulted in confusion. "The Definition of this council, which is to be seen not only in its creed but also in its recognition of Leo's letter to Flavian and Cyril's *epistola dogmatica*.

Without doubt, however, there is no real harmony between these different standards of faith."[28] Nestorius was doctrinally orthodox according to the Antiochene tradition and the Roman papal tradition but non-orthodox by the tradition of Alexandria and Cyril. The Henoticon of Emperor Zeno, which will be examined later, set aside the Tome of Leo in 482 C.E. which supported Cyril's position until it was abrogated in 519 C.E. At the Council of Constantinople in 553 C.E., the Emperor Justinian accepted as orthodox the two natures becoming one nature in Christ. Also the teachings of the Antiochene theologians Theodore of Mopsuestia, Theodoret of Cyrus, and Ibas of Edessa were posthumously anathematized. "This Cyrillian-Chalcedonian orthodoxy was supported by the emperor Justinian . . . The condemnation of Theodore of Mopsuestia and of the anti-cyrillian writings of Theodoret and Ibas, sanctioned by this council, clearly manifested the fact that an Antiochian interpretation of the Chalcedonian definition no longer was allowed." [29]

The Monophysite Belief of Eutyches

Eutyches is considered to be the father of Monophysitism. "Eutyches was an abbot in a monastery outside of Constantinople. "*Considered to be the father of Monophysitism*, a heresy condemned at the Council of Chalcedon in 451. Eutyches was abbot of an important monastery just outside Constantinople during the reign of Theodosius II."[30] This was during the reign of Theodosius II and while Nestorius was patriarch of Constantinople. The orthodox position at the time regarded Christ as true man and true God. The school of Alexandria stressed the divine nature of Christ as coming from the Logos. The Antiochene School stressed the humanity of Christ in order to preserve the redemptive nature of His incarnation and the belief which excluded any sin in His life. "With the extreme Alexandrian theologians, the humanity of Christ was ignored. It was the Logos who was born, the Logos who suffered and died. All about Christ was divine, even his body. The opposition between the Syrian and Egyptian bishops (Antioch and Alexandria) became so pronounced, that any distinction of natures in Christ was by the latter denounced as Nestorianism."[31] Eutyches lifespan was from 378-454 C.E. He opposed Nestorian doctrine but in doing so affirmed that Christ had only one nature after the union of the two natures. He further affirmed that Christ did not possess a human nature which was of the same substance with that of human beings which in effect lessened the effect of His redemptive sacrifice for our benefit. Eutyches was condemned at a local council of bishops in 448 C.E. In 449 C.E. another council was convened at Ephesus by Theodosius II which vindicated Eutyches which became known as the Robbers Council. "When summoned before the synod, Eutyches defended his position and was condemned by the bishops and deprived of his orders. Theodosius II, influenced by his favorite eunuch, Chrysophius, one of Eutyches' admirers, convoked another Ecumenical Council to vindicate Eutyches. The second synod of Ephesus, the Robber Council, met in August 449, during which all the old rivalries between Alexandria and Constantinople flared up."[32] Pope Leo I denounced Eutyches in a document known as the Tome of Leo. The argument was based on the papal position that Christ's flesh is consubstantial with human flesh. "The Council of Chalcedon endorsed the *Tome* of Pope Leo I, which spoke of Christ as one person having two natures—language repudiated by Dioscorus. Pope Leo I called Eutyches "an ignorant, imprudent old man" for holding that Christ's flesh was not consubstantial with ours. Even though the Robber Council rehabilitated Eutyches, he was exiled in 451 and nothing more is known of his life."[33]

Detailed Explanation of the Belief of Eutyches

Followers of Eutyches denied the distinction and coexistence of the two natures of Christ. They held that the two natures were blended into one nature thereby creating a third nature. "*The Eutychians* (condemned at Chalcedon, 451) denied the distinction and coexistence of the two natures, and held to a mingling of both into one, which constituted a *tertium quid*, or third nature. Since in this case the divine must overpower the human, it follows that the human was really absorbed into or transmuted into the divine, although the divine was not in all respects the same, after the union, than it was before."[34] Because the divine nature is superior to the human nature, the divine nature must in effect replace the human nature by mingling with and transforming the human nature into a third nature which has absorbed the divine nature. The resulting third nature is different from the original divine nature after the union. Eutychians are included as Monophysites because they believe in the transformation of the two natures into one nature. Several comparisons and metaphors were used to explain the fusion and transformation to describe the two natures of Christ. "Humanity joined to deity was as a drop of honey mingled with the ocean. There was a change in either element, but as when a stone attracts the earth, or a meteorite the sun, or when a small boat pulls a ship, all the movement was virtually on the part of the smaller object. Humanity was so absorbed in deity, as to be altogether lost. The union was illustrated by electron, a metal compounded of silver and gold."[35]

The Monophysite view of Eutyches denied the possibility of the redemptive work of Christ and the subsequent atonement accomplished. "And as the union of the two natures commenced from the beginning, the whole of Christ's human earthly life became an illusion, or empty show. Where then is his redeeming work and his bond of union or sympathy with us?"[36] If Christ did not suffer and redeem man as a human then it is a divine act by fiat and the sympathetic, suffering Christ who bore our sins and our sorrows did not take place as Scripture records the history of the crucifixion. Therefore man is not really made like unto Christ and he is not one with Him. The controversies over the person of Christ center on the reality of the two natures, the validity of the two natures, and the union of the two natures. "The decision against Nestorius, in which the unity of Christ's person was asserted; that against Eutyches, affirming the distinction of natures; and that against the Monothelites, declaring that the possession of a human nature involves of necessity the possession of a human will, have been received as the true faith by the Church universal, the Greek, Latin, and Protestant."[37]

The error of Nestorianism and Eutychianism lies in denying the appropriate union of the two natures. The error of Nestorius was to describe the two natures of Christ as if He were two persons. The Alexandrian school ignored the humanity of Christ in favor of the concept of the Logos as the divine in Christ which suffered and died. Eutyches viewed Christ before the incarnation as having two natures but afterward having only one nature based upon a union of the two where the human is swallowed up by the divine. The Tome of Leo I denounced Eutyches in language of condemnation. "When Eutyches responded to your questions by saying, 'I confess that before the union our Lord was of two natures, but after the union I confess one nature,' I am astounded that this quite absurd and quite perverse profession of his went uncensured by any rebuke from his judges and that an utterly foolish and blasphemous expression was passed over as if nothing offensive had been heard."[38] At this point Christ was no longer a man but became an illusion. In Christ the union of the two natures only seemed to be a joining into a new being. According to Eutyches, Christ was not both God and man as the orthodox believe. "Then Christ instead of being God and man, is neither God nor man."[39] Christ was neither God nor man but a third entity based on a hybrid status. Eutyches was condemned at the Council of Constantinople. His defenders from the school of Alexandria convened a council at Ephesus in 449 CE which excluded all orthodox theologians and voted to restore Eutyches to prominence and to condemn all of his detractors. This action was upheld by emperor Theodosius but lasted only two years. Theodosius died and the succeeding emperor called for the Council of Chalcedon in 451 CE which established the orthodox view of the two natures based upon the Tome of Leo written to emperor Flavian of Constantinople.

Analysis of the History of the Monophysite Belief

The Monophysite doctrine appeared first in the theology of the school of Alexandria. This school focused upon the incarnation of Jesus Christ as an act of redemption in the world. Cyril of Alexandria (375-444 CE) was the primary proponent that Christ retained only one nature after the union of the divine nature of Christ into the human incarnation nature of Christ. "This same one is coessential with the Father, as to his deity, and coessential with us, as to his humanity, for a union of two natures has occurred, as a consequence of which we confess one Christ, one Son, one Lord."[40] Cyril's main opponents were Pope Leo I of Rome and the theologians from the competing school of Antioch. At the time the school of Antioch dominated the theological principles which were dominant at Chalcedon. Opposed to this however were theologians residing in Syria, Egypt and Palestine who rejected the beliefs of the Antiochene School and preferred to follow the teachings of Cyril. "The term 'Monophysite' was first used in the aftermath of the Council of Chalcedon (451) to describe all those who rejected the Council's Definition that the Incarnate Christ is one Person 'in two Natures', and upheld, as their key formula the phrase of St Cyril of Alexandria, 'one Incarnate Nature of the Word'. It is still sometimes used to refer to the *Oriental Orthodox Churches."[41]

This group of churches was founded by Dioscorus who was Patriarch of Alexandria at the time of the Council of Chalcedon. These churches rejected the teachings of Eutyches, Apollinaris, Theodore of Mopsuestia, Nestorius, Theodoret of Cyrus, Ibas of Edessa, and the Creed of Chalcedon. They preferred to be called Miaphysites which is the belief that Christ has a single nature with both a divine and human character.

A leading theologian by the name of the Severus (465-538 CE) tried to explain the single nature of Christ by using an analogy taken from Platonism, where the body and soul are unique but form inseparable portions of the one nature of the human being. Thus the divine and human natures of Christ, subsequent to His incarnation, form the single nature of Christ. "So Severus is left with an unfamiliar sort of unity which is neither a confusion nor a juxtaposition, but which he justifies by pointing to the unity of man: the non-independent but real body and soul have somehow united to make up man."[42] There were variations of this understanding. For example, Julian of Halicarnassus held an extreme version regarding the person of Christ which stated that prior to the resurrection the body of Christ was incorruptible. "One group of disputing monks addressed a question to Severus and his fellow bishop in exile, Julian of Halicarnassus: was the flesh taken up by Christ corruptible? Severus answered yes; Julian, no."[43] The teaching of Julian denied the suffering and passion of Christ, in his humanity. Other Monophysites holding an extreme understanding of the divine nature of Christ held that the humanity of Christ was only an illusion and not a reality. This was the position of the Docetists.

Much of the controversy within Christianity during the fourth century centered on the concepts of the deity of the Logos and of the Holy Spirit. This controversy was to be resolved in the Councils of Nicaea and Constantinople in 325 and 381 C.E. respectively. In the fifth century the focus of the controversy was on the two natures of Christ. During the Council of Ephesus in 431 C.E. a controversy took place between Christians in the Eastern portion of the Empire. These controversies involved both the Nestorian controversy and the Monophysite controversy which were addressed at the Council of Chalcedon in 451 C.E. The position of the Council at Chalcedon was based upon a document known as the Tome of Leo the Great (440-461), who as pope in the West stressed the importance of the two natures of Christ without really attempting to unify these two natures. ". . . Leo dispatched his famous Dogmatic Letter, or Tome, to Flavian, and made his hostility to the One Nature doctrine clear."[44] A second position regarding the two nature's controversy was developed during the time of Emperor Justin I which has been called Neo-Chalcedonianism. This became the position and religious policy of this Emperor, whose desire was to reunite the Monophysites of Syria and Palestine to the Orthodox Church in Constantinople, as well as the Western church in Rome. "In 519 Justin welcomed the papal legates with all possible honor and offered to discuss terms. When the legates refused all discussion, the emperor acceded to their demands. The patriarch, all the bishops present in Constantinople and the heads of monasteries signed the papal formula of reunion."[45] The second modified position became the key concept promoted at the second Council of Constantinople in 553 C.E.

How the Monophysite Belief Originated

The term Monophysite was first claimed after the debates formed in the Council of Chalcedon in 451 C.E. This term was created in order to describe those who were opposed to the Council's orthodox position of the majority opinion regarding the incarnate person of Christ in two natures. The underlying phraseology was proposed by Cyril of Alexandria. "The term 'Monophysite' was first used in the aftermath of the Council of Chalcedon (451) to describe all those who rejected the Council's Definition that the Incarnate Christ is one Person 'in two Natures', and upheld, as their key formula the phrase of St Cyril of Alexandria, 'one Incarnate Nature of the Word'."[46]

A key position at the Council of Chalcedon was held by a church leader known as Eutyches. He maintained that after the incarnation Christ had only one nature, and that His nature was not consubstantial with us. "From his rejection of 'consubstantial with us' it has been inferred that Christ's humanity was in his eyes mere appearance; hence he must have been a Docetist. From his affirmation of two natures before and only one nature after the union the conclusion has been drawn that either the two must have been fused into a tertium quid or the humanity must have been swallowed up by the divinity."[47] As a result he was condemned, and his position was not widely held by most of the Monophysites. A more moderate form of the Monophysite belief was that the incarnate Christ became one nature out of two, which were divine and human at a point in time. One of the difficulties in coming to a compromise conclusion regarding the natures of Christ was due to the differing definitions of the term "nature". The Monophysite could not accept the term defining Christ as one person in two natures, because this implied to them a Nestorian position. The primary early defenders of the Monophysite position were Timothy Aelurus, Peter the Fuller, and Severus of Antioch. "Among the early leaders of moderate Monophysitism (which remained implacably opposed to the Chalcedonian Definition and to the Tome of Leo) were Timothy Aelurus and Peter the Fuller; the most important theologian was Severus of Antioch."[48]

Monophysitism included many varying definitional beliefs which historians have incorporated into the movement.

Many attempts were made during the fifth and sixth century to reconcile the definitional differences between the Monophysites and the orthodox position. Emperor Zeno who reigned from 474 until 491 C.E. authored a document known as the Henoticon, which was an attempt to set aside the declaration from the Council of Chalcedon. "Throughout the East, Zeno's Henotikon remained the imperially imposed official declaration of faith. But, outside of Egypt, partisans of Chalcedon were to be found everywhere."[49] But this was rejected by both the Pope and the representatives of the Monophysites which then resulted in a separation known as the Acacian Schism which will be examined later.

Justin I who was emperor from 527 until 565 C.E. also attempted to reconcile the two differing positions. He failed primarily based on political reasons as opposed to theological reasons. Other emperors also attempted reconciliation which included Justin II who reigned from 565 to 578 C.E., and Heraclius, who reigned from 610 until 661 C.E. both of whom were unsuccessful by the early seventh century. The different sub-definitions of the Monophysites were established such that the many ethnic churches had their own special definition of Monophysite doctrine. This included the Armenian, Coptic, Ethiopian, and Syriac churches. "As the eastern and southern provinces-Armenia, Syria, and Egypt-were regained to the Empire, the emperor had to face once again the religious question, how to reconcile the dissident Monophysites without alienating Chalcedonian Asia Minor."[50] These churches became estranged from the Byzantine Orthodox Church and formed a separate group of Christians following the Monophysite split within the greater Byzantine Empire. This of course made this group, non-supportive politically to the emperor of the Byzantine Empire.

The two earliest controversies were the debate and definition of the Trinity and the natures of Christ. The argument of the Trinity centered upon the relationship of the Son to the Father. The argument of the natures concerned the person of Christ. What was at stake, regarding the nature of Christ, was the efficacy of the act of redemption. Christian redemption must unite in the person of Christ the divine nature and the human nature. The orthodox requirements for this understanding concludes that Christ must be true man, true God, one person, and perfect in the union of the two natures.

The school of Alexandria mixed the divine nature of Christ with the human nature of Christ and then elevated the divine nature as more important than the human nature. "The Alexandrian school of theology, with its characteristic speculative and mystical turn, favored a connection of the divine and human in the act of the incarnation so close that it was in danger of losing the human in the divine, or at least of mixing it with the divine . . ."[51] The incarnation is a mystery which the church sought to understand during the early years of the church.

Detailed Explanation of the Alexandrian School

It is unclear how the school of Alexandria began. One view states that the disciple of the apostles, John Mark, founded the Alexandrian church. Other Jewish Christians from Palestine who had been baptized into the Christian faith relocated to Alexandria forming the backbone of the Alexandrian church. "Baptized Jews seem to have brought Christianity to Alexandria."[52] Subsequently leaders were chosen to initiate the work of the Alexandrian school during the apostolic age. Alexandria quickly became a mixture of Greeks and Jews who mixed both philosophy and culture into the community. "Among Alexandrian theologians there developed the close relationship with Greek philosophy which early Christianity achieved without entirely losing contact with the developing mainstream of the Church."[53] As the Alexandrian school developed in importance, the Bishop of Alexandria became a leading spokesman for the Christian faith.

Alexandria was an important city in Egypt and the second city to Rome in the Empire. It was a major center of Hellenism and of Jewish culture and thought. The importance of the city began with theologians like Basilides, Heracleon, Clement, and Origen. The school of Alexandria became increasingly important under bishops Athanasius and Cyril in the fourth and fifth centuries. "In size and importance, Alexandria in Egypt was the second city of the Roman Empire. It was a centre not only of Hellenism but also of Semitism, with the largest community of Jews in any single city of the ancient world . . ."[54] As the school of Alexandria competed with the school of Antioch in Syria for importance, Constantinople gained precedence over both cities as the seat of government and by the importance placed on the gatherings at the Council of Constantinople in 381 C.E. and the Council of Chalcedon in 451 C.E. Because most Christians in Egypt at the time were Monophysites, the school of Alexandria lost its standing of importance under the occupation and control of Egypt by foreign powers. "The great majority of Christians in Egypt supported the Monophysite schisms, and by the time Egypt passed under the Persians (616) and then under the Arabs (642), the Greek Orthodox Patriarchate of Alexandria had lost most of its influence."[55] Persia controlled Egypt from 616 until 642 C.E. when the Arabs took control of the territory. The church at Alexandria was influenced by the Platonic tradition as is evidenced by the writings of Origen including his use of allegory to explain Scripture. "This is a modern designation for a style of theology associated with the Church at Alexandria and markedly influenced by the Platonic tradition. Its characteristic emphases on the reality of the spiritual world and the allegorical exegesis of Scripture are clearly evidenced in the work of Origen."[56] Much of the writings emanating from the church at Alexandria prioritize the divine nature of Christ and the unity of his person. Cyril of Alexandria taught that the divine in the incarnate Christ suffered. ". . . even the orthodox among the Alexandrians (e.g. St Cyril) did not hesitate to say of the Incarnate Christ that 'God suffered', while the less orthodox, beginning with Apollinaris (who, though not in fact an Alexandrian, can be seen as belonging to the same theological tradition), undermined the completeness of Christ's humanity, holding that His highest human faculties were simply replaced by the Divine Nature, so that He could neither be tempted nor suffer."[57]

Detailed Explanation of the Antiochene School

The school of Antioch consisted of Dyophysites who believed in the two natures of Christ. Antioch, Syria was the third largest city in the Roman Empire. It dates in Christianity to the apostolic period of Peter and

Paul. Peter was considered by many as the first Bishop of Antioch. "According to tradition, the first bishop of the city was St Peter, and by the beginning of the 2nd cent. the Church had an organization, with the celebrated St Ignatius as its bishop."[58] Antioch continued in a position of prominence until the mid-fifth century when the Monophysite schism with Constantinople diminished the importance of the church and school at Antioch. The School of Antioch was primarily concerned with the human aspect and ethical terms regarding the nature of Christ. Those theologians from Antioch expressed a clear distinction between the divine and the human nature of Christ while avoiding any mixing such as suggested by Theodore of Mopsuestia and Theodoret of Cyrus. "He opposed the notion that in Christ the divinity absorbed the humanity as water absorbs a drop of honey."[59] Both of these theologians during their lifetimes were considered to be orthodox. Later they were condemned by association because the heretic Nestorius had taught their doctrines. The Antiochenes taught that the Logos became a human person at the advent of His birth. He was a perfect man with a human nature consisting of a soul, an intellect, and a body. This stress upon Christ's humanity implied a human personality. The term used to emphasize the union of the two natures was "indwelling" rather than a physical union. With this indwelling, the Logos imparted the fullness of the glory of the divine. The emphasis was always maintained on the real human history of Christ. Although the Logos indwelled the human Jesus, it did not replace or overpower the moral choices of Jesus. This view tends to lean toward an understanding of the indwelling as a possession by the divine Logos. "He dwelt in the *homo assumptus* 'as in a son'. This meant that 'He united the whole man assumed with Himself, causing Him to share with Him in all honour which He, the Son by nature indwelling him, enjoys'".[60] Clearly the Antiochenes taught the two complete natures in one person of Christ.

The Monophysite Belief of Cyril

Cyril of Alexandria believed that the divine nature was not subject to change or mixture as a result of the incarnation. He believed in the two perfect natures of Christ being both human and divine. "The humanity was as real as the divinity . . ."[61] His key concern with the Antiochenes was that they tended to preserve the full humanity of Christ while reducing the deity of Christ to only an appearance. Cyril believed that Nestorius taught that the events and actions of Jesus' life took place in his human nature.

Cyril believed that both God and man were united in Christ rather than joined, mixed, or associated. "This did not entail, however, that there was any confusion or mixing together of the two natures, hypostases or 'things' which coalesced in Him."[62] Cyril's objective was to elevate the deity of Christ to such an extent that the deity of Christ was the nature to be worshiped. His strongest point was that the deity and humanity of Christ were not to be mixed or changed. He maintained the real unity of the divine and human as true natures. "Aside from his partisan excesses, he powerfully and successfully represented the important truth of the unity of the person of Christ against the abstract dyophysitism of Nestorius."[63]

Cyril was misunderstood later by the Monophysites who maintained that the incarnation produced a third kind of nature. "The incarnate nature as seen by Cyril was not a real nature in the usual sense, i.e. not a third kind of nature, but as later Monophysites understood it to be so. Thus they claimed Cyril as the godfather of their doctrine."[64] He is best commended for his focus on the unity of Christ and his redemptive work. He is claimed as an original expositor of both the Monophysite and the Dyophysite positions. In a way the language of his definition of the unity of Christ without confusion or mixture became the hurdle which the Monophysites could not overcome and as a result they rejected Chalcedonian Orthodoxy. The Emperor Theodosius II and the Roman Pope Celestine accepted the doctrines as espoused by Cyril. After the Council of Ephesus in 431 C.E., Cyril agreed to a doctrine of union which was developed by Theodoret of Cyrus. ". . . Cyril himself admitted, as his correspondence after the act of union reveals, that it was possible to speak of two natures without dividing the one Christ."[65] This doctrine reaffirmed the consubstantial nature of Christ with the Father. Cyril's position did not satisfy the theologians of Alexandria. They continued to emphasize the one incarnate nature of Christ. The Antiochene theologians maintained that Christ had two natures full and complete in one single incarnate person. "Cyril's successor, Dioscorus . . . was determined . . . to reassert the One Nature doctrine which . . . had the authority of the fathers behind it and which had only been compromised by Cyril in a moment of weakness."[66]

Detailed Explanation of the Belief of Cyril
Cyril was named patriarch of Alexandria in 412 C.E. He succeeded his uncle Theophilus. He resisted the patriarchs of Constantinople and Antioch. He was the strongest opponent of Nestorianism when he argued against such beliefs at the Council of Ephesus in 431 C.E with a spirit of hatred and cruelty in defense of his beliefs.

From the year 428 to his death in 444 his life was interwoven with the Christological controversies. He was the most zealous and the most influential champion of the anti-Nestorian orthodoxy at the third ecumenical council, and scrupled at no measures to annihilate his antagonist. Besides the weapons of theological learning and acumen, he allowed himself also the use of willful misrepresentation, artifice, violence, instigation of people and monks at Constantinople, and repeated bribery of imperial officers, even of the emperor's sister Pulcheria.[67]

He was a powerful theologian of the Alexandrian school. His great theological adversary was Theodoret of the Antiochene School. He was a strong proponent of the elevation of Mary, the mother of Christ, far beyond what Scripture teaches. His works are primarily an apologetic against the writings of Theodoret and Nestorius.

Cyril of Alexandria was appointed Patriarch of Alexandria in 412 C.E. at the height of Alexandrian influence. His office had significant theological and political influence in the Christian Empire. His treatise entitled "That Christ is One" and his letters to Nestorius are what are best remembered of his writings. He wrote in the Alexandrian tradition of his predecessors including Demetrius (188-230), Peter (300-311), Alexander (311-328), Athanasius (328-373), and Theophilus (385-412). "In brief, Cyril's *Festal Letters* are his own adaptation of an Alexandrian tradition that began during the episcopate of Demetrius (188-230)."[68] He also wrote twenty nine annual Festal Letters between 414-442 C.E. which reflect his theology and teachings. He was the nephew of Theophilus and therefore an insider in the Alexandrian tradition.

His guiding principle was to explain the Christian theological economy from Scripture by describing the redemptive plan of God whereby Christ was the redeemer. "For he was, is, and will be God by nature, before the flesh and with the flesh. Paul supports this when he writes, 'Jesus Christ the same yesterday and today and forever.' You see that he is not to be found chopping Immanuel into a duality of Sons. . . ."[69]

From the time of Origen, the Alexandrian tradition used typology and allegory applied to Scripture to describe theological doctrine. This technique of exegesis was used by Cyril. This should not be confused, however, with the Origenists theology but rather just the technique itself of using typology and allegory. Cyril was influenced by the Egyptian monastic view advocating asceticism as a lifestyle which Christians should practice. "These years in the desert were critical for Cyril's intellectual development."[70] Cyril was concerned with the continued presence and influence of pagans and Jews in the Christian Empire but especially in Alexandria. "The Jews, that is, who practice impiety to the last degree, are scandalized at the cross of Christ our Savior, and exceed the madness of the pagans . . ."[71] He strived to denounce paganism and to emphasize the replacement of Old Testament Judaism with Christ and the New Testament. He virtually claimed ownership of the Old Testament by Christ and the Church.

Cyril wrote about his beliefs in the Festal Letters fourteen years before his controversies began with Nestorius in 428 C.E. and thirty seven years before the resolutions in 451 C.E. "When accordingly we think rightly, we do not speak of two Sons, nor of two Christs or Lords, but of one Son and Lord, both before the Incarnation and when he had the covering of the flesh."[72] He based his Christology on three Scripture passages including: Philippians 2:7 (nature of a servant), Hebrews 1:3 (radiance of God's glory), and John 1:14 (Word became flesh). "Cyril employed basically the same set of scriptural passages to support his Christological vision through his entire episcopacy . . ."[73] He tended not to use technical theological terms but rather biblical language. Many early church theologians were willing to accept any interpretation as acceptable as long as it reflected sound doctrine.

The Dyophysite Belief of Athanasius

Athanasius (298-373 C.E.) was born in Alexandria, Egypt. He was elevated to the position of Bishop of Alexandria. His most famous works were *"Apology against the Arians"*, *"On the Nicene Formula"*, *"Against the Heathen"*, and *"The Incarnation of the Word"*. Many of his arguments form the basis of the orthodox position regarding the issues which were pertinent to the Council of Nicaea in 325 C.E. Athanasius was the primary defender against Arianism. The School of Alexandria was influenced by Gnosticism and the allegorical methods of Origen which were both later deemed heretical. Those who were orthodox such as Athanasius were stressing the fullness of Christ's humanity and the historical importance of the Scriptural narrative of His life after the incarnation. "Unlike the Arians who were concerned primarily with the Son's place in creation, Athanasius begins with the firm conviction that the Word became flesh to redeem the human race, to make men godlike."[74]

The political career of Athanasius was one of turmoil. He was appointed Bishop of Alexandria in 328 C.E. by the Emperor Constantine following the death of Bishop Alexander. He was deposed in 335 C.E. and exiled. He returned to Alexandria but was driven out again in 339 C.E. Athanasius defended the view that Christ was (*homoousios*) of the same essence or substance as the Father. The Arian view was that Christ was (*homoiousios*) of a similar essence or substance as the Father which would make Him less than God. Athanasius prevailed in the defense of Christ's deity. Another heresy at this time was that of Marcellus the Bishop of Nicaea. His position was that the pre-incarnate Son was not personal until the incarnation occurred. "It was only in virtue of this humiliating separation from the Father that the Word acquired a sort of independent personality."[75] Athanasius successfully opposed this view. Once again Athanasius returned to Alexandria in 346 C.E. under emperors Constantine II and Constans but was deposed again in 356 C.E. as the political winds turned against him under emperor Constantius who was an Arian.

Detailed Explanation of the Belief of Athanasius

Athanasius lived in Alexandria under the leadership of the patriarch Alexander. After Constantine became emperor, he fell under the influence of the Arian Eusebius, Bishop of Nicomedia. Eusebius was openly hostile to Alexander and to Athanasius following Alexander's death. As an Arian, Eusebius taught that Christ was neither co-equal nor co-eternal with the Father. In 325 C.E., a total of 318 bishops met at the Council of Nicaea to determine by debate and vote the consubstantiality of Christ with the Father. Eusebius and his sixteen like-minded bishops argued that Jesus Christ was not God. The Council voted to condemn Arius and his writings. "This creed was recognized and acquiesced in by three hundred and eighteen (bishops); . . . Five only would not receive it, objecting to the term . . . .*consubstantial* : these were Eusebius of Nicomedia . . . .Upon this the Synod anathematized Arius . . ."[76] Eusebius was deposed by Emperor Constantine. Meanwhile Athanasius received training in the monasteries of Egypt where he was taught by Anthony and Pachomius. ". . . the West began to be influenced by Athanasius's *Life of Antony*, which had been translated about A.D. 380 by Evagrius, bishop of Antioch." [77] Upon the death of Alexander, Athanasius became Archbishop of the Eastern Church. Eusebius intrigued with Emperor Constantine falsely accusing Athanasius of usurping imperial powers for which he was summoned to Antioch to stand trial. "But before he came the Eusebian faction anticipating his arrival, added to their former accusation the charge of another crime . . . charging Athanasius with plotting against his sovereign. . ."[78] His accusers were nearly all Arians who judged him guilty whereupon Constantine banished him to Gaul. Constantine died in 337 C.E. and his three sons came to power. Constantius became sole ruler in 340 C.E. until his death in 361 C.E. Eusebius once again influenced this emperor to appoint Arian bishops and appointed the Arian Gregory as Patriarch of Alexandria. Julian the Apostate became emperor upon the death of Constantius in 361 C.E. He was a pagan who ruled the Empire until 363 C.E. when he was killed in battle against the Persians. Athanasius was allowed to return to Alexandria following Julian's death. His influence was centered on securing peace by offering forgiveness and reconciliation to anyone who would acknowledge the Nicene Creed.

Jovian became emperor in 363 C.E. He was a Western Catholic who supported Athanasius by returning him to the office of Bishop of Alexandria. Jovian died in 364 C.E, and was succeeded as emperor by Valentinian. His brother, Valens, was co-ruler in the East until 378 C.E. and was an Arian.

Valens attempted to convert the Empire to the Arian belief. The Western popes, who were non-Arian, became increasingly powerful. "In 366 Liberius died and was succeeded by Pope St. Damasus, a man of strong character and holy life. Two years later, in a council of the church, it was decreed that no Bishop should be consecrated unless he held the Creed of Nicaea. Athanasius was overwhelmed with joy on hearing this decision. The triumph of the cause for which he had fought so valiantly was now assured."[79] Athanasius was able to continue in his office having brought peace and the support of the divinity of Christ as expressed in the Nicene Creed of 325 C.E. to the orthodox position of the church which stated "Born of the Father before all ages, God of God, Light of Light, true

God of true God, begotten not made, consubstantial with the Father. . . ." He had served faithfully a total of 48 years.

During the period following the legalizing of Christianity by the Roman emperor Constantine and the advent of Islam into Christian lands in 632 C.E., the church was engaged in internal controversy when it should have been seeking to advance the kingdom for Christ. There was an opening to the East to spread and solidify the gospel outreach which was not the focus of the church. The traditions of the two leading schools in the Eastern portion of the empire were grounded in parochial approaches to biblical study. The school of Antioch focused on the humanity of Christ through His teachings. "It was the achievement of the Antiochene School (which) . . . deserves credit for bringing back the historical Jesus. . . .The 'Word-man' Christology . . ."[80] The school of Alexandria focused on the ability to explain and defend the Scripture in reference to Christ in terms of His relationship to deity. "The formula was evidently put forward at Alexandria by adherents of the Word-flesh Christology . . . since the Word . . . had united Himself with His flesh."[81] The background of each school was influenced by different outside sources. Antioch was influenced by the Eastern mystical religions whereas Alexandria was influenced by Greek philosophy. Explaining the mysteries of the Trinity and the Incarnation involved different methods of reasoning and differences in language which blurred agreement on these difficult concepts. At times the egos and power bases of leaders vied for supremacy by attempting to win the arguments and denounce their opponents in order to advance themselves. In advancing understanding through human endeavors, what has become the norm as orthodox is frequently seen as stagnant and rigid such that new concepts and explanations which are novel challenge the beliefs of the status quo. This becomes an internal battleground which saps the focus and energy from the purpose of spreading the gospel. The conflicts also cause division within the church resulting in animosities rather than unity in loving fellowship.

In summary we have examined the origin and basis of the Monophysite belief. In so doing the beliefs of two purely Monophysite theologians including Apollinaris and Eutyches were discussed. In addition the theology of Nestorius was examined. The history of the two leading schools of theology, Alexandria and Antioch, were described. Finally the opposing views of Cyril and Athanasius were presented where Cyril represented the Monophysite position and Athanasius represented the orthodox Dyophysite position.

CHAPTER 3

AN ANALYSIS OF THE DEBATE REGARDING THE NATURE (S) OF CHRIST

One of the key disputes regarding the nature of Christ is whether He suffered as God. Some argued that God suffered and others argued that God could not suffer. For example Luke 24:26 says "Was it not necessary that the Christ should suffer these things and enter into his glory?" If God suffers, then He is not omnipotent and not immutable. If God did not suffer, then He is not sharing human suffering and pain as we do and cannot be like us. For example Isaiah 53:4-5 says "Yet on himself he bore our sufferings/our torments he endured . . . but he was pierced for our transgressions, tortured for our iniquities. . ." "The premise that Christ who suffered is true God and true man does not require the conclusion that God suffers."[82] Jesus refers to Himself as a suffering servant and the Son of man. He reminds us in Luke 24: 46 that, "Thus it is written, that Christ should suffer and on the third day rise from the dead." The suffering is not done by just anyone but by the righteous One who knew no sin and therefore became our ransom and a substitute for fallen and sinful man. The whole unfolding of the offer of salvation to the Gentiles was opened when the Jews rejected Christ's coming in the flesh as the incarnate Christ.

Doctrinal Analysis of the Meaning and Importance of the One Nature of Christ

The doctrine of the one nature of Christ reflected the view of many theologians during the early years of the church. For example this would include Apollinaris, Eutyches, Cyril of Alexandria, Severus and many others. Any doctrine would be put to the test of argument and debate by theologians on both sides of the issue. After the debate, the issue would be voted on by the bishops attending a church council. The majority vote would usually decide the definition of the issue which would become the standard for the church. The winning definition would become orthodox and the losing definition would become heresy. For example during the Nicene controversy the party of Arius who were fewer in number were unable to convince the bulk of the attendees at the Synod of their view which opposed the views of the party of Alexander and Athanasius which became the basis for the Nicene Creed. However this activity did not always settle the debate. Some issues which were accepted as adequate and orthodox may later are challenged as inadequate. "As Christian communities came under increasing pressure, internal and external, to define themselves and to defend themselves against their alternatives, so there was growing interest in clarifying what were acceptable and unacceptable expressions of the faith . . ."[83] The real test became whether a definition could stand against the rigors of intellectual inquiry and successfully defeat alternative views. The definitions which were standardized into creeds which survived these tests through time were able to preserve the core beliefs of Christianity and best explain the Scriptural illustrations and statements which theologians posed to defend or to defeat the creed. Many of the heretical views, such as Arianism, were proposed from within Christianity rather than from without. Orthodox views became the authentic and normative view of the Christian faith and teaching. The progression of dangers to early Christianity began with persecution, followed by assimilation, and ended with fragmentation. Martyrdom of the faithful was the result of hostile persecution. The danger of assimilation to Judaism, Gnosticism, and paganism threatened the very existence of Christianity. The risk of fragmentation from within to any heresy threatened the core beliefs of Christianity which would result in dividing the church. The reasons for the controversies were usually: (1) local reactions to a practice acceptable to the greater church but unacceptable to a local church such as occurred with the Donatist controversy, (2) disagreement and strife between two competing individuals or schools such as between Arius and Athanasius and between Antioch and Alexandria, and (3) the explanation of a doctrine that threatened the core beliefs of the Christian faith. These latter threats were internal rather than external to Christianity. "Heresy renders the Christian faith incoherent and unstable, and thus undermines its longer-term prospects in a fiercely competitive world of ideas."[84] Eventually, the orthodox views would become the standard for the church, the beliefs propagated by the political authorities, and the hedge against the world outside the church where no salvation was thought possible outside of the Orthodox Church.

Description of the One Nature Belief Deemed Heretical

Severus (465-538 C.E.) was the patriarch of Antioch coming from the ranks of the monks. He was named patriarch by Emperor Anastasius in 512 C.E. He was deposed by Emperor Justin I in 518 C.E. and subsequently excommunicated in 536 C.E. by Emperor Justinian. He was the leading moderate Monophysite of his era. "The first important Monophysite, Severus, reiterated the traditional statements of orthodoxy and acknowledged two natures in Christ, but went on to assert that in the incarnation a synthesis occurs, producing a nature or *hypostasis*."[85]

Severus was born in Pisidia and trained in Alexandria, Egypt. He was an ascetic and a monk who was influenced by Basil and Gregory of Nazianzen. He opposed the Council of Chalcedon and the Henoticon of Emperor Zeno. He had several supporters which included Patriarch Macedonius, Patriarch Timothy, and Theodosius the Bishop of Alexandria. Severus was selected as Patriarch of Antioch in 512 C.E. He affirmed the Creeds of the Councils of Nicaea, Constantinople, Ephesus, and the substance of the Henoticon. He rejected the Creed of Chalcedon, the Tome of Leo, and the writings of Eutyches and Nestorius. Anastasius died in 518 C.E. and Emperor Justin attempted to arrest Severus which caused him to flee to Egypt. Severus was condemned in Constantinople in 536 C.E. by a synod which was confirmed by Emperor Justinian regarding him as guilty of Eutychianism and Nestorianism. Severus died in Egypt in 538 C.E.

Cyril of Alexandria was central to the Monophysite controversy. He did not intend to introduce confusion into the concept of union but unfortunately Monophysites confused the beliefs of the Chalcedonians with the Nestorians. Severus depended upon the writings of Cyril yet he also rejected the writings of both Eutyches and Nestorius. Severus did not claim to deny the manhood of Christ thus he was not a Monophysite in the sense of denying the human nature in the union.

Severus engaged in written debate on several occasions with Sergius. In all, Severus and Sergius exchanged seven letters on the subject of the nature of Christ. Severus insisted that Christ possessed two natures after the incarnation. He used the terms property, propriety, and particularity to define the nature of Christ. Sergius argued that Christ possessed only one nature following the Incarnation. "We do not speak of two natures or properties after the inexpressible union."[86] Sergius first argued that Christ could not have two natures because propriety is a nature and the flesh of a human is corruptible whereas Christ's flesh was not corruptible. Sergius believed that the hypostatic union requires mixing. If the natures are unmixed, then there is no union. In addition Sergius taught that the incarnate Christ would possess an independent nature. ". . . I will not cease repeating many times, and not that (which lies) in (independent) parts, and natures in independent existence are implied."[87] To Sergius, Christ was the union of divinity with perfect manhood. Sergius framed his argument around the technical concepts of a mixing which forms a composition of the natures of Christ in order to preserve the technical union of Christ's two natures.

Severus did not accept the concept of mixing but rather defined the union in Christ of the divinity and the humanity after the incarnation as both retaining their original properties. ". . . the different principle underlying the existence of the Godhead and manhood . . . This difference we in no wise assert that the union has removed."[88] He explained this by stating that the particularity of a nature retains its uniqueness. Therefore the integrity of each nature, but not its independence, in the union is maintained after the incarnation. The invisible divine Logos had united with the visible flesh without either nature losing its uniqueness. In the union which is hypostatic, neither nature is replaced, lost, mixed, or confused. "As the propriety of God identifies and implies the nature of God, and the propriety of flesh implies the nature of flesh, and the new unit, Christ, is truly new and different, neither of these proprieties apply to it."[89] Severus is arguing for the redemptive plan of God and the redemptive activity of the human Christ. While Sergius focused on the internal unity of the two natures of Christ, Severus focused on understanding the activity and ongoing process of the humanity of Christ. "The goal of the incarnation was to redeem mankind, and in his life on earth, God the Word was perpetually fulfilling that goal."[90] Severus concludes his argument by comparing the Trinity to the Incarnation. He indicates that the three hypostases in the Trinity are consubstantial whereas the two hypostases in the Incarnation are non-consubstantial.

Theodora I (500-547C.E.) the wife of Justinian I was a powerful empress who was supportive of the Monophysite position. "In the East many, including Justinian's wife, Theodora, supported the Monophysites, who emphasized Christ's divine nature."[91] Peter the Fuller was Patriarch of Antioch. He was trained as a monk and became a strong supporter of the Monophysite position. "Peter had been a monk of the convent of the Acoemetae at Constantinople, where he practiced the trade of a fuller. Expelled for his Monophysite leanings, he went to Chalcedon, but after a brief stay returned and became known to the Emp. Zeno the Isaurian, whom he accompanied to Antioch $c.470$."[92] He was deposed but subsequently returned to office. He was a supporter of Emperor Zeno and the Henoticon document, written by Zeno. Julian of Halicarnassus was an extreme Monophysite who taught that Christ's human body was incorruptible, impassible, and immortal. "An extreme Monophysite group, led by Julian, Bp. of Halicarnassus, and hence known also as 'Julianists'. They taught that from the first moment of the incarnation the earthly body of Christ was in its nature incorruptible (ἄφθαρτος), impassible, and immortal, though this fact did not preclude Him from accepting suffering and death by a free act of His will."[93] Julian taught that Christ possessed a glorified nature following the incarnation rather than following the resurrection. This minimized the pain and suffering of Jesus in His human nature.

Doctrinal Analysis of the Meaning and Importance of the Two Natures of Christ

Beginning with the Council of Chalcedon, those professing belief in the one nature of Christ were called Monophysites. By that time the Eutychian definition of the human nature having been absorbed into the divine nature had been rejected even by Monophysites. They maintained that Christ, following the incarnation, retained a single nature which was composed of both divine and human components. They argued that maintaining that Christ had two natures in effect means that He was two persons. To them the terms "nature" and "person" were synonymous. A nature must retain a personality and individuality. "Their main argument against Chalcedon was that the doctrine of two natures necessarily led to that of two persons, or subjects, and thereby severed the one Christ into two Sons of God. They were entirely at one with the Nestorians in their use of the terms "nature" and "person," and in rejecting the orthodox distinction between the two. They could not conceive of human nature without personality. From this the Nestorians reasoned that, because in

Christ there are two natures, there must be also two independent hypostases; the Monophysites, that, because there is but one person in Christ, there can be only one nature."[94]

The schism after the Council of Chalcedon set in motion serious controversies that weakened the church. The controversies based on the meaning of single words and empty formulas left a church in turmoil for a century. "Thus from the council of Chalcedon started those violent and complicated Monophysite controversies which convulsed the Oriental church, from patriarchs and emperors down to monks and peasants, for more than a hundred years . . ."[95] The results were riots, depositions, and divisions. The leaders in the patriarchates opposed their rivals. In Jerusalem, Theodosius opposed Juvenal. In Alexandria, Timothy Aelurus opposed Protarius. When Emperor Justin I came to power between 518-527 C.E., the Dyophysite position of the two natures was restored as the orthodox position and the Monophysites were deposed and many of them relocated to Alexandria. The division between Monophysite and Chalcedonian took place during the reign of Emperor Justin I (518-527) where the formula of 451 C.E. prevailed as the orthodox position... Following this event, the Monophysites splintered into two groups. Those who followed Severus maintained that the body of Christ before the resurrection was mortal and corruptible. Others who followed Julian of Halicarnassus maintained that the body of Christ was incorruptible before the resurrection.

The orthodox position is that Christ is both wholly God and wholly man. His deity is expressed in His essence but revealed in His attributes. Christ is eternal (John 8:58), omnipresent (Mathew 18:20), omniscient (Luke 6:80), omnipotent (Mathew 28:18), and immutable (Hebrews 13:8). Christ has the powers of deity which He has performed. He has acted in creation (Colossians 1; 16), preserves us (Hebrews1:3), forgives sins (Colossians 3:13), raised the dead (John 5:21), and will judge the world (II Corinthians 5:10). Christ has accepted the worship due only to deity (John 5:23). He has made the claim to be God (Luke 1:76).

The orthodox position was published in a manuscript produced at the Council of Chalcedon in 451 C.E. which stated:

> In agreement, therefore, with the holy fathers, we all unanimously teach harmoniously that we should confess

that our Lord Jesus Christ is one and the same Son, the same perfect in Godhead and the same perfect in manhood, truly God and truly man, the same of a rational soul and body, consubstantial with the Father in Godhead, and the same consubstantial with us in manhood, like us in all things except sin; begotten from the Father before the ages as regards His Godhead, in the last days, the same, because of us and because of our salvation begotten from the Virgin Mary, the Theotokos, as regards his manhood; one and the same Christ, Son, Lord, only-begotten, made known in two natures without confusion, without change, without division, without separation, the difference of the natures being by no means removed because of the union, but the property of each nature being preserved, and coalescing in one person (prosopon) and one hypostasis (hupostasis)— not parted or divided into two persons (prosopa), but one and the same Son, only begotten, divine Word, the Lord Jesus Christ, as the prophets of old and Jesus Christ himself have taught us about him, and the creed of our Fathers has handed down.[96]

This confession corrected various heresies regarding the deity of Christ. First, Ebionitism taught that Jesus was just an ordinary man, the literal son of Joseph and Mary, and possessed special but not supernatural powers. Second Arianism taught that Jesus was a created being who was similar to God but not of the same essence as God. It also corrected two heresies regarding the humanity of Christ. Docetism taught that Jesus only appeared to be a man in that His divinity just passed through Mary. Apollinarianism taught that although Christ had a human body and soul; He did not possess a human spirit. Rather the Divine Logos replaced His spirit making Him only partially human. Finally it corrected two different heresies regarding the natures of Christ. Nestorianism taught that Christ had two separate natures which in effect made Him into two separate persons. Monophysitism taught that Christ ended up with only one nature which was the result of mixing His divine and human natures into one new distinct and surviving third nature replacing the first two natures..." Five principles are helpful in formulating an exposition of the orthodox statement of Chalcedon.

1. The incarnation was more a gaining of human attributes than a giving up of divine attributes. This is directly related to the issue of the *kenosis*.
2. The union of the two natures means that they do not function independently. The divine nature of Christ was in some way limited by the circumstance of being in union with the human nature, but this is not a full limitation of his divine ability. Erickson provides an excellent illustration to make the point clear: if the world's fastest sprinter were running in a three-legged race, his union with another runner would limit his ability to run in that circumstance, but it would not limit his ability in himself to be the fastest sprinter in the world. In the same way Christ was limited by the circumstance of being in a human body, but this is not a real limitation of his deity.
3. Christ is fully God and fully human. This must be understood from the point of view that Christ reveals to us what *fully God* and *fully human* actually mean. Christ was not fully like us. We are fallen humanity, and he is full humanity. Christ has the same nature as Adam before the fall, which is not like our nature.
4. The incarnation is God becoming man, not man becoming God.
5. It is helpful to think of Jesus as a very complex person.[97]

Each of the formulas developed by man did not fully contemplate the mystery of Christ as God and as man. Each of these theological understandings over-emphasized either the deity or the humanity of Christ. When one nature is emphasized to the diminishment or replacement of the other then something is lost in our appreciation of Him. Also the redemptive plan of God is placed in jeopardy of fulfillment. Finally the Scripture references which speak of His deity or humanity are doubted, discounted or overlooked. The orthodox position of two complete natures of Christ allows for the redemptive plan of humanity and allows the truths of Scripture regarding his natures as both divine and human to be acknowledged. "There is no mixture of the divine and human attributes (as Eutychians taught), no change in either complex (as Apollinarians taught), no dividing of them and no separating them so as to have two persons (as Nestorians taught). Orthodoxy says two natures comprising one person or hypostasis forever".[98] However, the orthodox position does not explain the mystery of Christ as the God-man by a complete understanding to the human mind. As a definition one can agree that Christ is infinite and finite, unlimited and limited, eternal and temporal, Creator and creature, perfect and imperfect, and immutable and mutable. One can also accept these apparently conflicting attributes based on a firm and convicted faith which believes and acts upon these premises. But one cannot experience the mystery in life but must wait until the resurrection of life for oneself to occur as an actual experience. It is not possible to experience the mystery of Christ in a confession, creed, or formula which is based on the limitation of language and reason. It is a theanthropic process occurring in the incarnation which defies scientific investigation and proof and must be taken on faith.

The purpose of the incarnation of Christ is to redeem the human race. In this act the plan of God is put in motion to reconcile man back to God. The incarnation is the union of two natures into one person. It is not a transformation of God into man or man into God. It is not a mixing of the two but the union of the two where both retain all of their essence and attributes as we understand them as describing both God and man. The Logos is the second person of the Godhead. The Logos assumes the body, soul and spirit of a man. The man Jesus became like natural man in every way except that he neither assumed a sin nature nor actuated sin in His life. He was given to experience all of the deficiencies of human life such as suffering, pain, and death. The activity of the incarnation took place by an act of the Holy Spirit as the third person of the Godhead and a human being known as Mary.

Some of the controversy stemmed from the meaning ascribed to the words "nature" and "person". Some theologians used these two words interchangeably. A more appropriate word would be "being". "Nature" is the sum of the attributes of the "being". "Person" is the single self which is unique and personal. A "person" must have one or more natures. A "nature" need not be a "person". "The precise distinction between *nature* and *person*. Nature or substance is the totality of powers and qualities which constitute a being; person is the Ego, the self-conscious, self-asserting, and acting subject. There is no person without nature, but there may be nature without person (as in irrational beings)."[99] The Trinity is, by definition, three persons with a divine nature which is common to each divine person. The Logos is one person, the second member of the Godhead, who possesses a divine nature. The Logos did not unite with the human person Jesus but rather the nature of the Logos did unite with the human nature of Jesus. "It is primarily and pre-eminently a condescension and self-humiliation of the divine Logos to human nature, and at the same time a consequent assumption and exaltation of the human nature to inseparable and eternal communion with the divine person. The Logos assumes the body, soul, and spirit of man, and enters into all the circumstances and infirmities of human life on earth, with the single exception of sin, which indeed is not an essential or necessary element of humanity, but accidental to it."[100] The union is between two natures rather than two persons. The incarnation was an event initiated by the Godhead and acted upon by the second person of the Godhead which produced the God-man Jesus Christ. He was not the union of two persons as the Nestorians taught nor a mixture of two natures forming a single, separate, and unique nature as the Monophysites taught. Christ is one person, undivided, who has two complete natures consisting of the divine and the human.

The Eutychian Monophysites taught that Christ had two natures before the incarnation but afterwards had only one nature wherein the human nature was absorbed and replaced by the divine nature. The orthodox position was that the two natures were retained after the incarnation and remain so throughout eternity. This eternal union of the two natures in Christ is also maintained between the eternal unions of the three persons of the Trinity.

The person of Christ exists in a unity that is undivided and undiminished in eternity. The unity is theanthropic. Christ suffered and died as a man yet He rose and conquered death as God. The mystery of the incarnation is also seen in the mystery of the Trinity, the mystery of the body, soul, and spirit in man, and the mystery of the natural man and the spiritual regenerated man.

Christ's suffering occurred as the God-man. His person was not separated .The hypostatic union of the divine and human natures experienced the suffering and crucifixion. His redemption is an act of the divine because he conquered sin and death. His redemption is an act of the human because he suffered and died as humans do.

The Logos throughout eternity has been the second person of the Godhead. A person has a personality which is unique to that person and does not have the property of union with another person. However a divine person also took on the nature of man, thus becoming the God-man. God the Father is a separate person from Christ the Son but the divine nature in the Father is in union with the divine nature of the Son. The human nature of Christ originated at the incarnation based upon the union of the divine nature with the human nature. Thus the preexisting Logos is endowed with the perfect union of two natures at the incarnation whereby the result of this union is a God-man possessing the attributes of the divine and the attributes, excluding sin, of a human. The personality of the Logos is in union with the intellect and will of the human nature of Christ.

The development of the doctrine of the two natures of Christ was the result of differing attempts by theologians to explain the person and nature of Christ from Scripture and to build on the settled points of understanding while rejecting points of view which did not comply with the understanding which the theologians who argued successfully constituted as orthodox doctrine. The first to weigh in on the incarnation were the Gnostics. Because of their prior beliefs regarding the source of any matter and negative view of the flesh, the body, and the material; Gnostics rejected the doctrine that Christ had a human nature and therefore He was not a real person. Since anything which was a property of the physical creation was deemed evil, then it followed that Christ could not be interpreted as a man and still be God. Therefore, Christ was described as a spiritual being who only appeared to be a man. "The first group to challenge the traditional doctrine of the incarnation was the Gnostics, who in the 2nd century denied that Jesus was truly human. Their Greek belief that the physical creation was evil led them to deny the incarnation. They believed Christ to be a quasi-spiritual being who merely appeared human."[101] A leading spokesman for this view was Marcion who was influenced by his belief which rejected the history and truth of the Old Testament. Marcion was a leading Docetist whose views were accepted by many in the church during the first two centuries of the Christian era.

The second and third centuries were focused on three controversies which threatened the existence of Christianity. These were Arianism,

Apollinarianism, and Nestorianism. The Arian view of Christ argued that He was not fully God because in the incarnation He lost part of His divine nature. The Apollinarian view was that Christ possessed a real human body but that His soul was absorbed by the divine Logos. This was a unique way of explaining the incarnation by mixing component parts of the divine and human into the resulting person of Christ. Nestorius taught that the two natures remained separate and distinct in the one person of Christ.

The balance was found in the resulting orthodox position at the Council of Chalcedon which stated that Christ in the incarnation possessed a fully divine nature and a fully human nature in one person. This balance satisfied God's redemptive plan because as God in human form and flesh, Christ suffered and died as a perfect and sinless being for human beings. In this act, He became an innocent substitute and paid the penalty of guilty sinners to a righteous Father. "The NT teaching on the incarnation balances the humanity and divinity of Christ. Those two facts must harmonize in any theological system, for both are absolutely necessary parts of God's redemptive plan. In the incarnation, Jesus became a perfect human being. As God in human flesh, he suffered the divine penalty for sin as an innocent substitute. Being both God and a man, Jesus simultaneously revealed God's will for human life and reconciled sinful people to God through his own perfect life and death. Because of the incarnation, therefore, those who believe in Christ have peace with God and new life from God."[102]

The Two Nature Belief of Church Leaders Deemed Orthodox

The first challenge from the New Testament heretics came from the Docetists who claimed that Christ was a spiritual being and not a real person. Despite the Scriptural references to Christ's suffering and pain and the statements of the apostle John that Jesus had come in the flesh, this view maintained that Jesus was not a real, human person (I John 4:2-3;II John 2:7). The orthodox view stated that Jesus was fully human. The second person of the Godhead united with the human mind and body of Christ in perfect harmony. Christ could draw upon His divine nature to act on those powers as He sought fit to do while in the flesh. This did not diminish His compliance and sacrifice as a human in the flesh to suffer and die as all humans suffer and die. The only difference between Christ and human beings was that He knew no sin such that His death could be a substitute sacrifice for all others who did know sin. "Jesus, being divine, was impeccable (could not sin), but this does not mean he could not be tempted."[103] Jesus as a person could be tempted to sin but was able through His divine power to resist temptation in order to redeem humanity for all those who believe in Him (Hebrews 2:18). In this way Christ could fulfill the redemptive plan of God to restore humanity to fellowship with God.

Justinian I (482-565 C.E., emperor from 527-565 C.E.) spent most his life in Constantinople where he became an Orthodox Christian. Politically he was successful against the enemies of the Roman Empire. He sought to dominate the church by appointing and deposing various patriarchs and bishops of his liking. He believed in the divine right of kings with the purpose of protecting the church and spreading Christianity. He was the emperor who condemned the church father, Origen, as a heretic. "In 542 and 543 Justinian condemned the teaching of the church father Origen (c. 185-254), whose teaching was popular with Palestinian monks. The emperor's edict placed Origen himself under anathema, an action taken with the support of the bishops and Pope Vigilius."[104]

His major importance occurred in his interference in attempting to resolve the dispute which continued following the Council of Chalcedon in 451 C.E. regarding the two natures of Christ. Many theologians accepted the one nature of Christ argument of the Monophysite view. In order to attempt reconciliation, Justinian I condemned the writings of Theodore of Mopsuestia, Theodoret of Cyrus, and Ibas of Edessa for being Nestorian in separating Christ into two separate persons. This had been resolved in the condemnation of Nestorius at the Council of Ephesus in 431 C.E. This was known as the condemnation of the Three Chapters. "The whole incident proved fruitless, angering the Monophysites in the East and the pope in the West. The resulting schism between Rome and Constantinople lasted until 610."[105]

Leo the Great was a pope, who authored the Tome of Leo, condemned Eutyches, and denounced the Monophysites at the Council of Chalcedon. He was disappointed in the canon of the Council which elevated the Bishop of Constantinople to the position of Patriarch which threatened his own influence and importance in the Eastern portion of the Empire. Leo was active in political affairs as he convinced the advancing Attila the Hun and his armies to withdraw from the siege of Rome. He later convinced the Vandal leader Gaiseric to limit the looting of Rome and spare the city from destruction. He served in office as pope from 440-461 C.E. "Leo's leadership in these political crises helped begin the long process by which the bishop of Rome became the most powerful Western figure in the Middle Ages."[106] He was influenced by the positions of Tertullian and Augustine regarding the nature of Christ. "The notion determining the thinking of both Leo and the subsequent period was that the divine person Christ engaged his own humanity as an instrument of action for the sake of redemption, and in this situation Christ's human nature is conceived as being wholly passive and essentially determined only by sinlessness (the virgin birth!), while Christ himself acts in his capacity as the Divine Word. Chalcedon was thus quite correct in committing itself to the *anhypostasia* of the human nature."[107]

Simplicius succeeded Leo in 468 C.E. As pope he had to deal politically with the conquering barbarian king Odoacer who claimed rule over the western Empire from Rome in 476 C.E. which is the historical date for the fall of Rome. He was a strong supporter of the position of the Council of Chalcedon.

Pulcheria was Empress at Constantinople from 450 C.E. assuming power following her brother Theodosius II who served as Emperor from 408-450 C.E. "A palace coup on the death of Theodosius in 450 brought to power his formidable sister, Pulcheria, a bitter enemy of the 'one nature' theologians who had found political backing in Constantinople."[108] She was a strong supporter of the orthodox position which was not fully enunciated until 451 C.E. She arranged for the convening of that Council. She led the condemnation charge against Nestorius. The controversy over the explanation as to whether Christ following the Incarnation has one nature or two natures is important in determining a standard which marks the limits of accepted belief. This settled belief becomes normative and becomes a hedge guarding the central core understanding of Christianity. However the process which is based on debate and majority vote by flawed human beings with good intentions is divisive, leaves scars, and turns the focus away from spreading the gospel. The institutions of the schools and the church offices and councils lengthened the process of correspondence, debate, and voting resolution. Ultimately the orthodox Byzantine churches lost the opportunity to spread eastward and the unity within the empire in Egypt, Syria, Palestine, and Armenia was broken. With the loss of religious unity the political unity was jeopardized making first the southern portions of the empire vulnerable to the forces of a new religion known as Islam.

In summary we have discussed both the one nature and two nature beliefs of church leaders during the period. Those supporting the one nature view of Christ were deemed heretical. Those proposing the two nature's view of Christ were deemed orthodox.

CHAPTER 4

**HISTORICAL TIMELINE OF THE
MONOPHYSITE CONTROVERSY**

The historical timeline of the Monophysite controversy involves the progression of people and events which engaged Christian theologians and emperors preceding, during, and following the controversy. During the first century C.E., the Ebionites, who were Jewish Christians, rejected the Virgin Birth of Christ. Various theologians taught the belief in Gnosticism which was a dualistic philosophy consisting of good and evil cosmic forces. "The consequence of this mythology is that Gnosticism, which begins by affirming a single principle of all being, ends by asserting a radical dualism with reference to actual existence. Spiritual reality, which either resides in the eons or proceeds from them, is good, whereas material reality, coming as it does from the error of an eon, is evil."[109] Gnostics denied the incarnation of Christ as only an illusion. "Evil, therefore, was independent of God and resulted from the actions of another deity, namely the God of the Old Testament Yahweh, the chief of the creator angels. True Christians, therefore, would reject the Old Testament and confess Christ, but not Jesus as crucified as that was merely material worship."[110] Marcion denied any connection between Christ and Judaism as either ideology or history. "Marcion did not believe in a long series of 'eons'. He held, rather, that the God Yahweh of the Old Testament was not the same as the Father who sent Jesus to the world."[111] He further rejected the incarnation and resurrection of Christ. Irenaeus defended Christianity against Gnosticism. "God's purposes include not only the spiritual creation, but also the material. Irenaeus was convinced that, as part of the process of salvation, there will be an earthly kingdom 'which is the commencement of incorruption, by means of which kingdom those who shall be worthy are accustomed gradually to partake of the divine nature'."[112] Tertullian was the first church theologian to ascribe the term Trinity to the Godhead. "Tertullian's Christology, like his Trinitarian doctrine, is remarkable because he is the first to employ the terms which eventually became the hallmark of orthodoxy; two natures, or substances, in one person."[113] Several early heretical beliefs surfaced during the early church period prior to 300 C.E. Monarchianism taught that there was a single unity of the Father in the Godhead. Adoptionists taught the concept that the Father only adopted the Son. Modalism was the belief that God succeeds in modes from the Father to the Son to the Holy Spirit. This was also known as Sabellianism. The tradition of the theologians of Alexandria was rooted in Greek philosophy. An early Alexandrian theologian known as Origen taught several concepts which were prevalent until his condemnation in 400 C.E. Origen taught: (1) allegorical interpretation of Scripture to find the deeper meanings of the text, "Philo, on the contrary, saw an allegorical meaning in every single incident. Origen was influenced by him in this respect: he too held that *every* scriptural text without exception had a spiritual meaning."[114] (2) Christ as the Logos was subordinate to the Father, "Obedience, then, requires us too to say that if the Saviour and the Spirit transcend all creatures not in degree but in kind, they are in turn transcended by the Father . . ."[115] (3) salvation as a result of the Fall can be attained by human effort, "In the end, there will be a total restoration, so that the end will be just like the beginning."[116] (4) human freewill is good, "His universe is a world of free beings."[117] and (5) all humans will eventually be saved. "Origen regards the fall as universal. The second class are those in between, the *terrestria*, the human race, who are helped by the first class and thereby enabled to recover their lost happiness."[118]

During the period of the early church up until the time of the enthronement of the Emperor Constantine, Roman political authority accepted any religion if it had a lengthy prior tradition. "The fear of chaos if the Roman Empire fell was shared even by Jews and Christians. . . . Roman citizens were expected to revere and serve the roman gods and not to practice any alien cult . . . Common worship of the gods was both the symbol and the proof of a united Empire."[119] "Christianity was henceforth associated with 'evil religion' (*prava religio*) in the eyes of the ruling classes of the empire. It was not legal religion (*religio licita*)."[120] During this period of church persecution, Rome was suspect of Christianity due to: (1) lack of tradition, "To opt for Christianity was also to opt for a religion that had no claim to acceptance by the standards of antiquity or as a national cult, such as Judaism had."[121] (2) exclusivity claims, "Celsus accused the Christians of being a revolutionary sect, bound to each other by oaths, and intent on subverting the established order of society."[122] (3) refusal to honor the imperial cult, (4) and for refusal to join the military. " . . . typically one finds Clement of Alexandria condemning it as contrary to the Christian spirit. While Origen saw no place for Christians in the imperial armies . . ."[123] "The Romans were traditionally tolerant of the beliefs of others, willing to allow a wide diversity as long as believers supported the state and did not outrage the Roman sense of decency."[124] Challenges to Christianity during this period also came from the East. The Manichaean cult and the Sassanian religion of Zoroastrianism threatened the concepts of the Godhead. "Dualism, when it appeared in the West, came as an import from Persia, where the teachings of Zoroaster, and later of Mani (third century AD) provided the intellectual base for a dualistic religion of opposing forces."[125] In 313 C.E. Constantine succeeded to the throne of the Roman Empire and established his capitol at Constantinople. With this change, Christianity became both legal and the norm within the empire. Constantine had to deal with the Donatist controversy in North Africa. "When confronted with the choice of empire or Christian church in 250, the great majority of Christians played safe and sacrificed."[126] "The split was never healed, and it remained a source of weakness in North African Christianity for centuries until the Church there faded away."[127] This he did decisively in tolerating Christians who had fallen away from the faith during a period of martyrdom. His primary goal was to maintain peace and order within the Roman Empire. His next theological challenge came from the Egyptian theologian Arius. In doing so, he convened the Ecumenical Council at Nicaea in 325 C.E. Arius had maintained that the Logos did not share the same essence, or eternality as the Father, and was a created being.

Exposing these weaknesses was largely the work of Athanasius in the great anti-Arian treatises written some decades after the Nicene Council. He was able to show that the whole hierarchical approach was actually undermined by Arius' kind of subordinationism. The Logos could no longer be the Mediator because in principle he shared nothing of the divine nature, except by grace. He was not *essentially* one with God. God's own internal reason or Logos had no connection with the logos he created. His was not the true divine Wisdom but only a kind of image of it. So he had no real knowledge of God and could not really reveal him. He was not essentially god's son at all, simply a creature adopted by God as his agent. He could not communicate the divine, because he was not himself divine. This was inevitably the death-knell of a hierarchical approach: either the Logos was God or he was a creature and he could not be both.[128]

The Council Rejected the Ideology of Arius "If God is eternal and unknowable as Plato pictured him, Jesus Christ cannot be in the same sense God, since we know of him and of his deeds through the Gospels. This means, since the supreme God is one, that Christ must in some respect come after and be other than the Father, even if we accept that he was created or begotten before all the worlds."[129]

During this same period Latin Christianity, headquartered in Rome, was less influential than Greek Christianity in the East. The Bible was translated into Latin in 400 C.E. While the power of Western bishops was slow in developing, it finally emerged. Augustine was a Latin speaking theologian from North Africa. He saw original sin as passed on through the act of procreation. "All children were procreated in their parents' lust."[130] He saw evil as non-existence, which was in opposition to his previous belief in an active evil force as believed by the Manicheans. "He eventually found his solution in the teaching of the Neoplatonists—that evil is not an entity, but a deprivation of good."[131] He taught that the universal Church on earth was like the heavenly city. Augustine taught election, predestination, and the Trinity as three equal persons of the same substance. Pelagius taught that in our free will, we could lead moral lives worthy of salvation. "Pelagius did teach that once a believer had repented and begun moving toward good works, God's grace intervened, granting the repentant sinner forgiveness of sins and strengthening the will in its resolve to do good works. Thus sinners were not expected to erase their own sins, but simply to repent and correct their lives, whereupon God would grant forgiveness."[132] Rome became a pilgrimage destination. Martin of Tours formed the first monastery in the West about 361 C.E. John Cassian was a monastic leader who balanced the concepts of grace and responsibility.

The recordings of the councils of the church provided the narrative in a chronology of this period. Ecumenical councils are considered to produce binding authority. Doctrinal decrees are considered to be timeless, absolute, and unalterable. The primary statement of faith that would be the result of a given ecumenical council would be the publication of a creed.

In addition, any number of canons would be produced which would state either church discipline or organization. The ecumenical councils of the early church included Nicaea--325 C.E., Constantinople I--381 C.E., Ephesus--431 C.E., Chalcedon--451 C.E., Constantinople II--553 C.E., and Constantinople III--680-81 C.E. Conciliar tradition actually goes back to the apostolic age (Acts 15). The origin of the term "ecumenical" dates to 451 C.E. The term "ecumenical" implies producing binding authority. Generally the councils were attended by bishops, and on occasion by presbyters and deacons. The attendants were usually numbered in the hundreds and during these six councils were predominantly from the Eastern portion of the church. "The west, while it accepted the decisions of the Ecumenical Councils, did not play a very active part in the Councils themselves . . ."[133]Voting on any decree had to be by a significant majority decision. The Nicene Council of 325 C.E. was convened primarily to define the divinity of Christ in the Trinity, to denounce the teachings of Arius, and to define and determine the application of the term "consubstantial". "For the Nicenes, the Son, their head, consubstantial with God, true God from true God, was King of Kings and protector of the Church."[134] The Council of Constantinople of 381 C.E. was conducted in order to confirm the Nicene Creed and to further develop the concept of the Trinity. "It seems clear that the council's primary object was to restore and promote the Nicene faith in terms which would take account of the further development of doctrine, especially with regard to the Holy Spirit, which had taken place since Nicaea."[135]The Council of Ephesus in 431 C.E. considered the issues of Christology. "Theologically, what was the battle all about? It began . . . over the title 'Mother of God', but support of the title or opposition to it involved differing Christologies."[136]The Council of Chalcedon of 451 C.E. dealt with issues of divinity and humanity, was concerned with the doctrine of Christology, and focused on the usage of the words "same", "like", "essence", "substance", "person", and "nature". "The Council declared itself opposed to those who affirmed a double Sonship, who said that the Godhead of the Only-Begotten is passible who imagined a mixture or confusion of the two natures of Christ, who taught that the form of a servant, the flesh, of Christ is from heaven, and who feigned that the Lord had two natures before the union, but only one after."[137]The Council of Constantinople II of 553 C.E. centered on the acceptance of the Three Chapters which condemned the three supporters of Nestorius. "...the bishops condemned Theodore of Mopsuestia and his writings, certain writings of Theodoret, and the letter said to have been written by Ibas."[138] The Council of Constantinople III of 680--81 C.E. was concerned with the doctrine of two wills, which is known as Monothelitism. In all the Council of Nicaea produced a total of 20 canons and the Council of Constantinople III produced a total of 102 canons. As a result of these councils, the Nestorians broke from the orthodox church after the Council of Ephesus of 431 C.E. Likewise; the Monophysites broke from the orthodox church after the Council of Chalcedon 451 C.E.

Description of the Events During the Monophysite Controversy

The events leading up to the Council of Nicaea were many and varied. The Ebionites denied Jesus' Virgin Birth and his eternal preexistence. Some emphasized Jesus' name, such as "He is the Law" and "He is the Chief Angel," both of which are terms from the Old Testament. The Greek Gnostics emphasized Jesus as an emanation from Wisdom. The Demiurge emits the spirit into the human soul, which was consubstantial. "Valentinus, following Plato, uses the Greek term for 'creator' (*demiurgos*), suggesting that he is a lesser divine being who serves as the instrument of the higher powers."[139] Marcian taught that there were two gods; one Supreme of the New Testament, and one lesser Creator God of the Old Testament. "Yahweh was an inferior god who made the world either out of ignorance, or out of spite against the Supreme God, and placed us in it. Above Yahweh is the loving father of Jesus."[140] "Gnosticism took up a negative attitude to the world and formulated a theology which set over against this evil world with its evil creator a supreme God who had nothing to do with this world."[141] Irenaeus taught the preexistent Word became incarnate, fully divine and fully human. ". . . divinity and humanity are perfectly compatible, since humanity was made for communion with the divine."[142] Adoptionists taught that Jesus was a mere man uniquely indwelt by God. Monarchians taught the unity of God and the divinity of Christ, with no distinction from the Father. Adoptionists include Theodotus and Paul of Samosata, bishop of Antioch from 260-268 C.E. These theologians taught that Jesus' moral progress gained him the title of Son of God. They claim that Jesus and God are not consubstantial. Tertullian taught that the Father, Son, and Holy Spirit are conjoined, of one substance; but the phases, aspects, and manifestations are all of one indivisible God. He ultimately subordinated the Son to the Father. Novatian taught the Son was and is always in the Father, but the

Son returns divinity back to the Father as Son and is subordinate to Him. "According to Novatian, since the Son is begotten of the Father, he is always in the Father; otherwise the Father would not always be the father. Yet the Father is antecedent to the Son, and because the Son is in the father and is born of the Father, He must be less than the Father."[143] Dionysius, bishop of Alexandria from 248-265 C.E., had claimed that Jesus was a created being, where all three persons of the Godhead consist of three substances. "He wrote that' . . . that the Son of God is a work of God, a thing that was made, not by his own nature God, but other than the father in respect to His substance . . ."[144] "He spoke of three substances(hypostases), that is, three distinct subsistent beings in the Godhead."[145] Origen made the Son subordinate to the Father. "The Father is in consequence greater than the Son, for as Christ said, 'The Father is greater than I,' and the Son is in turn greater than the Holy Spirit."[146] The views of Arius included: the literal interpretation of Scripture, the unity of God, and the distinguishing between the Logos and God. God does not share his essence with any other. "Fundamental to his system is the absolute transcendence and unicity of God who is Himself without source but is the source of all reality."[147] The Logos is a non-eternal created being. "The Word had a beginning; though born outside of time, prior to the generation or creation he did not exist."[148] Arius was supported in his views by Eusebius of Nicomedia. All of these different views of the Trinity and the nature of Christ were prevalent preceding the Council of Nicaea. By the time of the Council of Nicaea in 325 C.E., attending theologians settled upon the publication of a creed which had several doctrinal points: First the creed declared that the Son was of the same substance as the Father. Second the Son was begotten rather than made out of nothing. Third the Son was co-eternal with the Father. Fourth the Son was immutable in His will. "It is clear that the Arians could easily accept the phrases 'begotten from the Father' and 'only begotten,' for they could understand begotten as the equivalent of made from nothing by the creative fiat of the Father."[149] "The vitally important phrase in the orthodox reply to Arianism was 'of one substance (homoousios) with the Father.' This phrase asserts that the Son shares the same being as the father, and is therefore fully divine."[150] There were those however who objected to the concept of the same substance for reason that: (1) if the Father and Son are of the same substance then this material must be able to be separated, (2) the Father and Son are of the same substance, which is indistinguishable, and (3) the term used to describe same substance, which is *homoousious*, is not found in Scripture. The arguments which were addressed at the Council of Nicaea were generally between a group demanding Alexandrian orthodoxy versus a group supporting the views of Arius. The Nicene claimed that the historical nature of Christ is such that he redeemed man in salvation. Arius believed the Logos reigned in heaven, while the emperor reigned on earth. Nicene bishops traced their heritage back to the apostles. Arian bishops were focused on appointment to office by the then current emperor. Nicenes valued a heavenly kingdom. Arian's valued an earthly kingdom. This chronology of events is focused on Constantine, Arius, Athanasius, and the Trinity.

The second major event was the Council of Constantinople I which occurred in 381 C.E. Western bishops in attendance avowed one hypostasis in the Godhead. Eastern bishops who attended avowed three hypostases in the Godhead. "The creed exemplifies the abiding concern of the East to safeguard the distinction of the Three as opposed to the West's insistence on the divine unity."[151] The leading theologian for the concept of one hypostasis was Athanasius who taught: (1) the Word became flesh to redeem humanity, (2) the Son existed from all eternity, (3) the Word is distinct from the Father, (4) the Father and Son possessed the same essence, (5), the divine nature is indivisible, and (6) the presentation of Father and Son are distinct. "Athanasius begins with the firm conviction that the Word became flesh to redeem the human race . . . He exists from all eternity . . . Nor does the Son come forth eternally from the Father. . . He belongs to the Father's very substance . . . The divine nature, however, is indivisible . . . the names denote distinct presentations of the divine being . . ."[152] During this council the Arians dominated the debate, which was conducted under the authority of Emperor Constantius. Apollinaris, bishop of Laodicea, from 361-390 C.E. taught the following: (1) the Son of God possessed one nature, (2) the Son did not possess a human mind or a rational soul, (3) the divine flesh is worthy of worship. "The flesh of the Savior, therefore, is not something super added to the Godhead; rather it constitutes one nature with the Godhead . . . The Word himself has become flesh without having assumed a human mind . . . Christ's flesh is the proper object of worship because there is in Him one incarnate nature of the Word . . ."[153] Emperors Jovian and Valentinian I were supporters of the Nicene Creed. Basil of Caesarea in Cappadocia accepted the formula of one essence and three hypostases in his understanding of the persons of the Godhead. "The only acceptable formula, he argued, is one *ousia,* three hypostases. *Ousia* meant for him the existence or essence or substantial entity of God; whereas hypostasis signified the essence in a particular mode, the manner of being of each of the three persons."[154] Theodosius became emperor in the East in 379 C.E., and he also supported the Nicene Creed. In 381 C.E., Theodosius convened the Council of Constantinople I with 150 Eastern bishops in attendance . . . therefore Theodosius proceeded to convoke a regional council of eastern bishops to ratify the new order. In May, 381, 150 eastern bishops assembled in the imperial palace at Constantinople . . ."[155] Timothy was bishop of Alexandria at this time. Gregory of Nazianzus was bishop of Constantinople. The Creed of Constantinople I was not published for 70 years until 451 C.E. Part of the Creed was intended to win support from the thirty-six Macedonian bishops who attended the council, but failed to do so. "It is possible that during Gregory's presidency the Council discussed the doctrine of the Holy Spirit and attempted to conciliate the Macedonian faction on the basis of a creed embodying the faith of Nicaea. In this the bishops failed, Eleusius of Cyzicus led the thirty-six Macedonian bishops out of the Council."[156] The Creed stated as follows: (1) the Holy Spirit's title is Lord, (2) the Holy Spirit gives life, (3) the Holy Spirit proceeds from the Father, and (4) the Holy Spirit should be worshiped. ". . . the Council declared its faith in the Holy Spirit in phrases drawn from the Bible. In II Cor. 3:17 the Holy Spirit is clearly called 'Lord;' in Rom.8:2 the Spirit is associated with life . . ."[157] ". . . the Holy Spirit proceeds or goes forth from the father in a manner different from that of the Son . . ."[158] At this time the see of Constantinople became primary over all other sees in the East. Flavian was elected Bishop of Antioch in 382 C.E. This chronology of events is focused on Theodosius, Apollinaris, the three Cappadocians, and the Holy Spirit.

    The Council of Ephesus was held in 431 C.E. Theodosius I had died in 395 C.E. The early to late fifth century was a period of invasion by German and Hun barbarians. "By the time of the Council of Ephesus, throughout much of the West the Germans were raising new kingdoms, replacing the majestic Roman law with primitive barbarian custom, worshipping according to their Arian Christian faith."[159] Theodosius II presided over this council. John Chrysotom of Antioch was appointed the bishop of Constantinople. Cyril became bishop of Alexandria in 412 C.E. Nestorius was appointed the bishop of Constantinople in 428 C.E.

Nestorius wanted to eliminate the term "Theotokos" from usage regarding Mary's title in favor of "Christotokos". Nestorius represented the Antiochene tradition where he was schooled. "By the end of 428, one of the Antiochene clergy whom Nestorius had brought with him to the capital began to preach against the *Theotokos,* the title Mother of God as applied to Mary . . ."[160] Cyril represented the Alexandrian tradition. "Nestorius represented the Antiochene tradition; Cyril, the Alexandrian"[161] The Antiochene tradition focused on how Jesus the man became God. "Nestorius this time replied with force, retorting that the Nicene Fathers did not teach that the consubstantial Godhead was passible or that the one co-eternal with God had been begotten. The very phrase 'one Lord Jesus Christ, his only –begotten Son' showed how the Fathers had carefully laid side by side the names belonging to each nature so that one Lord is not divided, while at the same time the natures are not in danger of confusion because of the singleness of Sonship."[162] The Alexandrian tradition explained how the Logos described in the Gospel of John took on human flesh. Apollinaris supported the one nature concept of Christ. "Diodorus decisively rejected the one nature theory of the Apollinarians." [163] Theodore of Mopsuestia taught the complete humanity of Christ. "More remains of the controversial Theodore of Mopsuestia who against the Arians and Apollinarians stoutly defended the full humanity of Christ."[164] God indwelt both the body and soul of Christ. Christ is a single person, where the two natures are neither confused nor the person divided. "For Theodore, the Word took to Himself not just a body but a complete man, body and soul . . . The coming together of the Word as man resulted in a single person or *prosopon* 'Thus there results neither any confusion of the natures nor any untenable division of the person; for in our account the natures must remain unconfused, and the person must be recognized as indivisible'."[165] Nestorius taught that: (1) Christ had two natures, (2) each nature was objectively real, (3) each nature remained unaltered and distinct in the union, (4) there was no mixture or confusion of the natures, (5) there is one person in Christ with two natures as God and man, (6) the two natures are conjoined, (7), the divine nature is immutable, (8) the human nature suffered.

Nestorius held that in Christ there are two natures . . . These metaphysical distinctions meant in the end not that each nature was an actually subsistent entity but that each nature was objectively real. These two natures remained unaltered and distinct in the union. . . . Divinity and humanity remained objectively real . . . 'Christ is indivisible in His being Christ, but He is twofold in His being God and man. . . . ' The two natures, then, are not for Nestorius two persons juxtaposed in loose connection but are conjoined in one . . . Nestorius shared with all the Fathers the conviction that the divine nature is immutable . . . real redemptive life on earth, the suffering, death and resurrection cannot be predicated of the Word Himself but only of Christ . . .[166]

Cyril wrote to Nestorius a letter containing Twelve Anathemas about 430 C.E. Cyril's remarks to Nestorius were as follows: (1) Mary is Theotokos, (2), the Word was personally united to the flesh, (3) Christ cannot be divided into divine and human, (4) the single person Christ is worshiped, (5) the Word suffered but only in its human nature, (6) there was no confusion or mixing of natures, (7) the external Word was the same before and after the incarnation, (8) Christ had one nature with two different properties.

". . . the Word, having for us and our salvation personally united to Himself a human nature . . . We do not say that God the Word suffered in His own divine nature, for the Godhead is impassible. But inasmuch as that which had become His own body suffered, we say that he Himself suffered for us . . . we worship one and the same Lord . . . So the Virgin is called *Theotokos* . . . The human and divine in the one Christ cannot be divided . . . Yet there was no confusion or mingling of the divine and human . . . he preferred to talk of two natural properties or qualities."[167]

The Council of Ephesus opened in 431 C.E. with 160 bishops attending. Nestorius was condemned and deposed with the opposition led by Cyril. John of Antioch and his forty-three likeminded bishops supported Nestorius. Bishop Nestorius and those bishops of the East Oriental church accepted Theotokos as Mary's title. Theodoret of Cyrus reluctantly accepted this Creed but refused to condemn Nestorius. Theadore of Mopsuestia was the mentor of Nestorius. Ibas of the Edessa propagated the views of Nestorius. The Nestorians moved to Nisibis in Persia. They were expelled from Edessa in 489 C.E. by Emperor Zeno. Cyril's radical followers became Monophysites in Syria. " . . . Nestorians still live on. After the Council Ibas continued to propagate Nestorius' view at Edessa. As the Monophysites, the more radical followers of Cyril, began to win over Syria, the Nestorians gradually moved into Persia and established a center at Nisibis."[168] This chronology of events is focused on

Theodosius II, Cyril of Alexandria, Nestorius, Christological nature, and the Virgin Mary.

The Council of Chalcedon was held in 451 C.E. Eutyches was an Eastern monk and advocate of Cyril. He taught: (1) before the incarnation, Christ had two natures, but afterward he had one nature, (2) the flesh of Christ was not consubstantial with human beings, (3) the two natures were in effect equal to two persons. "Eutyches began to teach that before the incarnation Christ was of two natures, but after it there was one Christ, one Son, one Lord in one hypostasis and one prosopon . . . the flesh of Christ was not in his view consubstantial with ordinary human flesh. . . . to affirm two natures was for him to affirm two concrete existences, two hypostases, two persons in Christ."[169] At this time, Pope Leo wrote a Tome to Flavian which provided that the Antiochene position of the reality and independence of the two natures should be accepted and the Alexandrian position that the person of the incarnate is identical with the Divine Word. "Leo agreed to send legates and provided them with letters to the Emperor, Flavian, the Council and the monks of Constantinople. Among these letters was the famous Tome to Flavian in which Leo summarized the Christology of the West."[170] "The Antiochenes could find here insistence on the reality and independence of the two natures; the Alexandrians, Cyril's basic insight that the person of the Incarnate is identical with that of the Divine Word."[171] He hoped to reconcile the two opposing parties at the council. A prior council was called at Ephesus in 449 C.E., which was termed the Robber Council. This council was called by Flavian, patriarch of Constantinople, with 170 bishops in attendance. At this council Eutyches was declared orthodox while Flavian and Ibas of Edessa were deposed. "Then with Dioscurus leading the chorus, the assembly approved Eutyches' profession of two natures before the Incarnation, one afterward."[172] Cyril's Twelve Anathemas were accepted denouncing Nestorius. Pope Leo denounced the council's findings. Emperor Theodosius II died in 450 C.E. Pulcheria, his sister, became empress and married a general named Marcian who became emperor as a result. They denounced both Eutyches and Flavian in 450 C.E. The Council of Chalcedon was held in 451 C.E. with 500 bishops in attendance. Dioscurus, a proponent of the one nature view, was deposed. The council reaffirmed the Nicene Creed, the Constantinople I Creed, Cyril's three letters to Nestorius, and the Tome of Leo. "Then after investigating the authenticity of the Creed of Constantinople I with which many bishops were not familiar, the Council accepted that Creed not as supplying any omission but as an authentic interpretation of the faith of Nicaea . . . The definition also stated that the Council 'has accepted the synodal letters of the blessed Cyril . . . Coupled with Cyril's letters was the Tome of Leo . . ."[173] The Chalcedonian Creed included the following definitions: (1) Christ is to be distinguished as one person with two natures, (2) there is no separation, division, or confusion in Christ, (3) Christ is immutable and impassable, (4) Christ's natures are joined, (5) Mary is to be called Theotokos.

Wherefore, following the holy Fathers, we all with one voice confess our Lord Jesus Christ one and the same Son, the same perfect in Godhead, the same perfect in manhood, truly God and truly man, the same consisting of one substance with the Father as touching the Godhead, the same of one substance with us as touching the manhood, like us in all things apart from sin; begotten of the Father before the ages as touching the Godhead, the same in the last days, for us and for our salvation, born from the Virgin Mary, the Theotokos, as touching the manhood, one and the same Christ, Son, Lord, Only-begotten, to be acknowledged in two natures, without confusion, without change, without division, without separation; the distinction in natures being in no way abolished because of the union . . .[174]

This Creed by definition was lacking in the following ways according to its opponents: (1) it left confusion over the meaning of the phrase "hypostatic union", (2) it required the believer to accept the suffering and death of the divine Word, (3) it postulated the deification of the humanity of Christ. "But the East found it wanting in clarity about the hypostatic union, the problems of predication, the single subject of suffering and death in Christ and the deification of the human begun in Christ."[175] Theodoret of Cyrus and Ibas of Edessa, who had been deposed as Nestorian, were restored based on the definition which they supported. Thirty church discipline canons were agreed to at this council. The patriarch of Constantinople was given authority over all Eastern bishops and Constantinople was elevated in status to second place after Rome. "Besides it was declared, as the see of the capital of the eastern Empire, to have equal privileges in ecclesiastical matters with the see of Rome but occupying second place in honor."[176] Timothy Aelurus and Peter Mongus, from Alexandria, supported Cyril's doctrine of one nature, thereby forming the Monophysite party. "Resistance centered in a faction headed by the priest Timothy (Aelurus) the Cat and the deacon Peter (Mongus) the Hoarse. They had no sympathy with the muddled theology of Eutyches but were stalwart Cyrillians. This party came to be known as the Monophysite, for adhering to the Cyrillian formula—one incarnate nature (*physis*) of the Divine Word."[177] They denounced the idea that Christ had two natures, which they defined as two persons. They thought the Chalcedonian definition was Nestorian. These post-Chalcedonian Cyrillians believed: (1) that hypostasis equaled "prosopon" (person), (2) Theodoret and Ibas should not have been restored, (3) Cyril's doctrine of one incarnate nature of the divine Word was wrongly omitted, (4) there was no mention of the hypostatic union, (5) Chalcedon added to the Nicene Creed, which was forbidden by the findings of the Council of Ephesus, (6) the person of the union was the preexistent person of the Word, and (7) the Word united with the flesh, which was consubstantial with our flesh.

Timothy complained that in the Definition of Chalcedon no mention was made of hypostatic union; nor of the phrase 'out of two' to show that Christ existed out of two disparate elements, the divine and the human, but not 'in two' natures which would be to separate the One Christ into two persons, as did Nestorius . . . The restoration of Nestorian-tainted Theodoret of Cyrus and Ibas of Edessa to their sees was further indication that the Council of Chalcedon was Nestorian. Finally, Chalcedon had added to the faith of Nicaea, something that the Cyrillian Council of Ephesus had forbidden . . . Timothy and the Cyrillians believed that without change in His divinity the eternal Word, consubstantial with the Father, truly became man in Jesus Christ . . . This is what the Council of Chalcedon had not clearly declared: that the person of the union was the pre-existent person of the Word.

Pulcheria died in 453 C.E. and Marcian died in 457 C.E. Timothy Aelurus was finally banished in 460 C.E. Emperor Zeno came to office in 474 C.E. Peter the Fuller, a Monophysite, became patriarch of Antioch in 475 C.E. Timothy Aelurus was restored as patriarch of Alexandria in 477 C.E. Rome was overthrown by Odovacar in 476 C.E. and was invaded in the Western provinces by Arian or pagan Germanic peoples. Emperor Zeno approved the Henoticon written by Acacius confirming the Nicene, Constantinople I, and Ephesian creeds; and the Twelve Anathemas of Cyril against Nestorius. Nestorius and Eutyches were both condemned. Peter the Fuller accepted the Henoticon. This chronology of events is focused on Pulcheria, Leo the Great, Eutyches, Christological natures, and the Monophysite controversy.

The Council of Constantinople II was held in 553 C.E. The Acacian schism began in 484 C.E. Anastasius I became emperor in 491 C.E. as a Monophysite. The Chalcedonian view was supported by patriarchs Macedonius of Constantinople, Flavian of Antioch, and Elias of Jerusalem. Severus was a Cyrillian Monophysite. His views opposed any mingling of natures in Christ and any manhood as a distinct nature. "In his Christology Severus was purely and simply Cyrillian, though more rigorous and obstinate in presentation. He opposed any mingling of natures in Christ, any manhood as a distinct nature."[178] He supported the following: (1) the Word is not transformed into flesh nor the flesh transformed into the Word (2) Christ had a single nature, (3) the single nature possessed a duality of qualities, properties, and characteristics, (4) hypostasis should be understood as "physis" (real, physical), (5) one concrete being sharing the essence of God and man, (6) there is a composition and union without confusion, "The flesh does not cease to exist as flesh, even if it becomes God's flesh, and the Word does not abandon His own nature . . . the Word is not changed into flesh. Christ was for Severus not a single essence, a single *ousia,* for to say this would be to deny all duality in the qualities and Christ's consubstantiality with us. Christ was rather a single nature. Severus taught a real duality within the one nature while avoiding all confusion between humanity and divinity . . . *Hypostasis* and *physis* Severus regarded as synonymous in the case of Christ, for He was one concrete, unique being sharing in the essence of God and the essence of man."[179] and (7) the hypostasis of union is the preexistent hypostasis of the Logos. "Chalcedon did not stress firmly enough for Severus that the hypostasis of union is the preexistent hypostasis of the Logos."[180] Severus was appointed patriarch of Antioch in 512 C.E. He accepted the Nicene, Constantinople I, and Ephesian creeds, and the Henoticon; but rejected Nestorius, Eutyches, the Council of Chalcedon, and the Tome of Leo. "In his place Severus himself was chosen patriarch. At his consecration, he solemnly professed the faith of Nicaea, Constantinople and Ephesus, and accepted the Henotikon, while condemning Nestorius, Eutyches, the Council of Chalcedon, Leo's Tome and all who held two natures in Christ."[181] John the Grammarian supported the Cyrillian view and the Monophysite view that Christ's single nature was constituted of two substances. John became patriarch of

Jerusalem. Anastasius died in 518 C.E. Justin I became emperor as an orthodox Chalcedonian. Severus left Antioch for Alexandria, which was a Monophysite stronghold. The Acacian schism ended in 519 C.E. when Justin accepted the Tome of Leo and the excommunication of emperors Zeno and Anastasius.

The Theopaschite Formula sought to unite the two opposing groups by stating that one of the Trinity suffered for us. "The colloquy seemed to have convinced Justinian that the Theopaschite Formula—One of the Trinity suffered for us—a formula designed to integrate Chalcedon and Cyril, was key to the reconciliation of the Monophysites."[182] An earthquake destroyed Antioch in 526 C.E. The Monophysites residing there fled to the safety of Egypt. Severus and Julian of Halicarnassus debated over the issue of the corruptibility of Christ's flesh. Severus taught the body suffered, whereas Julian taught that Christ's body suffered for the redemption of humanity and his body was like that of the pre-fallen Adam. "For Julian, pushing the doctrine of one nature in Christ to extremes, by nature Christ could not suffer. From the union of Word and flesh in Mary's womb, Christ was impassible. He admitted, however, that Christ had suffered, because he willed to do so for the sake of the economy of redemption, not because His body was subjected to the necessity of natural laws. In Julian's view, the capacity to suffer is a result of sin; Christ's body was consubstantial with the body of Adam before his fall into sin and not with man in his present sinful state."[183]

Justinian became emperor in 527 C.E. Justinian was orthodox, whereas his wife Theodora was a Monophysite. He codified the primacy of the Roman pope and secondary authority of the bishop of Constantinople. The pagan University of Athens was closed in 529 C.E. Justinian persecuted the Jews in Palestine, along with the Manicheans, Montanists, and Arians. Justinian accepted the Theopaschite Formula and the Twelve Anathemas of Cyril. Theodora placed two Monophysites in the bishop seats, Theodosius in Alexandria, and Anthimus in Constantinople in 535 C.E. "The Monophysites, centered in Egypt, controlled the grain exporting regions of the empire. And then there was Justinian's beloved Theodora: a Monophysite. In 544 Justinian published a tract, known as "The Three Chapters," in which he tried to find ground for compromise, but this satisfied nobody. Even after forcing his views through a church council, the Second Council of Constantinople (553), the issues were left unresolved."[184]

Severus was chased out of office by Menas, patriarch of Constantinople. Theodosius was deposed in 538 C.E. but spread Monophysitism to the Ghassanid Arabs and appointed Jacob Baradeus bishop of Edessa. The Three Chapters condemned the writings of the Antiochenes: Theodore of Mopsuestia, Theodoret of Cyrus, and Ibas of Edessa. "After consultation, it was agreed to condemn the person and whole works of Theodore of Mopsuestia (d. 428), the writings of Theodoret of Cyrus (d. 458) against the Cyrillians and the Letter to Maris the Persian of Ibas of Edessa (d. 457)."[185] Justinian supported this condemnation in 543 C.E. The patriarchs of Alexandria, Antioch, and Jerusalem also supported the condemnation. The pope and Western bishops refused to support the condemnation. Justinian supported: (1) the Chalcedonian definition, (2) the Twelve Anathemas of Cyril, (3) the Theopaschite Formula, and (4) the two natures of Christ, which are distinguished only in thought. "The emperor insisted on the Theopaschite Formula but not to the detriment of the Definition of Chacedon . . . Yet the two natures of Christ can only be distinguished 'by way of speech and thought and not as two distinct things' . . . the Theopaschite Formula (was) proclaimed; Cyril's Twelve Anathemas accepted."[186] The Council of Constantinople II was held in 553 C.E. with 151-68 bishops in attendance. The findings of this Council were as follows: (1) condemnation of the three Antiochenes, (2) the Trinity is consubstantial, (3) Christ had two births, from eternity and at the incarnation (4) Christ suffered in the flesh, (5) the unions proposed by Apollinaris, Eutyches, Theodore, and Nestorius were rejected, (6) the natures were not separated or confused, (7) the Word and flesh are hypostatically united in one person, (8) Mary is Theotokos, (9) Christ is consubstantial with the Father and with humanity, and (10) Arius, Apollinaris, Nestorius, Eutyches, and Origen were anathematized posthumously.

. . . the bishops condemned Theodore of Mopsuestia and his writings, certain writings of Theodoret and the letter said to have been written by Ibas . . . the bishops condemned first of all those refusing to confess a consubstantial Trinity . . . they rejected anyone who does not admit that the Word of God had two births . . . they were condemned who do not say that one and the same Lord Jesus Chris . . . . endured sufferings in His flesh . . . The union of divinity and humanity proposed by Apollinaris and Eutyches which produced a mixture of natures was rejected as was the relative union proposed by the followers of Theodore and Nestorius . . . 'the synthetical union not only preserves unconfusedly the natures which are united, but allows no separation' . . . the Word of God is united with the flesh hypostatically, and that therefore there is but one hypostasis or only one person . . . Mary' is exactly and truly Mother of God' . . . there is one Christ, both God and man, consubstantial with us touching his manhood . . . The eleventh canon gathered up the heretics of the previous three hundred years in a blanket condemnation—Arius, Eunomius, Macedonius, Apollinaris, Nestorius, Eutyches and Origen.[187]

The Christology of Evagrius was condemned. Hellenism and the Gospel were deemed to be incompatible. The Western church did not accept the findings of this Council. The Monophysites in Egypt and Syria were not satisfied with the findings of this Council either. Emperor Justin II issued a new Henoticon in 571 C.E. stating that there is only one real nature but with two natures existing in thought. ". . . Justin prepared a new Henotikon in 571, which recognized one sole incarnate nature, and a difference only in thought between the two natures, divine and human. Chalcedon was again ignored."[188] The imperially appointed orthodox bishops in Syria were called Melchite's and were replaced by Jacobites in 575 C.E. Syrian and Egyptian Monophysites were in dispute in 578 C.E. The Nestorians who had located in Persia condemned all Monophysites. Armenia remained Monophysite. The West did not accept the council's views until Constantinople III in 680-81 C.E. The chronology of events focused on Anastasius I, Justin I, Justinian, Theodora, Severus, and Theopaschism.

The Council of Constantinople III was held in 680-81 C.E. During the early seventh century Slavic peoples (Avars) flooded into the Balkans and Greece. Persia in 611 C.E. conquered Syria, Armenia in 613 C.E., Jerusalem in 614 C.E., and Egypt in 619 C.E. as a Zoroastrian power. The Byzantine counter offensive defeated the Persians in 628 C.E. Heraclius became emperor from 610-641 C.E. Sergius became patriarch of Constantinople beginning in 610 C.E. Sergius held to the two nature's doctrine, but insisted upon the one activity of Christ. "What Sergius evidently had in mind was to hold to the Chalcedonian definition of 'in two natures' but to reconcile this with a declaration of one activity in Christ."[189] This was known as Monoenergism. "In 624 conferences of the Monophysite leaders with the Emp. Heraclius resulted in producing a formula seemingly acceptable to both, which asserted two natures in Christ but only one mode of activity . . ."[190] Maximus the Confessor and

Sophronius both argued against Monoenergism. "Sophronius insisted that activity proceeds not from the person of Christ as the sole agent but from the two natures."[191] The argument proceeded from "activity" to "will" and by the time of 636 C.E. Pope Honorius and Patriarch Sergius taught that there was only one will in Christ. "For what Sergius and the emperor had decreed was that there is in Jesus Christ only one will and one truly free and spontaneous activity, the divine activity and will."[192] Maximus taught the Orthodox view of two natures, two operations, and two wills. "Christ has therefore two natures, two operations, two wills really proceeding from the divine and human natures but always in harmony because the single divine Person assures their goodness of choice."[193] Honorius died in 641 C.E. as did Heraclius. The two wills concept was deemed orthodox and accepted by the West. "Then coming to the heart of the matter, they declared that in Christ there are 'two natural wills and two natural operations indivisibly, incontrovertibly, inseparably, inconfusedly'."[194] The Council of Constantinople III was held in 680-81 C.E. with 174 bishops in attendance. The Monophysites rejected the two wills doctrine, which was the finding of this Council. "The controversy was finally settled by the Council of Constantinople in 681, which confirmed the decisions of a synod held at Rome in 680. The Council condemned the Monothelite formulas and their adherents, and proclaimed the existence of two wills in Christ, Divine and human, to be the orthodox faith."[195]

Arab Muslims conquered Syria in 634 C.E., Palestine in 639 C.E., Egypt in 642 C.E., Mesopotamia in 641 C.E., and Persia in 642 C.E. The sees of Alexandria and Jerusalem were eliminated forever. "During Justinian's rule and that of his son, the Empire shrank further as Armenia in eastern Asia-Minor and all North Africa were lost to the Arabs."[196] Monophysites and Nestorians were free to pursue their own beliefs as a result of the Muslim invasion. The Byzantine Empire was reduced to include Asia-Minor, Greece, and the Balkans. This chronology of events focused on Heraclius, the Muslim invasion, Cyrus of Alexandria, and Monothelitism.

Brief Explanation of the Events

Christianity initially began among the Jews. Jews believed in the continual revelation emanating from the Old Testament. This allowed that any new religion could be explained by the history of the Old Testament. In the first century, there were one million Jews in Alexandria and twelve synagogues in Rome. Mingled in with Jews in the synagogues were many Gentiles who were known as God-fearers who were not circumcised. During the Third Century B.C.E. the Greek speaking Jews of Alexandria had translated the Old Testament from the Hebrew into the Greek language. Many Christians in this early period believed in the concept that the Roman Empire had been providentially given by God. This was an age of persecution for Christians. Many church fathers were martyred for their faith including: Ignatius bishop of Antioch, Polycarp bishop of Smyrna, and Justin Martyr. Alternate religious beliefs, such as the Gnostics, believed in the Platonic concept of the immortality of the soul rather than the Christian concept of the resurrection of the body.

Whether or not the struggle began as early as Paul's lifetime the first to clarify the fundamental issues was Irenaeus, bishop of Lyons at the end of the second century. The different groups he criticizes certainly had different positions in detail. But the common features were (1) a distinction between the Creator God (the Demiurge) and the ultimate Father; (2) an account of the origin of all things which involved a pre-cosmic 'fall', so treating the material universe as the result of an accident or of sin; (3) an estimate of human nature which offered re-union with the divine for the spiritual elite, who were sparks trapped in the material universe, and who would be released by the secret 'knowledge' purveyed by the esoteric group, but dismissed the 'material' as beyond redemption, and regarded ordinary church members as second class.[197]

During this transition period following the death of the apostles, the central issue became who had the authority to interpret the Bible. Ignatius thought that it should be by a local bishop. "No amount of ingenuity can fully reconcile the differing accounts of the ministry to be found in *I Clement, the Letters of Ignatius and the Didache* respectively. Ignatius writes as though the norm of Church government was the bishop, priest and deacon, with absolute power in the hands of the bishop."[198] Clement of Rome taught that it should be from a succession of bishops following the apostles. The written letters of the New Testament began to replace the oral tradition of the apostles. The leadership of the church was formalized into specific offices such as bishops, presbyters, and deacons. "There were also 'prophets and teachers' as *Didache* shows, and in certain circumstances these could take precedence over the bishop in the administration of the Eucharist (*Didache* 10:7)."[199] But the regional leaders with apostolic authority were dying out and the power of the prophets was already on the wane."Unity in the early church was maintained by a mutual trust among Christians amidst persecution and martyrdom. Christianity was at first a *religio illicita,* a religion forbidden and persecuted by the government . . ."[200] Threats to Christianity from the outside included Judaizers, Gnostics, mystics, and pagans. Some of the early church fathers held beliefs which would later affect the future doctrines of the church. For example, Justin Martyr believed in the Platonic concept of the divine Logos linked to but separate from the Father. "He uses the concept of the divine Logos or Reason both to explain how the transcendent Father of all deals with the inferior, created order of things, and to justify his faith in the revelation made by God through the prophets and in Christ."[201] Justin's belief influenced Clement of Alexandria and his successor Irenaeus of Lyons. Irenaeus denounced Gnostic beliefs as heresies which were written to satisfy a person's curiosity. "Once more against the Gnostics, Irenaeus defined the basis of the Christian faith. God was one. The same God who created the universe was the God of Israel in the Old Testament. With him, Jesus Christ was united as his word and Son, and his coming had been predicated through the Holy Spirit by the Hebrew prophets. Moreover, Christ truly ministered, suffered and died and was received into Heaven, would rise at the Last day and be judged."[202] Irenaeus influenced Tertullian of Carthage. Tertullian taught that God is one substance consisting in three persons. "Here African theology, as defined by Tertullian in his attack on the Monarchian Praxeas by the neat formula of God as 'one substance' though of 'three persons' would have encountered opposition."[203] His writings on the Trinity influenced the document known as The Tome of Leo.

    Clement of Alexandria also denounced Gnosticism. He was influenced by Platonic concepts. His central principle centered on the fall of man following creation and man- kind's progression in life toward redemption. " . . the enlightened Christian advanced from faith toward knowledge . . . Like his Gnostic opponents, Clement saw spiritual perfection in intellectual terms . . ."[204] Origen was willing to use Greek philosophy to interpret Scripture. Origen taught that evil is the privation of goodness based on the misuse of free will. 'For Origen, therefore, Christ was the guide, educator and leader of mankind, revealing the whole essence of God so that man might rise toward god and be united to him."[205] He allegorized the interpretation of Scripture suggesting that there were deeper levels of meaning beneath the literal words. "And, just as the human frame consisted of the trinity of body, soul, and spirit, so interpretation of Scripture was to be understood under three headings, the literal, moral and spiritual. The moral meant the drawing out of some lesson from a text quite intelligible to the ordinary Christian, but the spiritual meaning was a higher and different order."[206] Origen believed that Christ was the pre-existent Logos. "It is important to realize that his own theology of the Logos (Word) was involved in answer to practical issues of the day."[207] Origens' writings influenced Jerome. Two early heretical beliefs included the writings of Dionysius of Alexandria and Paul of Samosata. Dionysius taught that the Father and the Son consist of different substances. "In one of his letters to a colleague explaining his views Dionysius himself had pressed his reasoning too far. The Son was described as a 'creature' and the three essences of father, Son and Holy Ghost were so separated as to be capable of being understood as three gods."[208] Paul taught that God and the Word are not differentiated but that Jesus is merely an inspired man. "In Antioch, the new Bishop, Paul of Samosata, 261-272 . . . asserted among other things that the Virgin Mary gave birth to a man . . ."[209]

Cyprian of Carthage wrote that the unity of the church was based on the authority of the bishop. Novatian claimed the bishop could not forgive a person guilty of apostasy. Cornelius and Cyprian claimed the opposite. Cyprian claimed sacraments administered by an apostate bishop were invalid. "It stood to reason that a minister who was himself outside the Church could not convey the Spirit in baptism, and thus an ex-heretic or schismatic would have to be baptized anew when he came into the Church."[210] The Donatist Schism in Africa lasted through the fourth century C.E.

Bishop Alexander of Alexandria was opposed by Arius, Eusebius of Caesarea, and Eusebius of Nicomedia. The Nicene Council denounced the Arian view that Christ was a created being inferior to the Father. Church organization was determined to be based on the secular provincial system. Those deposed by Eusebius of Nicomedia were Eustace bishop of Antioch, Athanasius bishop of Alexandria, and Marcellus bishop of Ancyra. Arius died in 336 C.E. and Constantine in 337 C.E. Emperor Constantius was an Arian. The leading Arian bishops succeeded in declaring the essence of Christ like that of the Father. "In the reign of Constantius they allied themselves with others, who were prepared to go further along the road of separation between God and Christ and substitute the term 'of like essence' (*Homoiousios*) instead of 'of the same essence' (*Homoousios*)."[211] Arianism was the norm in the East from 361-381 C.E. Macedonianism argued against the divinity of the Holy Spirit. Apollinaris of Laodicea was an anti-Arian who held that Christ's human mind was replaced by the Divine Logos. Basil and the two Gregory's affirmed three hypostases in one essence. The Council of Constantinople in 381 C.E. was called by Emperor Theodosius. The Holy Spirit was elevated to divinity as proceeding from the Father. Constantinople was elevated to second see. By 381 C.E., selecting bishops by local congregations was replaced by senior bishops selecting others. Pagan temples were destroyed around 380-415 C.E. under Emperor Theodosius's reign.

Diodore taught that the incarnation was merely an act of grace and denied the Virgin birth. Theodore taught that the redemption of man was dependent on the perfection and obedience of Christ as a man. "Jesus Christ really went through the normal experiences which man must live. He was a true man. But his Sonship to God meant that God dwelt in him to a unique degree, indissolubly united with him, and enabling him to offer a perfect pattern of virtue and redemption to humanity. But despite all, the Antiochenes thought of Christ 'in two Persons' or '*hypostases*' (individualities) whose union must be conceived more as a conjunction of opposites (i.e., God and man0 brought about by a harmonization of wills, rather than a union of essences as taught by the Alexandrians."[212] Apollinaris denounced this view as implying that there were two sons of God i.e. one by nature and one by grace. Apollinaris demanded the one nature and one hypostasis of Christ. "Apollinaris of Laodicea had attempted to establish that the human and divine element of Jesus' nature were united, but united in such a way that the human element was partly sacrificed. There were not two persons or natures, but only the divine nature, which possessed, however, human aptitudes corresponding to the functions of the body and soul in a man."[213] Cyril of Alexandria attacked the doctrines of Nestorius in 429 C.E. accusing him of denying the divinity of Christ. "He also sent Nestorius a long and not altogether discourteous letter setting out his views, namely that Jesus was 'One Christ and Lord, not as worshipping a man conjointly with the Word. . . . but as worshipping one and the same person."[214] Nestorius was supported by Empress Eudokia but was opposed by Emperor Theodosius's sister

Pulcheria. He believed in the two nature's Christology of Antioch. Cyril had to accept a Formulary of peace in 431 C.E. which supported Antiochene theology. "This Formulary of reunion protected Antiochene theology in all essentials. It declared that Christ was 'perfect God and perfect man consisting of rational soul and body, of one substance with the Father in the Godhead, of one substance with us in his Manhood, so that there is a union of two natures; on which ground we confess Christ to be one and Mary to be mother of God'."[215] Cyril died in 446 C.E. Eutyches sought to impose the Twelve Anathemas of Cyril on the church as orthodox. The Robber Council of 449 C.E. in Ephesus affirmed the doctrine of Cyril of one nature after the union. In 450 C.E. Theodosius ll died and Pulcheria exiled Eutyches. The Council of Chalcedon condemned Nestorius, accepted Leo's Tome, and Theodoret of Cyrus and Ibas of Edessa were restored to office. The Monophysites were ousted in 451 C.E.

Alexandria and Syria were still Monophysite. The Henoticon remained as the orthodox standard in the East (482-518 C.E.). "The Henoticon condemned both Nestorius and Eutyches, explicitly approved Cyril's Twelve Anathemas, declared that 'one of the Trinity was incarnate', avoided any mention of either one nature or two, and concluded by condemning any heresy 'whether advanced at Chalcedon or at any other synod whatever'."[216] The extreme Monophysite doctrine of Bishop Julian of Halicarnassus taught that the physical body of Christ was incorruptible before the resurrection. "The heresy of *Aphthartodocetae*, whose leader was the sixth century theologian Julian of Halicarnassus, conceived Christ's humanity as incorruptible, and they were accused of a docetic understanding of the Incarnation."[217] Timothy Aelurus, an ultra Monophysite, became bishop of Alexandria in 457 C.E. Leading Monophysite intellectuals included Severus of Antioch and John Philoponus (490-570 C.E.). Leontius of Byzantium was a leading two natures intellectual. Emperor Justinian (527-565 C.E.) was two nature's orthodox but his wife Theodora was a Monophysite. Origens' writings were condemned in 542 C.E. The Council of Constantinople in 553 C.E. condemned Origen posthumously and the Three Chapters as well. The Monothelite doctrine of two wills in Christ was proposed between 625--638 C.E. but rejected at the Council of Constantinople in 680--81 C.E. "In spite of the support given to it by Heraclius and his successors, Monotheletism was finally condemned by the Sixth Ecumenical Council in 680, which restated the Chalcedonian affirmation that in Christ each nature keeps the entirety of its characteristics, and therefore, there are two 'energies' or wills, the divine and human, in Christ."[218] The key opponent of Monothelitism was Maximus the Confessor (580--662 C.E). John of Damascus (675--749 C.E.) wrote an anthology of orthodox theology.

Augustine (354--430 C.E.) became the West's greatest intellectual. Donatists wanted a puritanical Catholic church whereas Catholics were willing to forgive lapses in ethical or political judgment by persons seeking to avoid martyrdom. "This time 'traitors' (i.e. those who surrendered the Scriptures) replaced 'collaborators'. We hear of the deposition of bishops and the rebaptizing of clergy who had lapsed. Foremost in this move was a priest from the southern edge of the great plains of Numidia, Donatus of Casae Nigrae."[219] Augustine backed the Catholics. "Augustine knew that the motives which bring men to the truth are often complex, and may include elements of fear or self-interest that have to be regarded as a temporary stage towards a full, glad, and willing assent."[220] Augustine taught the following concepts: (1) original sin, (2) predestination, (3) irresistible grace, (4) human perseverance, (5) absence of free will, (6) the Trinity with no subordination, and (7) double procession of the Holy Spirit from the Father and the Son. "He was convinced of the primacy and priority of grace in redemption . . . We do not have freedom not to sin . . . he declares that the number of the predestined is exactly the number needed to fill the ranks of the fallen angels . . ."[221] "According to Roman catholic theology as expressed, for example, by St Augustine of Hippo (360—430) . . . the Holy Spirit proceeds eternally from the father and the Son (*Filioque*)."[222]

Rome was the guardian of the Peter and Paul apostolic tradition. Within the church, the bishop in Rome was considered first among equals. This was stressed in 382 C.E. by Pope Damasus. "Four years later, in 382, an even more important council was summoned perhaps in reply to the canons of the second Ecumenical Council. At this, Damasus seems to have claimed formally the possession of 'a primacy over all the other churches in virtue not of conciliar decisions, but of the lord's promise to St. Peter . . . ."[223] Pope Leo the Great dissuaded Attila the Hun from sacking Rome in 452 C.E. The Vandals captured Carthage in 439 C.E. The Goths were converted to Arian Christianity by Ulfila (311-383 C.E.). Theodoric, the Ostrogoth king, (493-526 C.E.) became an Arian Christian. The Franks and Visigoths of Spain were converted to Catholicism in the early sixth century C.E.

Description of the Relevant Persons
During the Monophysite Controversy

There are no references to the Triadic God in the Apostolic Fathers writings. The Apologists refer to Christ as the Logos who was preexistent before the incarnation. The Logos functioned as the Father's agent in creation, revealed truth, and was distinct from the Father. The Apologist's insight was limited to an understanding of the eternal plurality and unity of the Godhead. Irenaeus of Lyon taught the Son and Holy Spirit were divine. "Finally, by the Church's sacraments Christ's divine life was imparted to humanity, and by sharing it, man himself would become divine."[224] Monarchianism is the belief that God is an absolute monad without distinction in the unity. "On the other, were the Monarchians, a general term for those who stressed the unity of God in such a fashion that they acknowledged the divinity of Christ but denied His distinction from the Father."[225] This was the view of Paul of Samosata bishop of Antioch.

Origen and Paul of Samosata had in different ways ensured that Eastern theology had a deep and endemic hostility to any kind of Modalism, and conceived of God and his relationship with the world in terms of a hierarchy with the 'one Lord Jesus Christ' having the nature, status and role of mediator between the 'one God' who was ultimately Father and source of all, and everything else that exists. The one Lord Jesus Christ was the incarnation of the pre-existent Logos, the creative instrument used by God to generate his creation and communicate with it. He was a second *hypostasis*, a distinct existence, never to be confused with the one ultimate, ingenerate God.

Tertullian was the first to introduce the Latin term "trinitas" Trinity. "To him (i.e. Tertullian) belongs the honor of first having employed the formula that later became classic—'one substance and three persons'."[226] The three in the Godhead are numerically distinct and are disposed in roles in an economy to create and redeem in three persons. Each of the three is one in substance. Novatian taught the Father generated a Son where the Son is subordinate to the Father. "According to Novatian, since the Son is begotten of the Father, He is always in the Father, otherwise the Father would not always be Father. Yet the Father is antecedent to the Son, and because the Son is in the Father and is born of the Father, He must be less than the Father."[227] Clement of Alexandria taught that God is transcendent, ineffable, and incomprehensible. The Son is the image and mediator of the Father. "It must be admitted that Clement's Christ was an abstraction, and no more than his Gnostic opponents could he conceive of a wholly human savior."[228] Origen taught that God created spiritual beings which required a mediator as a continuous act of the Father's will. The union of Father and the Word is based on love and action. The Father is of a different substance than the Son. The Son is subordinate to the Father. "Obedience, then, requires us to too to say that if the Saviour and the Spirit transcend all creatures not in degree but in kind, they are in turn transcended by the father . . . They thus form an intermediate category, which though much nearer to the father than to the rest of creation, is still separate from him because their essence, power and other attributes are different from his."[229] He was influenced by Plato through Philo. The Son is preexistent with the Father as the Word. Arius from Alexandria taught in 319 C.E. that Christ the Logos had a beginning and was a creature created out of nothing i.e. "there was when he was not." "The Son has a beginning, but God is without beginning." Because of this we are persecuted because we say, "The Son has a beginning, but God is without beginning." "He is from nothing." But we speak thus inasmuch as he is neither part of God nor from any substratum." [230] Alexander of Alexandria taught the divinity of the Logos, eternally generated by the Father, but with a distinct hypostasis. "Alexander was himself an Origenist, and although he held to the divinity of the Word, eternally generated by the Father, he regarded him as a distinct person."[231] Eusebius of Caesarea was a historian reflecting the Origenists view that the Son is subordinate to the Father. Also the Logos is not coeternal with the Father. "In his theological outlook, Eusebius was a follower of Origen."[232] "Given his markedly subordinationist view of the Logos, Eusebius of Caesarea saw both Christ and Constantine as instruments of the Logos."[233] Athanasius bishop of Alexandria from 328--373 C.E defended the Nicene Creed. He taught the eternal existence of the Son who could not have a Father unless there was a Son. Only a Son who was truly God can save man.

Gregory of Nazianzus and Gregory of Nyssa taught the Godhead exists in three modes consisting of one nature i.e. divine. Augustine, bishop of Hippo, taught the unity of God, distinct in three, and of one substance. The Trinity possesses the same will and action but maintains distinct roles and characteristics.

Biographical Description of Relevant Persons

John the Grammarian was an educator-theologian during the early part of the sixth century C.E. He was from the city of Caesarea. He took up the challenge of defending the findings of the Council of Chalcedon by supporting the writings of Cyril and denying the claims of the Monophysites that Cyril's works had been abandoned by the council. "This position involved an insistence that the one hypostasis of the incarnate Christ is identical with the Second Person of the Trinity, and a consequent justification of the Theopaschite formula."[234]

Peter Mongo became patriarch of Alexandria in 477 C.E. as a Monophysite succeeding Timothy Aelurus in that position. He accepted the statements in the Henoticon over the objections of his Monophysite supporters in order to gain the acceptance of the emperor Zeno to his appointment to the patriarchate. "Peter the Hoarse promptly accepted the Henotikon and was recognized by Acacius as the legitimate patriarch of Alexandria."[235]

Jacob Baradaeus was a Syrian monk during the late sixth century C.E. He was a leader in the Syrian Monophysite church. His teaching was based on the ignorance manifest in the human soul of Christ. He was later condemned as teaching heresy.

Gelasius I became the pope in Rome serving from 492--496 C.E. His contribution was to defend the right of the Roman see based upon apostolic succession to primacy in church matters. He supported the power of the pope to excommunicate anyone who maintained the one nature position of the Monophysites. "He admonished the Eastern church for denying Rome the right to excommunicate those who believed Christ had only one nature (Monophysites) and the secular authorities for attempting to meddle in religious disputes. Gelasius insisted that there are two powers, "the consecrated authority of the bishops and the royal power."[236] He was the first pope to be named Vicar of Christ.

Zeno was emperor at Constantinople during the late fifth century C.E. He was emperor during the war with Theodoric and the Ostrogoths. He sponsored the Henoticon which was an attempt to reconcile the orthodox with the Monophysites which was not acceptable to either side. "...his Henoticon (482) did nothing to bring about the reunion for which it was devised, and occasioned a new schism between Constantinople and Rome."[237]

Theodosius II was emperor at Constantinople during the late fifth century C.E. He called for the Council of Ephesus to be held in 431 C.E. He was a Monophysite supporter who was influenced in his reign by the monk Simeon Stylites and his Minister, Chrysaphius, due to the incompetence of his leadership skills. "But Theodosius formally approved the Council of Ephesus and assured the West that 'peace reigned and pure truth supreme'."[238]

Facundus was an African bishop during the mid-sixth century C.E. He argued in support of the Three Chapters' writings which were in support of the teachings of Theodore of Mopsuestia, Theodoret of Cyrus, and Ibas of Edessa. "Facundus pointed out forcefully that in his opinion the Letter of Ibas had been pronounced orthodox at Chalcedon."[239] He taught that the Three Chapters was a necessary interpretation and support for the findings of the Council of Chalcedon.

Anatolius was patriarch of Constantinople during the mid-fifth century C.E. He followed the wishes of Pope Leo I in condemning both Nestorius and Eutyches and endorsing the Tome of Leo. He became an advocate of the findings of the Council of Chalcedon especially when he sensed the orthodox beliefs of Emperor Marcian and Empress Pulcheria. "The Emperor Marcian and the Patriarch Anatolius wrote asking Leo to approve canon twenty—eight which merely sanctioned a custom of 60 to 70 years in the dioceses of Pontus, Asia and Thrace."[240] During his term in office, the Monophysite party was kept from power in Constantinople.

Vigilius became pope in Rome in the mid sixth century C.E. He intrigued with the Empress Theodora in the East in promising to restore Monophysite control of the Eastern Church but he declined becoming a supporter of the Council of Chalcedon. "At Rome the wily Pope Vigilius, who was imposed on the Romans as pope through the influence of Empress Theodora after the Byzantine general Belisarius had removed Pope Severius on a trumped up charge of treason, hesitated."[241]

Honorius served as pope in Rome during the mid-seventh century C.E. He was instrumental in converting many of the former pagan European kingdoms from Arianism to orthodoxy. He backed the two nature orthodox views of Chalcedon but also supported the one will view of Monothelitism. "In various writings, Honorius upheld Christ's two distinct natures, but he also specified that proper depictions should ascribe

Christ only "one will" and not "two wills." Honorius also declared that the dispute was a problem in semantics and not basic doctrine. Nonetheless, not long after his death, the Council of Constantinople (681) pronounced monothelitism heretical and named Honorius along with Sergius among its proponents. This declaration was then ratified by Pope Leo II in 682."[242]

Gregory I became bishop of Rome between 590-604 C.E. He took the title of pope. The first Leo and the first Gregory are the two greatest bishops of Rome in the first six centuries. "Between them no important personage appears on the chair of Peter; and in the course of that intervening century the idea and the power of the papacy make no material advance. In truth, they went farther in Leo's mind than they did in Gregory's. Leo thought and acted as an absolute monarch; Gregory as first among the patriarchs; but both under the full conviction that they were the successors of Peter."[243]

Brief Explanation of Relevant Persons

The patristic era was the age of the Church Fathers who lived between 96-451 C.E. Church Fathers were given the honor of the title based upon : (1) living and serving during the critical period following the last apostle and the Council of Chalcedon, (2) an accepted belief in the person's holiness as a servant of Christ, (3) the compliance of the person's teachings and writings which were considered to be orthodox, and (4) acceptance and approval by the councils and church authorities. "The same careful work in trying to establish continuity with the faith of the first Christians has had to be done again and again, as the old questions arose afresh in each generation. The first of these to attempt a comprehensive statement of faith or Creed was the Council of Nicaea in 325."[244]

Four significant Church Fathers in the East were Athanasius, Gregory of Nazianzus, Basil the Great, and John Chrysotom. Athanasius defended against the heresy of Arianism. Gregory also defended against Arianism. Basil defended against sects which over-utilized allegorical interpretation. John defended the literal as opposed to the allegorical interpretation of the Scriptures.

Athanasius lived approximately from 295-373 C.E. He was the first person to settle on the twenty-seven books of the New Testament as canonical. He was at various times bishop of Alexandria. He was the strongest supporter of the findings of the Council of Nicaea. His view became the orthodox view of the church which was based upon the concept that Jesus Christ was of the same essence or substance as the Father. "His strength lay in his single-minded attachment to the creed of Nicaea, and his perception that the Christian doctrine of redemption required the sharing of the same substance by Father, Son and Spirit."[245] He viewed the role of Jesus the man as required in order to save humanity. "The fact that the Word had taken on flesh and sacrificed his mortal body for humanity meant that death was henceforth no more than the passage of joyful resurrection, for Christ had overthrown sin and death once and for all."[246] This was based upon the reasoning that only God could save from sin whereas a man cannot save another man. The divine nature appropriated the human nature in Christ making Him the God-man. The Son joined in union with flesh like ours so that he could experience our human condition, excluding sin, as a substitute for us. He is worthy of our worship because he is God. "The incarnation of the Son of God was the great mystery that Athanasius defended for all his life. God the Son, true God with the Father and the Holy Spirit, had in great love willingly joined his divine nature to human nature in the wonder of the incarnation."[247]

Gregory of Nazianzus lived from 329-390 C.E. He served for eight years as bishop of Constantinople. Gregory had profound insight into Scripture believing that god reveals Himself and His plans through progressive revelation in the Scriptures. He defended against the Arian claims that Christ was: (1) divine but a created being, (2) not of the same essence or substance as the Father, (3) not consubstantial with the Father, and (4) was of similar substance as the Father. "There are, he said, three individualities or hypostases or persons, but they are one in respect of substance or Godhead."[248] He further defended against a heretical group known as the Macedonians who believed that Christ was of a different essence from the Father and that the Holy Spirit is not equal in deity. "For Gregory, 'all things' includes the surprising, wondrous revelation that the Spirit is also divine, sharing the same divine essence with the Father and Son."[249] In the incarnation, the Son has willingly assumed the human condition of limitations in order to redeem us. He has become what we are while remaining what He has always been.

Basil the Great lived from 330-379 C.E. He was born and served in Cappadocia along with his close associates Gregory of Nazianzus and Gregory of Nyssa. ". . . basil determined to increase the number of sees subject to him as metropolitan by installing his brother Gregory as bishop of Nyssa and his friend Gregory of Nazianzus at the remote relay station of Sasma . . ."[250] His voice was critical of the allegorical method of interpretation of Scripture. He defended against the heresies of the Manicheans, Marcionites, and Gnostics. He was a frequent user of animal analogies to explain human behavior. "What animal of the ocean, Basil asks, can match the rancor of the camel? 'The camel conceals its resentment for a long time after it has been struck, until it finds an opportunity, and then repays the wrong.' Are humans any different?'"[251]

John Chrysotom lived from 347-407 C.E. He trained at Antioch along with the two previous Church Fathers. He was more of a preacher than a theologian. "The Byzantine bishop was not only a distant figure who attended councils; he was also in many cases a true father to his people, a friend and protector to whom people confidently turned when in trouble. The concern for the poor and oppressed which John Chrysotom displayed is found in many others."[252] His primary contributions were oratorical and behavioral. "During these last year's John wrote a final work titled *On the Providence of God*, an extended biblical, theological and devotional exploration of suffering in the life of the faithful Christian." [253]

In summary we have developed an historical timeline before, during, and after the Monophysite controversy. The earliest issues involved combating other religions and preventing syncretism. Very soon the issues became internal to Christianity. The beliefs which would become orthodox versus those beliefs which would be deemed heretical were established as the position of the church. "So it is not easy with hindsight to identify some positions confidently as 'orthodox', conforming in their thinking with the settled view of the continuing Christian community, and others as 'divergent', or 'unorthodox'."[254] Christological issues such as the deity of Christ, the nature(s) of Christ, the title of Mary, and the deity of the Holy Spirit were resolved in ecumenical councils called to settle these disputes. What followed was the publication of creeds expressing in words the beliefs agreed to by the majority of bishops attending a given council. These steps did not finalize the debates to everyone's satisfaction causing schism and separation of theologically or politically defeated theologians and their followers. "There is another way of 'dealing with heresy' and that is to regard it as legitimate difference and live with it. A willingness to 'live with difference', unthinkable in the first Christian centuries, could and did have a number of causes."[255] Many of the relevant persons involved in these controversies have been discussed.

CHAPTER 5

ANALYSIS OF THE CANONS, CREEDS, AND COUNCILS DURING THE MONOPHYSITE CONTROVERSY

The developing Christian Church was organized based upon patriarchates. There were five during the period studied located at Rome, Constantinople, Alexandria, Antioch, and Jerusalem. Each patriarchate was divided into metropolitan sees. The sees were responsible for dioceses. The patriarchates, sees, and dioceses were led and officiated over by a bishop. Councils were called either by the emperor, the pope, or the leading bishop of a patriarchate. Councils were held to determine acceptable Christian belief, doctrine, and practice which would be applicable to the universal church. "The life of the Church in the earlier Byzantine period is dominated by the seven general councils. These councils fulfilled a double task. First, they clarified and articulated the visible organization of the Church, crystallizing the position of the five great sees or *Patriarchates,* as they came to be known. Secondly, and more important, the councils defined once and for all the Church's teaching upon the fundamental doctrines of the Christian faith. . . ."[256] These beliefs would determine what was to be considered orthodoxy worthy to be taught and what was considered to be heresy and set outside the teachings of the church. Councils were considered ecumenical if the attendance and acceptance of the findings of the bishops were deemed representative of the universal church. "Orthodoxy has always attached great importance to the place of councils in the life of the church. It believes that the council is the chief organ whereby God has chosen to guide His people, and it regards the Catholic Church as essentially a conciliar Church."[257] Some of the councils were considered only local in attendance and application of the issues debated. Some meetings of a local nature were referred to as synods. Many forms of documents and writings were used before, during, and after the councils to influence an issue, to denounce a belief, teaching, or person; or to state the agreed to findings of the council by a majority of the bishops attending. "A major source of our knowledge of Byzantine ecclesiological ideas is constituted by ancient canonical texts; conciliar decrees, commentaries, and later synodal legislation."[258] These publications were officially in two forms. The publication of a creed was intended to establish as settled doctrine the acceptable beliefs and teachings of the universal church. "They were generally aware that at least certain canons reflected the eternal and divine nature of the Church, and that it was a Christian and absolute duty to obey them."[259] The publication of church canon was intended to establish acceptable and normative church discipline and organization. A creed acted as a statement of faith which was used and built upon by later councils to serve as a boundary or limit of acceptable belief. "By the end of the second century, the greater Churches were standardizing their statements of belief in set terms which were to become the creeds."[260] Canons served to regulate the functioning, practices, and organizational issues of the church.

The Conciliar tradition began at Jerusalem in 49 C.E. with the bishop James, the brother of Jesus, presiding (Acts 15). "For the next eighteen years, until 62, this office was the prerogative of Jesus' brother, James, and Jerusalem was the center and directing arm of the Christian mission."[261] During the age of persecution, no ecumenical councils were held. The ecumenical councils were considered to produce binding authority. In addition, the doctrinal decrees were considered to be timeless, absolute, and unalterable. "The doctrinal definitions of an Ecumenical Council are infallible. Thus in the eyes of the Orthodox Church, the statements of faith put out by the seven councils possess, along with the Bible, an abiding and irrevocable authority."[262] Voting by the bishops in attendance was required to be by significant majorities in order to formally adopt a decree. There were six ecumenical councils held between 300-700 C.E. One further council was held in 787 C.E. and accepted by the West.

The Council of Nicaea was held in 325 C.E. It has been recorded that 318 bishops were in attendance. Emperor Constantine presided over the council. The purpose of the council was to define the divinity of Christ in the Trinity. "The Nicenes held tenaciously to the historic Christ who by His divine self-sacrifice secured the salvation of humankind and established the law to which even the Christian sovereign is subject."[263]

The writings of Arius were deemed heretical. The Nicene Creed was produced. "What the Council of Nicaea did in its creedal statement was simply to attend to what the Scripture asserts as true about the Word of God, reduce that multitude of true statements to the one judgment which is the foundation of all the rest . . ."[264]

The Council of Constantinople I was held in 381 C.E. Approximately 150 bishops were in attendance. Emperor Theodosius I presided over the council. The result of the council was to denounce Arianism and Macedonianism, to define Christ as co-eternal with the Father, and to define the Holy Spirit as deity. A revision to the Nicene Creed was produced. "The present text of the Creed of Constantinople made its first appearance as an official formulary at the second session of the Council of Chalcedon in 451."[265]

The Council of Ephesus was held in 431 C.E. Approximately 160 bishops were in attendance. Emperor Theodosius II presided over the council. The results of the council were to denounce Nestorianism and Pelagianism and to declare Mary as "Theotokos" Birth –giver of God. No creed was produced from this council but rather a profession of faith was agreed to. "Cyril argued that the solution to the whole controversy should be based on the affirmation that Mary is truly Theotokos because the Body of Christ did not come from heaven but from Mary."[266]

The Council of Chalcedon was held in 451 C.E. Approximately 500-600 bishops were in attendance. Emperor Marcian and Empress Pulcheria presided over the council. The findings of the council were to denounce Eutychianism, to define the two natures of Christ as a hypostatic union of the divine and human, and to re-instate some theologians who were wrongly deposed in 449 C.E. The Chalcedonian Creed was produced. "In their Definition the bishops at last clearly distinguished between person and nature; the person of Christ being one, his natures two. They rejected decisively the view that Christ is from two natures and in one by affirming that Christ subsists in two natures."[267]

The Council of Constantinople II was held in 553 C.E. Approximately 151-68 bishops were in attendance. The results were to clarify the Chalcedonian Creed, to denounce the Three Chapters, to condemn the writings of Origen, and to define the Theopaschite Formula. Eleven Anathemas were produced in lieu of a creed. "…the bishops condemned Theodore of Mopsuestia and his writings, certain writings of Theodoret and the letter said to have been written by Ibas."[268]

The Council of Constantinople III was held in 680-81 C.E. Approximately 174 bishops were in attendance. The Emperor Constantine IV presided over the council. The outcome of this council was to denounce Monothelitism and Monoenergism and to define Christ as having two wills. A statement of faith was produced instead of a creed. "Then, coming to the heart of the matter, they declared that in Christ there are 'two natural wills and two natural operations indivisibly, inconvertibly, inseparably, inconfusedly.'"[269]

The Council of Nicaea II was held in 787 C.E. Anywhere from 258-335 bishops were present. Emperor Constantine VI presided at the council. The findings were to allow the veneration of sacred images. No creed was produced. "For the honor which is paid to the image passes on to that which the image represents, and he who reveres the image reveres in it the subject represented."[270]

These first seven ecumenical councils were accepted by both the Roman Catholic and Eastern Orthodox Churches as authoritative. "Today Roman Catholics accept twenty ecumenical councils; the Orthodox and some Protestants only seven."[271] The Nestorians broke with the Orthodox Church following the Council of Ephesus in 431 C.E. The Monophysites broke with the Orthodox Church after the Council of Chalcedon in 451 C.E.

Analysis of Church Canons

The issuance of church canons represents the church's position on organization and discipline. "besides doctrinal definitions, the Ecumenical Councils drew up *Canons,* dealing with Church organization and discipline . . ."[272] Four of the first six ecumenical councils published canons. These were Nicaea I, Constantinople I, Chalcedon, and Constantinople III.

Nicaea I produced twenty canons. ". . . the bishops turned to matters of church discipline and drew up twenty canons dealing with actual problems affecting the orderly administration of ecclesiastical affairs."[273] The first canon prohibits eunuchs from the clergy. The second canon restricts elevation to the bishopric too soon after conversion or baptism. The third canon prohibits the clergy to house a woman within one's abode. The fourth canon requires written consent by other bishops in the diocese to the ordination of any bishop in the province. The fifth canon requires bishops to convene two provincial councils each year. The sixth and seventh canons provide the organizational hierarchy of patriarch, metropolitan, and bishop. Canons 8-14 state the methods of reconciliation for lapsed clergy. Canon 15 forbids the transfer of clergy without church approval. Canon 16 forbids recruiting clergy between dioceses. Canon 17 forbids the clergy to collect usury. Canon 18 states the local organizational hierarchy as bishop, priest, and deacon. Canon 19 defines the ordination of women as lay persons. Canon 20 restricts communicants from kneeling at worship services on Sundays. "They were not meant to be a comprehensive code covering all aspects of canon law . . . Rather they touch on particular points that seem to need attention."[274]

Constantinople I produced four-six canons. "At the end of its deliberations the Council issued four canons; the fifth and sixth canons sometimes attributed to Constantinople I are in fact from the local Council of Constantinople of 382 . . . ."[275] The first canon anathematized the Arians and several other sects as heresies. The second canon established boundaries between dioceses in order to avoid confusion of authority. "They further decreed that as necessity required it, the ecclesiastical affairs of each province should be managed by a Synod of the province."[276] The third canon denounced Maximus the Cynic and deposed him as bishop. The fourth canon provide for the acceptance of anyone who accepted the unity of the Trinity. The fifth canon prescribes the terms of reconciliation to former heretics for re- admittance into fellowship.

Chalcedon produced thirty canons. "The assembled fathers then debated thirty disciplinary canons."[277] The first canon reaffirmed the prior canons. The second canon prohibited the clergy from buying his office. The third canon prohibited the clergy from engaging in worldly gain. The fourth prohibited the establishment of a monastery without the permission of the local bishop. The fifth canon reaffirmed the rules regarding the transfer of clergy. The sixth canon required all ordinations to be titled. The seventh canon prohibited the clergy from engaging in military or secular service. The eighth canon required clerics to be subject to the will of their bishop. The ninth canon required clerics having a judicial claim against another cleric to seek resolution from the bishop. "Canon nine provided that bishops or clerics who had a dispute with their provincial metropolitan could appeal over his head to the exarch of the diocese or directly to the patriarch of Constantinople."[278] The tenth canon prohibited appointment of a cleric to two cities at the same time. The eleventh canon prohibited travel of paupers with ecclesiastical letters of commendation.

The twelfth canon prohibited bishops from seeking secular approval to divide an ecclesiastical province. The thirteenth canon prohibited foreign clerics to serve in another city without permission by the appropriate bishop. The fourteenth canon prohibited functionaries in the local church from marrying a heretic and remaining in service. The fifteenth canon forbad the ordination as a deaconess of a woman under the age of forty. The sixteenth canon prohibited a declared and dedicated virgin from marrying. The seventeenth canon exhorted rural parishes to remain in association with their local bishop. "Canon seventeen allowed anyone wronged by his metropolitan to appeal to the exarch of the diocese or to the patriarch of Constantinople."[279] The eighteenth canon forbad clerics from joining secret societies. The nineteenth canon reaffirmed the convening of twice yearly local councils. The twentieth canon reaffirmed the prohibition of clerics transferring to another city. Canon 21 prohibited clerics from bringing allegations against a cleric without establishing a credible reputation based upon examination. Canon 22 prohibited a cleric from seizing the assets of a deceased bishop. Canon 23 condemned the behavior of disaffected clerics who cause a disturbance in Constantinople. Canon 24 required an established monastery to remain in monastic service. Canon 25 required the ordination of a metropolitan bishop to occur within three months following a vacancy. Canon 26 established that every church which has a bishop must also have an administrator. Canon 27 reaffirmed the prohibition for a cleric to cohabitate with a woman. Canon 28 elevated the see of Constantinople to second in prerogatives to Rome. "Most controversial of all, canon twenty-eight read that the fathers of the Council of Constantinople 'properly gave the primacy to the Throne of elder Rome, because that was the imperial city'."[280] Canon 29 stated the terms of deposing and restoring a cleric to office. Canon 30 pertained to the status of bishops in Egypt. The final three were enacted at a later session. "Before disbanding, the council passed twenty-seven canons, establishing Constantinople as a court of appeal from provincial synods, and, at a session from which the Roman legates were absent, enacted a resolution reasserting the privileges of Constantinople on the ground of imperial status and the analogy to the dignity of old Rome."[281]

Constantinople III produced 102 canons published ten years later which became the first attempt to establish a canon law for the church which was more comprehensive than the prior publications of canons. ". . . in 692 a Council, which was later named the Quinisext, was called in

Constantinople to reform ecclesiastical law neglected in the fifth and sixth councils . . . In the end the Council agreed on 102 canons."[282] Only the important canons will be referred to. Canon 3 prohibited bigamy by a cleric. Canon 6 prohibited any cleric from marrying after ordination to office. Canon 14 required a minimum age for ordination of thirty for a Presbyter and twenty-five for a Deacon. Canon 23 prohibited a cleric from receiving funds in payment for offering Communion. Canon 27 prohibited a cleric from wearing secular clothes in public. Canon 31 forbad a cleric from holding church services in a residential or commercial building. Canon 36 established the hierarchy of patriarchates. Canon 40 required examination for persons seeking to join a monastery. Canon 50 prohibited gambling by a cleric. Canon 55 prohibited fasting on Saturday or Sunday. "The Saturday fast during Lent, practiced at Rome, was forbidden."[283] Canon 64 prohibited a layman from teaching divine facts in public. Canon 69 prohibited a layman from entering the place of the altar. Canon 70 prohibited any woman from speaking during Mass. Canon 72 prohibited marriage between a believer and a heretic. Canon 74 prohibited the conducting of a love-feast at the Lord's Supper. Canon 81 forbad the addition of certain words in the utterance of the Trisagion. Canon 84 prescribed the necessity of infant baptism. Canon 87 prescribed some penalties for marital abandonment. Canon 91 forbad procuring drugs for an abortion. Canon 98 prohibited adultery by any lay person. Canon 102 defined the process of clerical examination for a person's sin. The mere number and comprehensiveness of these canons suggests the development of rules for organization and discipline. The fact that these canons are developed and approved during council meetings shows the conciliar nature of decision making which was consistent during this period of church history. ". . . the Council (Nicaea 325) confirmed the precedent already established in the previous century, that the Holy Spirit would guide and direct the Church best through a council of bishops each of whom was individually a partaker of the Spirit."[284]

    The writings of the church theologians and emperors became the influential views which dominated the church councils and formed the critical parts of the church creeds. These writings were known by various names such as Tomes, Chapters, Epistles, and Canons. A Tome was a large scholarly work. A Chapter was a main section of a collected writing. "The Fifth Ecumenical Council (553) . . . approved Justinian's earlier posthumous condemnation of the Three Chapters . . . anathema 13 gave formal approval to the Twelve Chapters of Cyril against Nestorius . . . *The Gnostic Chapters of Evagrius* help greatly in the understanding . . . against non-existent heresies attributed to Origen . . ."[284] An Epistle was a writing directed to a group of people which was intended to teach. Canons were either judicial decrees of the church or synodal decrees which may only be accepted by a group outside of the Orthodox Church. "Viewed from a juridicial point of view, the entire body of Byzantine canonical sources hardly constitutes a coherent whole."[285]

The Tome of Leo the Great was a letter sent by the Western pope to Flavian who was patriarch of Constantinople in 449 C.E. The Tome represented the approved views of Emperor Justinian I. The purpose of the Tome was to clarify the Orthodox position that Christ was one person with two natures. "The person of the God-man is for Leo identical with that of the Divine Word . . ."[286] This clarification was effective in laying the groundwork for denouncing the views of Eutyches which tended to confuse the composition of the natures. This Tome became the Orthodox definition of Chalcedon in 451 C.E. where Eutyches was condemned and exiled. "Thus the properties of each nature and substance were preserved entire, and came together to form one person."[287]

The Three Chapters were a collection of writings in 543-44 C.E. which condemned the writings of three church leaders who were accused of supporting Nestorianism. These were Ibas of Edessa, Theodore of Mopsuestia, and Theodoret of Cyrus. "The theological authority of the School of Antioch was shattered by the condemnation of Nestorius, a pupil of Theodore of Mopsuestia, at Ephesus in 431, and by the anathemas against the Three Chapters (Theodore of Mopsuestia, and the anti-Cyrillian writings of Theodoret of Cyrus and Ibas of Edessa) pronounced by the Second Council of Constantinople in 553."[288] These three had been teachers of Nestorius. Emperor Justinian issued this writing as an imperial edict in order to attempt reconciliation with the Monophysites who objected to the writings of Nestorius. The Three Chapters stood amidst controversy until the condemnation document was accepted in 553 C.E at the Council of Constantinople II. Neither the ten year acceptance nor the subsequent condemnation of the Three Chapters satisfied the Monophysites. "If any one . . . says that of those two characters introduced by him there is one personality in respect of worth and honour and adoration, as Theodore and Nestorius have written in their madness . . ."[289]

Canon LXXXI was issued as an instruction concerning an important ecumenical hymn known as the Trisagion. Peter Fullo, a Monophysite, had inserted the words "who [290] was crucified for us" into the hymn in 478 C.E. which meant that Christ suffered as God. "To the venerated Trisagion—Holy God, Holy and Mighty, Holy and Immortal— Peter added the phrase; crucified for us." "Peter Fullo had been deposed for the insertion of this clause, because he intended to imply that the true God had suffered death on the cross. This sentence was a confirmation of one already pronounced against him by a synod held at Antioch which had raised a man, Stephen by name, to its episcopal throne. Such is the history of a matter which, while it seemed at first as of little moment, yet for many years was a source of trouble in the church."[291] By 518 C.E the issue was in dispute among Monophysites and Orthodox. Those favoring retention of the clause were called Theopaschites. The clause was removed at the Council of Constantinople in 553 C.E.

Epistle L was a letter from Gregory the Great who was pope in Rome to Eulogius who was patriarch of Alexandria approximately 600 C.E. It was written to the patriarch in Alexandria requesting fellowship to be extended to several clerics who had renounced Monophysitism. This correspondence showed the mutual support between like-minded believers where the "natures" issue was the basis of support or rejection. "The bearers of these presents, coming to Sicily, were converted from the error of the Monophysites, and united themselves to the holy universal Church."[292]

The Syriac Canon was a compilation of the New Testament written in the Syriac language. It variously contained different writings of the apostles. ". . . the *Doctrine of Addai*, a 5th-century document which in its account of the beginnings of Christianity in Edessa mingles legend with trustworthy tradition. The next stage in the closer alignment of the Syriac Canon with the Greek was the production of the 'separated gospels'. . ."[293] It was compiled between the compilation of Marcion's New Testament canon in approximately 150 C.E. and Athanasius's New Testament canon in approximately 368 C.E. The existence of the Syriac Canon in a different language from the Greek and Latin became one of the reasons for confusion of the meaning of the biblical text between different theologians especially in the Eastern churches. "…theological differences were made more bitter by cultural and national tension. Egypt and Syria, both predominantly non-Greek in language and background, resented the power of Greek Constantinople, alike in religious and political matters."[294]

The Epistle LXVII was a letter written by Gregory the Great from Rome to Quiricus who was bishop of Hibernia. The purpose of the letter was to inform church leaders regarding the terms under which someone who has been turned out of the church may be received back into fellowship. It served both as instruction in the matter as well as a teaching tool of orthodox belief which needed to be constantly defended and continually clarified. "And indeed we have learnt from the ancient institution of the Fathers that whosoever among heretics are baptized in the name of the Trinity, when they return to holy Church, may be recalled to the bosom of mother Church either by unction of chrism, or by imposition of hands, or by profession of the faith only."[295]

The Henoticon was a document written by Emperor Zeno in 481 C.E. The purpose was to end the disputes between Monophysite and Orthodox. "By this date (484) almost everywhere in the East the Henotikon of Emperor Zeno and the patriarch Acacius was accepted by the bishops, at least formally, as the definition of orthodox faith."[296] The language used stated that Christ was one person who was both God and man. This avoids the inclusion of language asserting the two natures of Christ. "Moreover we confess that the Only-begotten Son of God, himself God, who truly took upon himself manhood, our Lord Jesus Christ, who in respect of his Godhead is consubstantial with the Father, and consubstantial with us in respect of his manhood . . ."[297] It also condemns the teachings of Nestorius and Eutyches but incorporates the Twelve Anathemas of Cyril. No one was completely satisfied with the Henoticon.

The Acacian Schism was developed under Pope Felix III (483-491) who repudiated the Henoticon in 484 C.E. "Outraged, Felix III convened a synod of seventy-seven bishops in Rome in 484 at which both Acacius and the legates were deposed."[298] He repudiated Acacius and excommunicated Peter Mongus. Anastasius I became emperor in 491 C.E. He supported the Henoticon as he was in sympathy with Monophysitism. Anastasius I died in 518 C.E. and was replaced as emperor by Justinian I. Justinian I was sympathetic to the Orthodox position but attempted reconciliation with the Monophysites which ended the current schism but did not bring reconciliation between the parties. "In the Monophysite controversy, a temporary schism (482–519) between Rome and the E. which arose out of the Emp. Zeno's Henoticon (q.v.). It began during the

Patriarchate of Acacius (471–89) at Constantinople. Despite the attempts of Flavitas (490) and Euphemius (490–6), Acacius' successors, to heal it, it continued till the accession of Justin (518)."[299]

The Tome of Leo set the standard for orthodox belief in the one person in two natures of Christ. "In their Definition the bishops at last clearly distinguished between person and nature; the person of Christ being one, his natures two."[300] It is the one document that best defines the meaning of Chalcedon. It is the document most rejected by the Monophysites. So the proper character of both natures was maintained and came together in a single person. Lowliness was taken up by majesty, weakness by strength, mortality by eternity. To pay off the debt of our state, invulnerable nature was united to a nature that could suffer; so that in a way that corresponded to the remedies we needed, one and the same mediator between God and humanity the man Christ Jesus, could both on the one hand die and on the other be incapable of death. Thus was true God born in the undiminished and perfect nature of a true man, complete in what is his and complete in what is ours. By "ours" we mean what the Creator established in us from the beginning and what he took upon himself to restore. There was in the Saviour no trace of the things which the Deceiver brought upon us, and to which deceived humanity gave admittance. His subjection to human weaknesses in common with us did not mean that he shared our sins. He took on the form of a servant without the defilement of sin, thereby enhancing the human and not diminishing the divine. For that self-emptying whereby the Invisible rendered himself visible, and the Creator and Lord of all things chose to join the ranks of mortals, spelled no failure of power: it was an act of merciful favour. So the one who retained the form of God when he made humanity, was made man in the form of a servant. Each nature kept its proper character without loss; and just as the form of God does not take away the form of a servant, so the form of a servant does not detract from the form of God.[301]

The Three Chapters were proposed to anathematize the writings of three Antiochene theologians. These were Theodore of Mopsuestia, Theodoret of Cyrus, and Ibas of Edessa. Under Justinian's edict of 543-44 C.E., the Three Chapters were anathematized. The hope of the emperor was to reconcile the Monophysites to the Orthodox Church. The claims against the three theologians were both regarding their writings which sounded like the ideas of Nestorius but also their guilt by association with this man whom orthodoxy had declared a heretic.

At the end of 543 or the beginning of 544 an edict was issued in the name of the Emperor Justinian in which the Three Chapters were anathematized. Justinian's purpose was to facilitate the return of the Monophysites to the Church. These heretics accused the Church of Nestorianism, and, when assured that Nestorius was regarded as a heretic, pointed to the writings of his teacher Theodore of Mopsuestia, which were quite as incorrect, and yet had never been condemned. They added that Theodoret, the friend and defender of Nestorius, had been restored to his see by the Council of Chalcedon, and that the epistle of Ibas had even been treated as harmless by the council. It was sincerely hoped by Justinian that when grounds of complaint against the council had been removed, the Monophysites might be induced to accept the decisions of the council and the letters of St. Leo, which they now insisted on misinterpreting in a Nestorian sense. As a temporal ruler he wished to heal religious divisions which threatened the security of the empire, and as a good amateur theologian he was probably rather pleased with himself at being able to lay his finger upon what seemed to him an important omission on the part of the Council of Chalcedon.[302]

Canon LXXXI was an attempt to suppress those who wanted to insert the words "Who was crucified" into a popular church hymn which was a hope of the Monophysites to introduce a supportive phrase to their one nature doctrine. "'Whoever adds to the hymn Trisagion these words 'Who wast crucified' shall be deemed heterodox.'"[303]

Epistle L showed the efforts of the Western Church to restore any theologian who would separate from heretics as welcome in the church.

Gregory to Eulogius, & c
The bearers of these presents, coming to Sicily, were converted from the error of the Monophysites, and united themselves to the holy universal Church. Having proceeded to the church of the blessed Peter, Prince of the apostles, they requested of me that I should commend them by letter to your Blessedness, to the end that they may not now be allowed to suffer any wrong from the heretics that are near them. And because one of them says that the monastery in which he was had been rounded by his kindred, he desires to receive authority from your Holiness that the heretics who are in it may either return to the bosom of holy Church or be expelled from the same monastery. Let it be enough for us to have indicated this to you: for we know of your Blessedness that whatever pertains to zeal for

Almighty God you hasten with all fervour to do. But for me I beg you to pray, since amid the swords of the Lombards which I endure I am excessively afflicted by pains of gout.[304]

The Syriac Canon was an example of the New Testament in a language other than Greek or Latin. ". . . doubt contributed to the continued mistrust with which it was viewed by the Gk. churches, and it's very late acceptance in the Syriac and Armenian churches. In the W, on the contrary, it was very early accorded a high place; it was translated into Latin on at least three different occasions, and numerous commentaries were dedicated to it from the time of Victorinus of Pettau (martyred 304) onwards."[305]

Epistle LXVII provided for the conditions to be met to restore a follower of a heretic back into fellowship. The Epistle also re-affirmed the orthodox beliefs regarding the incarnation.

But we say that the Word was made flesh not by losing what He was, but by taking what He was not. For in the mystery of His Incarnation the Only-begotten of the Father increased what was ours, but diminished not what was His. Therefore the Word and the flesh is one Person, as He says Himself, *No man hath ascended up to heaven, but he that came down from heaven, even the Son of man which is in heaven* (Joh. iii. 14). He Who is the Son of God in heaven was the Son of man who spoke on earth. Hence John says, *We know that the Son of God is come, and hath given us an understanding* (1 Job. v. 20). And as to what understanding He has given us, he straightway added, *That we may know the true God.* Whom in this place does he mean as the true God but the Father Almighty? But, as to what he conceives also of the Almighty Son, he added, And that we may be in his true Son Jesus Christ. Lo, he says that the Father is the true God, and that Jesus Christ is His true Son. And what he conceives this true Son to be he shews more plainly; *This is the true God, and eternal life.* If, then, according to the error of Nestorius the Word were one and the man Jesus Christ were another, he who is true man would not be the true God and eternal life. But the Only-begotten Son, the Word before the Ages, was made man. He is, then, the true God and eternal life.[306]

The Henoticon was a publication by the emperor Zeno which was intended to end the schism between the Orthodox and Monophysites. It failed and was replaced in 518 C.E. by a re-affirmation of the findings of Chalcedon. The anathema issued against Acacius in 484 C.E. separated the Eastern Church from the Western Church until 518 C.E.

As an attempt at conceding what both parties most desired, the Henoticon is a very skillful piece of work. It begins by insisting on the faith defined at Nicaea, confirmed at Constantinople, followed faithfully by the Fathers at Ephesus. Nestorius and Eutyches are both condemned, the anathemas of Cyril approved. Christ is God and man, one, not two. His miracles and Passion are works of one (whether person or nature, is not said). Those who divide or confuse, or introduce a phantasy (i.e. affirm a mere appearance) are condemned. One of the Trinity was incarnate. This is written not to introduce a novelty, but to satisfy everyone. Who thinks otherwise, either now or formerly, either at Chalcedon or at any other synod, is anathematized, especially Nestorius, Eutyches, and all their followers. It will be noticed that the Henoticon carefully avoids speaking of nature or person, avoids the standard Catholic formula (*one Christ in two natures*), approves of Peter Fullo's expression (*one of the Trinity was incarnate*), names only the first three councils with honor, and alludes vaguely but disrespectfully to Chalcedon. There is no word against Dioscurus of Alexandria. Otherwise it offends rather by its omissions than by its assertions.[307]

The Acacian Schism was the result of the difference in belief between the West who supported the two natures position and the east which supported the one nature position. The interference by the emperor Zeno in publishing the Henoticon exacerbated the conflict which was not abated until the Emperor Justin intervened in 518 C.E. accepting the Tome of Leo and excommunicating Emperors Zeno and Anastasius. Pope Felix III of Rome and Patriarch Acacius of Constantinople excommunicated each other. "In 519 Justin welcomed the papal legates with all possible honor and offered to discuss terms. When the legates refused all discussion, the emperor acceded to their demands. The patriarch, all the bishops present in Constantinople and the heads of monasteries signed the papal formula of reunion. The Acacian Schism was over at long last."[308]

Analysis of the Church Creeds

Creeds became the product of church councils where a large representative body of bishops had gathered to decide a doctrinal matter. ". . . the Creed is the common possession of the whole Church, and if any change is to be made in it, this can only be done by an Ecumenical Council."[309] The formularies which were produced as creeds were intended to define what correct orthodox teaching was and what incorrect heretical teaching was. In addition since most doctrinal teachings were attributed to an author, the creed may also determine who was orthodox and who was heretical. There were many creeds published in the early church. Many of these creeds sourced from the traditions of words spoken during the conduct of baptisms. "Baptize thus: having first recited all these things, baptize' in the name of the father, and of the Son, and of the Holy Ghost,' in running water."[310] Others developed as traditional words spoken during the activity of a communion service. "In worship, particularly at the Lord's Supper or Eucharist, the congregation could affirm the faith of the community together in a single form of words . . ."[311] Eastern creeds were more theological than Western creeds. Eastern creeds focused more upon ideas whereas Western creeds paid more attention to facts. Eastern creeds were more interested in the cosmic realm of the divine whereas western creeds placed more emphasis on the apostolic ideas coming from Scripture. Eastern creeds developed more independently due to the lack of a strong central authority. Western creeds developed more progressively as expressing consistent themes. This may be due to the exercise of Rome's centralized authority. The early attempts to develop baptismal creeds and statements of faith were at times local efforts. In these early creeds theologians experimented with different words to express the meanings of their faith which later sometimes found their way into the creeds produced by the church councils. "Thus formularies of different types were existing side by side in friendly competition, and no one type had the monopoly. This is exactly the situation which we should expect at this early date on the assumption that there was no one original stock from which all creeds derived, but their roots were embedded in the act of baptism and the catechetical rule of faith."[312]

     The creeds produced by church councils are likened to statements of faith and distinguished from the church canons which are concerned with the rules of discipline and organization within the church. At times the creed was later amended at an ensuing church council providing the historian with original and amended versions of a given creed. The creeds produced at the councils between 300-700 C.E. will be described and then analyzed. Some are preliminary to the Monophysite controversy. Some are directly relevant and some are successive to the controversy. The creeds which will be described are the: Nicene, Constantinople I, Ephesian profession of faith, Chalcedon, Constantinople II anathemas, and Constantinople III.

Description of Church Creeds

The first official church formulary was produced in 325 C.E. and was known as the Nicene Creed. The purpose of the creed was to declare that: (1) Christ was of the same substance as the Father, (2) Christ was not made or created, and (3) Arius' teachings which were contrary to this teaching were anathema. "Several of its clauses are directed against those with doubts over the true divinity and humanity of Christ, such as the followers of the contemporary heretic Arius . . . These clauses emphasize the divinity of Christ, the fact that he is eternal, and that his substance is the same divine substance as that of the Father."[313] The combatants during the debate over these two points of doctrine were Arius and Athanasius. The wording submitted by Athanasius became the accepted doctrine of the creed. "The final triumph of the Nicene faith, and its ratification at the Council of Constantinople in 381, is due to Athanasius more than to any other man."[314] Arius had stated in 318 C.E. that the Father could not have transferred His substance or essence to Christ because that would require the Father to be divisible and mutable. "The Son of God is begotten according to his personal relationship with the Father, but not according to his participation in the divine essence. This is an important point which was frequently denied in the early church, notably by the arch-heretic Arius (d. 336)."[315] He believed that the Word and Christ were first-born and begotten of all creation but that each was created "ex nihilo" out of nothing. This would result in Christ being before time and space but not co-eternal with the Father. "Arius maintained that the Word and the Spirit were not eternally latent in God but had been created . . ."[316] Further Christ would be finite, mutable, and capable of sin. Finally the three persons of the Trinity would be unequal in their essence and authority. "To Arius this meant that the three persons could not share equally in the same divine *ousia,* which by definition was unique."[317] The position of Athanasius was that Christ was of the same substance as the Father which meant that Christ was equal to the Father in essence and authority. "With unflagging energy he defended the formula of the *homoousion,* as expressing this truth, that if Christ is God, then he must be God in the same sense as God the Father is God; divinity is one 'substance'."[318] Secondly Athanasius declared that Christ was co-eternal with the Father because He was begotten not made. ". . . He is God's offspring, and since God is eternal and He belongs to God as Son, He exists from all eternity . . ."[319] This position reflected the full deity of Christ with the Father which meant that Christ was infinite, immutable, and incapable of sin. "The divinity of the Father is identical to the divinity of the Word."[320] The intent of this creed was to unify the position of the church regarding the deity of Christ in the Trinity, set the boundaries of acceptable teaching by the bishops of the church, and to clearly denounce the teachings and person of Arius as outside of the boundaries of the church. The introduction of the key word "homoousious" to describe a hypostatic union however caused subsequent confusion over the critical meaning of the term as applied to the God-head. ". . . Athanasius has no word to express the subsistence as persons of Father and Son. For him even in 369 hypostasis which designates the three is the same as ousia which designates the one. This lingering impression in terminology will continue to bedevil theological discourse."[321] The term could alternatively mean essence, substance, being, person, or nature. It could be applied to the God-head either universally, individually, or materially. "Sometimes the term was generic: it stood for the universal. . . Sometimes, however, the dominant meaning was 'individual'. . . But, thirdly . . . ousia might suggest just matter . . ."[322]

The second official creed was the amended creed of Constantinople I in 381 C.E. which revised and updated the Nicene Creed. This activity took place at the Council of Constantinople I. The purpose of the revision was to reflect the incarnation of Christ as attributed to both the Holy Spirit and the Virgin Mary. "There are ten additions to the Constantinopolitan Creed, most of them slight. Only two—'from the Holy Spirit and the Virgin Mary' following 'was incarnate', and 'sits at the right hand of the Father' after 'ascended into heaven'—have doctrinal significance."[323] The second purpose was to refute the teachings of Apollinaris. Apollinaris taught that Christ was not wholly human having a single divine nature. ". . . the one Son of God is not of two natures but is 'one incarnate nature of the divine Word'."[324] The revised creed re-affirmed the full deity of Christ and His consubstantiality with the Holy Spirit. In addition the Holy Spirit was defended as deity proceeding from the Father. "Athanasius argues that the Spirit is the spirit of Christ within us, and his divinity is therefore the correlate of Christ's divinity. Furthermore our sanctification and deification depends on the work of the

Spirit within us, and if the Spirit is a creature, he could not make us divine. As in the debate with the Arians, the argument is based on what is necessary for salvation to be real, and it leads to uncompromising statements about the whole Triad being one God. "[325] During the years 361-381 C.E., the Arians dominated the Eastern bishoprics and with Emperor Constantius. The Creed of Constantinople was not published until 451 C.E. The creed defended the Holy Spirit as: (1) retaining the title of Lord, (2) giving life, (3) proceeding from the Father, and (4) worthy of worship. Apollinaris and his teachings were denounced as a result. "Apollinaris taught that the flesh was assumed into heaven, and also, it seems, that the Logos' flesh preexisted in heaven. He was the 'Man from heaven', as Paul said. It is not easy to see exactly what he meant, but his opponents certainly expended much energy refuting the idea that the flesh of Christ was eternal. What lies behind this may be an objection on Apollinaris' part to the Trinity becoming 'four' by the assumption of the flesh, but it seems more likely to relate to his endeavour to give a satisfactory account of the union of the divine Logos with human flesh."[326] A long lasting dispute arose from this creed which reflected the eastern view that the Holy Spirit proceeded from the Father alone. The Western view was that the Holy Spirit proceeded from both the Father and the Son. "When the council of Constantinople met in 381, one of its express objects was to bring the Church's teaching about the Holy Spirit into line with what it believed about the Son."[327]

    The third council met in Ephesus in 431 C.E. The council was called by Emperor Theodosius II. The two points of discussion were over the title to be applied to Mary and the teachings of Nestorius. Representatives of Antioch wanted to call Mary "Christotokos" Mother of Christ rather than "Theotokos" Mother of God. Nestorius favored Christotokos because he and other Antiochenes believed in the two separate and distinct natures in Christ resulting in their understanding that Mary as a human being could only be the mother of Christ the human not the divine. "Nestorius began to attack the title at every opportunity; he seemed, says one account, scared of the term, as though it was a terrible phantom. Others in the city took up Mary's defense, even interrupting Nestorius' sermons to shout that Mary is the Mother of God."[328]The more comprehensive debates at Ephesus were between the teachings of Nestorius and of Cyril. Nestorius taught that Christ's two natures existed as real persons each containing its own reality. "Nestorius this time replied with force, retorting that the Nicene Fathers did not teach that The consubstantial Godhead was passible or that the one co-eternal with God has been begotten. The one co-eternal with God had been begotten. The very phrase 'one Lord Jesus Christ, his only-begotten Son' showed how the Fathers had carefully laid side by side the names belonging to each nature so that the one Lord is not divided, while at the same time the natures are not in danger of confusion because of the singleness of the Sonship."[329] He was strongly opposed to the idea of Apollinaris of any mixing or confusing of the natures of Christ. The approach of the Antiochenes to understanding the incarnation was to explain how the Word became man. The approach of the Alexandrians, including Cyril was to explain how the Word became flesh. "Nestorius represented the Antiochene tradition; Cyril, the Alexandrian . . . all theologians are in Christology either Antiochene, beginning with Jesus . . . and attempting to explain how this man is also God, or Alexandrian beginning with the Word . . . and attempting to understand the implications of the Logos taking flesh."[330] The Alexandrians described the union of the two natures metaphorically as like that of the union of the body and soul within a human being. Nestorius was supported in his teachings by the Empress Eudokia but opposed by the emperor's sister Pulcheria. Nestorius and the Antiochenes "were blamed by their opponents for not having brought these two ideas to such an agreement, that the oneness of the person of Christ became comprehensible. They were said to have divided Christ into two persons and two sons-the eternal son of God and the son of Mary,-the first being Son of God by nature and the other only by adoption."[331] Cyril was from the Alexandrian tradition. He often explained his understanding of Christology from references to the Scriptures using the allegorical method of interpretation. During the fourteen previous years before the council of Ephesus, Cyril published fourteen Festal Letters which defined his beliefs. "When accordingly we think rightly, we do not speak of two Sons, nor of two Christs or Lords, but of one son and Lord, both before the Incarnation and when he had the covering of flesh."[332] "In the incarnation, two realities which were philosophically and theologically impossible to combine, have been demonstrably united in Christ."[333] Even though Nestorius was denounced, Cyril was forced to sign a Formulary of Peace which preserved Antiochene theology. "It declared that Christ was 'perfect God and perfect man consisting of rational soul and body, of one substance with the Father in his Godhead, of one substance with us in His

Manhood, so that there is a union of two natures; on which ground we confess Christ to be one and Mary to be mother of God'"[334] Cyril also corresponded with Nestorius and in his second letter to him incorporated twelve anathemas which thereafter were endorsed by the church fathers at the Council of Council of Ephesus. These Twelve Anathemas were:

1. If anyone will not confess that the Emmanuel is very God, and that therefore the Holy Virgin is the Mother of God, inasmuch as in the flesh she bore the Word of God made flesh [as it is written, "The Word was made flesh"] let him be anathema.
2. If anyone shall not confess that the Word of God the Father is united hypostatically to flesh, and that with that flesh of his own, he is one only Christ both God and man at the same time: let him be anathema.
3. If anyone shall after the [hypostatic] union divide the hypostases in the one Christ, joining them by that connexion alone, which happens according to worthiness, or even authority and power, and not rather by a coming together, which is made by natural union: let him be anathema.
4. If anyone shall divide between two persons or subsistences those expressions which are contained in the Evangelical and Apostolical writings, or which have been said concerning Christ by the Saints, or by himself, and shall apply some to him as to a man separate from the Word of God, and shall apply others to the only Word of God the Father, on the ground that they are fit to be applied to God: let him be anathema.
5. If anyone shall dare to say that the Christ is a Theophorus [that is, God-bearing] man and not rather that he is very God, as an only Son through nature, because "the Word was made flesh," and "hath a share in flesh and blood as we do:" let him be anathema.
6. If anyone shall dare say that the Word of God the Father is the God of Christ or the Lord of Christ, and shall not rather confess him as at the same time both

God and Man, since according to the Scriptures, "The Word was made flesh": let him be anathema.
7. If anyone shall say that Jesus as man is only energized by the Word of God, and that the glory of the Only-begotten is attributed to him as something not properly his: let him be anathema.
8. If anyone shall dare to say that the assumed man ought to be worshipped together with God the Word, and glorified together with him, and recognised together with him as God, and yet as two different things, the one with the other (for this "Together with" is added [i.e., by the Nestorians] to convey this meaning); and shall not rather with one adoration worship the Emmanuel and pay to him one glorification, as [it is written] "The Word was made flesh": let him be anathema.
9. If any man shall say that the one Lord Jesus Christ was glorified by the Holy Ghost, so that he used through him a power not his own and from him received power against unclean spirits and power to work miracles before men and shall not rather confess that it was his own Spirit through which he worked these divine signs; let him be anathema.
10. Divine Scripture says, that Christ became High Priest and Apostle of our confession, and that he offered himself for us a sweet-smelling savour to God the Father. Whosoever shall say that it is not the divine Word himself, when he was made flesh and had become man as we are, but another than he, a man born of a woman, yet different from him, who is become our Great High Priest and Apostle; or if any man shall say that he offered himself in sacrifice for himself and not rather for us, whereas, being without sin, he had no need of offering or sacrifice: let him be anathema.
11. Whosoever shall not confess that the flesh of the Lord giveth life and that it pertains to the Word of God the Father as his very own, but shall pretend that it belongs to another person who is united to him [i.e., the Word]

only according to honour, and who has served as a dwelling for the divinity; and shall not rather confess, as we say, that that flesh giveth life because it is that of the Word who giveth life to all: let him be anathema.
12. Whosoever shall not recognize that the Word of God suffered in the flesh, that he was crucified in the flesh, and that likewise in that same flesh he tasted death and that he is become the first-begotten of the dead, for, as he is God, he is the life and it is he that giveth life: let him be anathema.[335]

The next council in 451 C.E. produced the Chalcedonian Creed. This creed was the primary statement of faith of the Orthodox Church. From this time forward they were known by the term Chalcedonians. The creed produced a central thesis that Christ existed in two natures which were in union as inseparable and distinct. "By using a series of four Greek negative adverbs—without confusion, without change, without division, without separation—the bishops showed their concern for the mysterious and incomprehensible nature of the subject matter with which they were dealing."[336] Those who rejected this doctrine insisted that the two natures of Christ had become one which became the central doctrinal theme of the Monophysites. ". . . if then there are two natures, there are of necessity two persons, but if there are two persons, there are two Christs."[337] The creed also: (1) accepts the Nicene Creed, (2) states that the Holy Spirit proceeded from the Father, and re-asserted that Mary is the Mother of God. Following the publication of the creed, there remained confusion over the exact meaning of the term "hypostatic union", doubts about the suffering of the Divine Word, and the potential deification of the humanity of Christ. "The council declared itself opposed to those who affirmed a double Sonship, who said that the Godhead of the Only-Begotten is passible, who imagined a mixture or confusion of natures of Christ, who taught that the form of a servant, the flesh, of Christ is from heaven, and who feigned that the Lord had two natures before the union, but only one after."[338]

The Council of Constantinople II was held in 553 C.E. The struggle over doctrine reached a high point between Chalcedonians and Monophysites. During the sixth century leading up to this council, the writings of the three Antiochene theologians had been condemned in 509, prominent patriarchs such as Severus of Antioch and Theodosius of Alexandria had written eloquently defending Monophysite doctrines. The Three Chapters and Origen were condemned in 543, and fifteen anathemas were published at the conclusion of the council. "Associated with the Second Council of Constantinople are fifteen anathemas directed against Origenist doctrine."[339] Eutyches and former heretics were anathematized. "Eutyches was accused of preaching, equally subversively, that the Incarnate Christ possessed but a single nature, and that nature was divine. Found guilty and degraded, Eutyches appealed to Pope Leo (the Great), to the Emperor and to the monks of Constantinople; and in so doing he unleashed a storm of unimaginable ferocity."[340] The definitions in the form of anathemas were intended to clarify the findings as published in the Chalcedonian Creed.

The creed from the third council of Constantinople in 680-81 C.E. was directed toward the issue of whether Christ had two wills or one. Those who were Monophysites such as Sergius and Honorius were condemned for their belief in the one will of Christ. "Patriarch Sergius propagated a new formula . . . that although Christ had two natures, the human and the divine, these natures possessed a single active force, or energy."[341] Maximus the Confessor taught the orthodox view that Christ had two wills. "The idea is developed in the theology of Maximus the Confessor, when he argues, against the Monophysites, for the existence in Christ of a human 'will,' or 'energy,' stressing that without it authentic humanity is inconceivable."[342] The subsequent ruling as expressed in the creed affirmed the two wills doctrine.

The Athanasian Creed was a statement of orthodox faith which is attributable only to the influence of Athanasius and is unconfirmed as to its authorship and date of original publication.

1. Whosoever will be saved, before all things it is necessary that he hold the catholic faith;
2. Which faith except every one do keep whole and undefiled, without doubt he shall perish everlastingly.
3. And the catholic faith is this: That we worship one God in Trinity, and Trinity in Unity;
4. Neither confounding the persons nor dividing the substance.

5. For there is one person of the Father, another of the Son, and another of the Holy Spirit.
6. But the Godhead of the Father, of the Son, and of the Holy Spirit is all one, the glory equal, the majesty coeternal.
7. Such as the Father is, such is the Son, and such is the Holy Spirit.
8. The Father uncreated, the Son uncreated, and the Holy Spirit uncreated.
9. The Father incomprehensible, the Son incomprehensible, and the Holy Spirit incomprehensible.
10. The Father eternal, the Son eternal, and the Holy Spirit eternal.
11. And yet they are not three eternals but one eternal.
12. As also there are not three uncreated nor three incomprehensible, but one uncreated and one incomprehensible.
13. So likewise the Father is almighty, the Son almighty, and the Holy Spirit almighty.
14. And yet they are not three almighties, but one almighty.
15. So the Father is God, the Son is God, and the Holy Spirit is God;
16. And yet they are not three Gods, but one God.
17. So likewise the Father is Lord, the Son Lord, and the Holy Spirit Lord;
18. And yet they are not three Lords but one Lord.
19. For like as we are compelled by the Christian verity to acknowledge every Person by himself to be God and Lord;
20. So are we forbidden by the catholic religion to say; There are three Gods or three Lords.
21. The Father is made of none, neither created nor begotten.
22. The Son is of the Father alone; not made nor created, but begotten.
23. The Holy Spirit is of the Father and of the Son; neither made, nor created, nor begotten, but proceeding.
24. So there is one Father, not three Fathers; one Son, not three Sons; one Holy Spirit, not three Holy Spirits.
25. And in this Trinity none is afore or after another; none is greater or less than another.
26. But the whole three persons are coeternal, and coequal.
27. So that in all things, as aforesaid, the Unity in Trinity and the Trinity in Unity is to be worshipped.
28. He therefore that will be saved must thus think of the Trinity.

29. Furthermore it is necessary to everlasting salvation that he also believe rightly the incarnation of our Lord Jesus Christ.
30. For the right faith is that we believe and confess that our Lord Jesus Christ, the Son of God, is God and man.
31. God of the substance of the Father, begotten before the worlds; and man of substance of His mother, born in the world.
32. Perfect God and perfect man, of a reasonable soul and human flesh subsisting.
33. Equal to the Father as touching His Godhead, and inferior to the Father as touching His manhood.
34. Who, although He is God and man, yet He is not two, but one Christ.
35. One, not by conversion of the Godhead into flesh, but by taking of that manhood into God.
36. One altogether, not by confusion of substance, but by unity of person.
37. For as the reasonable soul and flesh is one man, so God and man is one Christ;
38. Who suffered for our salvation, descended into hell, rose again the third day from the dead;
39. He ascended into heaven, He sits on the right hand of the Father, God, Almighty;
40. From thence He shall come to judge the quick and the dead.
41. At whose coming all men shall rise again with their bodies;
42. and shall give account of their own works.
43. And they that have done good shall go into life everlasting and they that have done evil into everlasting fire.
44. This is the catholic faith, which except a man believe faithfully he cannot be saved.

Detailed Description of Church Creeds

The Nicene Creed used metaphysical terms to describe who Christ was in relation to the Trinity. Terms such as begotten and substance were intended to convey a distinction that Christ was not created like all humanity and that He was of the same essence in His being as that of the Father. "he is no demigod or superior creature, but God in the same sense that the Father is God: 'true God from true God,' the council proclaimed in the Creed which it drew up, 'begotten not made, *one in essence* with the

Father'."³⁴³ The creed was written to confront the teachings of Arius who denied the full deity of Christ. Arius' claims concerning Christ were: (1) He was divine but created, (2) He was not of the same essence as the Father, and (3) He was not consubstantial with the Father.

Arius was certainly a monotheist:

> he confessed one God, alone ingenerate or unbegotten, alone everlasting, alone unbegun, who begat an only-Begotten Son before eternal times through whom he made both the ages and the universe, perfect creature of God, not as one of the creatures. The Father alone is God, according to Arius; the Son is the first and greatest of the creatures. He is 'divine', one might say but not God as God is God. There are therefore three hypostases, three existent beings, Father, Son and Spirit, but the Father is the Monad, the only true God: the others are derivative not ingenerate beings. Certainly the Monad cannot be divided as Sabellius suggested, speaking of a 'Son-and-Father', nor can the Son be regarded as a 'portion' of the Father, consubstantial with him. Such are the views expressed by Arius in a letter to his bishop, Alexander.

Athanasius was the primary defender of the deity of Christ during this debate and thus he was responsible for formulating the response which is represented by the Nicene Creed. The mystery of the Trinity had been accepted on Biblical terms for three hundred years but many theologians sought to go deeper into the understanding of Christ in the Trinity. The controversy itself centered upon the meaning of Proverbs 8:22-23 "The Lord possessed me in the beginning of his way, before his works of old. I was set up from everlasting, from the beginning, or ever the earth was." Pelikan describes the implications of the divinity of Christ by reference to Scripture which suggests several understandings including: (1) adoption, (2) identity, (3) distinction, and (4) derivation. Adoption suggested that the Father adopted Christ to become a member of the Trinity. Identity suggested that there was a sequence to the three-in-one Trinity. Distinction suggested that there were three persons but of only one substance. Derivation suggested that Christ was an angel as described in the theophanies. Pelikan describes this as follows, "The use of the titles

Logos and Son of God to interpret and correlate the passages of adoption, passages of identity, passages of distinction, and passages of derivation was a theological tour de force accomplished by the theologians of the second and third centuries . . ."[344] The concept underlying the teachings of Arius was that Christ was a created being, only the Father was eternal and unbegotten, and therefore God is monadic. "Before the time of Origen, and even to some extent after it, it was generally believed that only the Father had 'being' in the absolute sense; the other two hypostases of the Trinity had something less, corresponding to temporal 'existence'."[345] The result of the council was in producing the Nicene Creed which affirmed the triadic nature of the Godhead.

We believe in one God the Father all powerful, maker of all things both seen and unseen. And in one Lord Jesus Christ, the Son of God, the only-begotten begotten from the Father, that is from the substance [Gr. ousias, Lat. substantia] of the Father, God from God, light from light, true God from true God, begotten [Gr. gennethenta, Lat. natum] not made [Gr. poethenta, Lat. factum], CONSUBSTANTIAL [Gr. homoousion, Lat. unius substantiae (quod Graeci dicunt homousion)] with the Father, through whom all things came to be, both those in heaven and those in earth; for us humans and for our salvation he came down and became incarnate, became human, suffered and rose up on the third day, went up into the heavens, is coming to judge the living and the dead. And in the Holy Spirit.

And those who say "there once was when he was not", and "before he was begotten he was not", and that he came to be from things that were not, or from another hypostasis [Gr. hypostaseos] or substance [Gr. ousias, Lat. substantia], affirming that the Son of God is subject to change or alteration these the catholic and apostolic church *anathematises*.[346]

The Creed of Constantinople I was written to denounce both Arius and Apollinaris. Apollinaris taught that Christ had one incarnate nature. This nature he believed was dominated by the Divine Logos. ". . . the logical mind of Apollinaris saw difficulties, and by 370 he was already beginning to teach the one, divine, nature of Christ, and to oppose clergy who disagreed with him."[347] His focus was on the aspect of the union of the body of Christ with the Godhead. He taught that Christ is: (1) bodily conjoined in union with the Godhead, (2) co-essential with God, (3) preexistent with the Father, (4) 'like" a human being but not actually a human being, (5) the body of Christ did not unite with God, and (6) the divine nature and the human body are mingled together in a unity. "Thus he is both coessential with God in the invisible Spirit (the flesh being comprehended in the title because it has been united to that which is coessential with God), and again coessential with men (the Godhead being comprehended with the body because it has been united to what is coessential with us)."[348] Apollinaris rejected the ideas that Christ possessed a human mind, that Christ had two natures that Christ had two wills, and that Christ could not have voluntarily become fallible in his humanity. ". . . the Apollinarist doctrine which accounted for the subjective unity of Christ by teaching that the divine Logos dispensed with a human mind or consciousness in Christ, because the superior displaced the inferior."[349] Rather Christ was composed of a composite union wherein the divine portion is impassible and the human portion is passible. Therefore in the composite union it is acceptable to worship Christ in the flesh because it has been deified. He was opposed by the two Gregory's who objected that Christ did not only "appear" to be a man, which the two natures may have united without becoming a "composite", that Christ was not just a mere man, and that Christ had to be incarnate as a man who suffered so that the redemption he provided would be efficacious for humanity. "The Council of Constantinople reaffirmed the doctrine of Nicaea regarding the divinity of the Son, and added that the same ought to be said about the Holy Spirit. Thus, it was this council that definitively proclaimed the doctrine of the Trinity. Its decisions and the theology reflected in them, were in large measure the result of the work of the Great Cappadocians."[350] The Creed of Constantinople revises the Nicene Creed as follows:

We believe (I believe) in one God, the Father Almighty, maker of heaven and earth, and of all things visible and invisible. And in one Lord Jesus Christ, the only begotten Son of God, and born of the Father before all ages. (God of God) light of light, true God of true God. Begotten not made, consubstantial to the Father, by whom all things were made. Who for us men and for our salvation came down from heaven. And was incarnate of the Holy Ghost and of the Virgin Mary and was made man; was crucified also for us under Pontius Pilate, suffered and was buried; and the third day rose again according to the Scriptures. And ascended into heaven, sits at the right hand of the Father, and shall come again with glory to judge the living and the dead, of whose Kingdom there shall be no end. And (I believe) in the Holy Ghost, the Lord and Giver of life, who proceeds from the Father (and the Son), who together with the Father and the Son is to be adored and glorified, who spoke by the Prophets. And one holy, catholic, and apostolic Church. We confess (I confess) one baptism for the remission of sins. And we look for (I look for) the resurrection of the dead and the life of the world to come. Amen."[351]

The Council of Ephesus was called to denounce the teachings of Nestorius and to determine the appropriate title for Mary in relation to the Godhead. ". . . Nestorius was saying that Mary could not be called Theotokos but only Christotokos because Jesus was not fully divine but only a man adopted by the Divine Word."[352] The concept of Christotokos was suggested in order to disclaim a connection of Mary to the Godhead as had been implied in the term Theotokos. Theotokos was adopted as the orthodox title. Nestorius taught that the two natures of Christ remained unaltered and distinct in union. Further, Christ's two natures existed together each with its own reality and concrete existence forming a single person. "This conjunction resulted in a single prosopon, Christ, that is, one object of perception, one external undivided appearance. This is the one *prosopon* of Jesus Christ in whom God is transparent in the manhood and the manhood is glorified in the Godhead. This single *prosopon* resulting from conjunction of natures is one in dignity and honor and worshipped by all creation."[353] The concept that was rejected by Cyril and the council was of the two concrete realities which implied to them that Nestorius taught that Christ was two persons. Cyril taught that the single, unique Christ became one out of two natures. "He argued for a union in the strict sense of the word, yet a union that was of the type that did not destroy its constituent elements."[354] The council produced a Profession of Faith reaffirming their beliefs. Cyril produced a document containing Twelve Anathemas rejecting Nestorian teachings. The Profession of Faith was as follows:

> So we shall confess one Christ and one Lord. We do not adore the man along with the Word, so as to avoid any appearance of division by using the word "with". But we adore him as one and the same, because the body is not other than the Word, and takes its seat with him beside the Father, again not as though there were two sons seated together but only one, united with his own flesh. **If, however, we reject the hypostatic union as being either**

impossible or too unlovely for the Word, we fall into the fallacy of speaking of two sons. We shall have to distinguish and speak both of the man as honoured with the title of son, and of the Word of God as by nature possessing the name and reality of sonship, each in his own way. We ought not, therefore, to split into two sons the one Lord Jesus Christ. Such a way of presenting a correct account of the faith will be quite unhelpful, even though some do speak of a union of persons. For scripture does not say that the Word united the person of a man to himself, but that he became flesh. The Word's becoming flesh means nothing else than that he partook of flesh and blood like us; he made our body his own, and came forth a man from woman without casting aside his deity, or his generation from God the Father, but rather in his assumption of flesh remaining what he was. [355]

The statement of faith concerning Mary was as follows:

Therefore, because the holy virgin bore in the flesh God who was united hypostatically with the flesh, *for that reason* we call her **mother of God**, not as though the nature of the Word had the beginning of its existence from the flesh (for "the Word was in the beginning and the Word was God and the Word was with God", and he made the ages and is coeternal with the Father and craftsman of all things), but because, as we have said, he united to himself hypostatically the human and underwent a birth according to the flesh from her womb. This was not as though he needed necessarily or for his own nature a birth in time and in the last times of this age, but *in order that* he might bless the beginning of our existence, in order that seeing that it was a woman that had given birth to him united to the flesh, the curse against the whole race should thereafter cease which was consigning all our earthy bodies to death, and in order that the removal through him of the curse, "In sorrow thou shalt bring forth children", should demonstrate the truth of the words of the prophet: "Strong death swallowed them Up", and again, "God has wiped every tear away from all face." It is *for this cause* that we say that in his economy he blessed marriage and, when invited, went down to Cana in Galilee with his holy apostles. We have been taught to hold these things by the holy *apostles* and evangelists and by all the divinely inspired *scriptures* and by the true confession of the blessed *fathers*.[356]

The Chalcedonian Creed defended against the extreme version of Monophysitism espoused by Eutyches. "He combined the two natures so intimately that the human nature appeared completely absorbed by the divine one, Just 'as a drop of honey, which falls into the sea, dissolves in it,' so the human nature in Christ is lost in the divine. Thus, Eutyches denied the central prerequisite for the mystery of Christ and his mission as Savior and Redeemer."[357]

"According to Eutyches, Christ took human nature from the Virgin, but that humanity was not consubstantial with ours and was taken up into the one nature of the Incarnate Word. It was not Apollinarianism, but like Apollinarianism it showed up some of the potential implications of an extreme Alexandrian position. For the West there was one nature before the incarnation, namely that of the pre-existent Son, and after their union in the incarnation, two natures united in Christ. Even after Chalcedon the Alexandrian tradition would continue to affirm that there were two natures before the union, and one after (hence the label "Monophysite')."

In addition the council reaffirmed the Nicene Creed, the Constantinople Creed, two of Cyril's letters, and the Tome of Leo. The most significant finding was the statement that Christ was one person with two natures.

The phrase which became the focus of contention was 'in two natures'; the anti-Chalcedonians wanted to amend it to 'out of two natures'. It is easy to laugh at the slight difference between the Greek prepositions *en* and *ek*, just as it was to mock the fight over an 'iota' when disagreement over *homoousios* and *homoiousios* was at issue in the previous century. But the accounts so far should have alerted us to the ramifications of that apparently slight difference. The affirmation that two natures persist after the union was vital to the Antiochenes and assumed by the West, but it was precisely this that the Alexandrians distrusted as 'dividing the Christ'. The alternative touched the heart of Antiochene suspicions: if you spoke of two natures prior to the union but not after, it suggested a pre-existent humanity and a subsequent 'mixture'."

The Creed of Chalcedon was as follows:

> Following, then, the holy fathers, we unite in teaching all men to confess the one and only Son, our Lord Jesus Christ. This selfsame one is perfect both in deity and in humanness; this selfsame one is also actually God and actually man, with a rational soul {meaning human soul} and a body. He is of the same reality as God as far as his deity is concerned and of the same reality as we ourselves as far as his humanness is concerned; thus like us in all respects, sin only excepted. Before time began he was begotten of the Father, in respect of his deity, and now in these "last days," for us and behalf of our salvation, this selfsame one was born of Mary the virgin, who is God-bearer in respect of his humanness.
>
> We also teach that we apprehend this one and only Christ-Son, Lord, only-begotten -- in two natures; and we do this without confusing the two natures, without transmuting one nature into the other, without dividing them into two separate categories, without contrasting them according to area or function. The distinctiveness of each nature is not nullified by the union. Instead, the "properties" of each nature are conserved and both natures concur in one "person" and in one reality {hypostasis}. They are not divided or cut into two persons, but are together the one and only and only-begotten Word {Logos} of God, the Lord Jesus Christ. Thus have the prophets of old testified; thus the Lord Jesus Christ himself taught us; thus the Symbol of Fathers {the <u>Nicene Creed</u>} has handed down to us.[358]

The Council of Constantinople II held in 553 C.E. repudiated the Three Chapters, condemned Origen, and decreed the Theopaschite Formula. The Three Chapters denounced the writings of three Antiochene theologians as Nestorian. Theodore of Mopsuestia was born in Antioch in 350 C.E. He was declared orthodox at the Council of Chalcedon but later due to the complaints of Cyril he was declared a heretic posthumously. "When the great exegetes of Antioch—Diodore of tarsus, Theodore of Mopsuestia, Nestorius, and even Theodoret of Cyrus—emphasize the full humanity of the historical Jesus, they understand this humanity not merely as distinct from the divinity, but as 'autonomous' and 'personalized'."[359] He was a Dyophysite whose writings were held in high esteem by the Nestorian Church. "The strict Dyophysites were Chalcedonians who still rigidly maintained the Antiochian Christology, and who objected to some of Cyril's propositions, such as the Theopaschite formula. . . ."[360] Theodoret of Cyrus was born in Antioch in 393 C.E. He was another leading theologian who disputed with Cyril and supported Nestorius. "Theodoret of Cyrus and other Oriental bishops were horrified at John's surrender to Cyril who had not expressly withdrawn his Twelve Anathemas."[361] He was also the primary critic of Eutyches. Ibas of Edessa was born in Syria. He became head of the School of Edessa. He was the third theologian condemned at the council in 553 C.E. "…they examined 'the letter which is said to have been written by Ibas to Maris the Persian,' whose 'impiety was manifest to all'." [362] The plan of Emperor Justinian was to conciliate the Monophysites. "One of the principal Monophysite objections to Chalcedon was that it had acquitted the Nestorianizing sympathizers, Theodoret of Cyrus and Ibas of Edessa. Might not the Monophysites be reassured if the assertion of the Chalcedonian definition, as interpreted in the light of Cyril of Alexandria, were to be combined with a condemnation of objectionable propositions ('chapters') cited from Theodore of Mopsuestia, Theodoret, and Ibas?"[363]

The Creed of Constantinople III of 680-681 C.E. denounced the attempts of the Monophysites to introduce Monothelitism and Monoenergism into the findings of the council. "What Sergius evidently had in mind was to hold to the Chalcedonian definition of 'in two natures' but to reconcile this with a declaration of one activity in Christ."[364] Maximus taught the orthodox view of the two wills of Christ. "Christ has therefore two natures, two operations, two wills really proceeding from the divine and human natures but always in harmony because the single divine Person assures their goodness of choice."[365]

The Creed or statement of faith was as follows:

> We also proclaim two natural willings or wills in him and two natural operations, without separation, without change, without partition, without confusion, according to the teaching of the holy Fathers -- and two natural wills not contrary to each other, God forbid, as the impious heretics

have said they would be, but his human will following, and not resisting or opposing, but rather subject to his divine and all-powerful will. For it was proper for the will of the flesh to be moved naturally, yet to be subject to the divine will, according to the all-wise Athanasius. For as his flesh is called and is the flesh of God the Word, so also the natural will of his flesh is called and is God the Word's own will, as he himself says: "I came down from heaven, not to do my own will, but the will of the Father who sent me," calling the will of the flesh his own, as also the flesh had become his own. For in the same manner that his all-holy and spotless ensouled flesh, though divinized, was not destroyed, but remained in its own law and principle also his human will, divinized, was not destroyed, but rather preserved, as Gregory the divine says: "His will, as conceived of in his character as the Saviour, is not contrary to God, being wholly divinized." We also glorify two natural operations in the same our Lord Jesus Christ, our true God, without separation, without change, without partition, without confusion, that is, a divine operation and a human operation, as the divine preacher Leo most clearly says: "For each form does what is proper to it, in communion with the other; the Word, that is, performing what belongs to the Word, and the flesh carrying out what belongs to the flesh." We will not therefore grant the existence of one natural operation of God and the creature, lest we should either raise up into the divine nature what is created, or bring down the preeminence of the divine nature into the place suitable for things that are made. For we recognize the wonders and the sufferings as of one and the same person], according to the difference of the natures of which he is and in which he has his being, as the eloquent Cyril said. Preserving therefore in every way the unconfused and undivided, we set forth the whole confession in brief; believing our Lord Jesus Christ, our true God, to be one of the holy Trinity even after the taking of flesh, we declare that his two natures shine forth in his one hypostasis, in which he displayed both the wonders and the sufferings through the whole course of his dispensation, not in phantasm but truly, the difference of nature being recognized in the same one hypostasis by the fact that each nature wills and works what is proper to it, in communion with the other. On this principle we glorify two natural wills and operations combining with each other for the salvation of the human race."[366]

Analysis of the Church Councils

Arius of Alexandria around the year 318 C.E. began to teach that Jesus was created by God which resulted in a rift in the church. Alexander, who was bishop of Alexandria, disputed with Arius. He taught that Jesus was co-equal and co-eternal with God. "Though we know little about its results it seems evident that Arius was condemned, Eusebius of Caesarea severely censured and a confessional formula drawn up which conformed to Alexander's views. The son was not *homoousios* but the very image, not of the will or of anything else, but of his Father's very substance (*hypostasis*)."[367] The dispute was elevated to Emperor Constantine for resolution. Constantine called a council at Nicaea to resolve the dispute in 325 C.E. with 318 bishops in attendance. As a result, Arius was excommunicated and the Nicene Creed was adopted which upheld the deity of Jesus within the doctrine of the Trinity. "Only if Christ is truly God, the council answered, can He unite us to God, for none but God Himself can open to humans the way of union."[368] This creed became the bedrock of the Roman Catholic, Eastern Orthodox, and later the Anglican churches. Athanasius succeeded to the bishopric of Alexandria and clarified and supported the Nicene Creed by defending the concept that god is in three persons. "If you contemplate the father, who is one distinct presentation of the deity, you obtain a mental view of the one true God. If you contemplate the Son or the Spirit, you obtain a view of the same God; though the presentation is different, the reality is identical."[369] Constantine wanted to bring peace and order to the empire which he had recently won militarily. The result of the council was to conclude that Christ is truly divine and that He is of the identical essence as the Father.

The second council was held in Constantinople in 381 C.E. The Alexandrian school emphasized the divine nature of Jesus wherein the two natures are intertwined. The Antiochene School emphasized the human nature wherein Jesus had a free will subject to human weaknesses but not lapsing into sin. "To the Alexandrians, the Antiochenes taught 'Two Sons'; to the Antiochenes, the Alexandrians taught an Apollinarian 'mixture'."[370] In 381 C.E. the Emperor Theodosius called for the council to meet at Constantinople. The council rejected the teachings of Apollinaris. He taught that Jesus' body was human but His soul became divine by infusion of the Spirit. The Nicene Creed was expanded to include wording that the Holy Spirit was divine and an equal person of the Trinity.

In 428 C.E Nestorius, the bishop of Constantinople had taught that the separation of Jesus' two natures were brought together by agreement into a union. He believed that Jesus was born as a human being with a human soul and human body. "Refusing to attribute the frailties of humanity to a member of the trinity, he preached that Christ was not, as the Nicaens believed a single person but that he possessed two distinct persons, one human and the other divine."[371] He was challenged on theological and political grounds by Cyril of Alexandria and excommunicated at the Council of Ephesus in 431 C.E. His followers were successful in establishing monasteries and in missionary outreach to Syria, Iraq, Persia, and India. The council was called by the Emperor Theodosius II with 160-198 bishops in attendance.

The issue before the church in the fifth century was focused on Jesus' incarnation in the flesh. The Council of Chalcedon met in 451 C.E. to formulate a statement about Jesus' divinity and humanity. The doctrinal result was to affirm that Christ was wholly God and wholly man, two natures in one person. Eutyches had taught that Jesus possessed only one nature wherein the human nature had been absorbed into the divine nature. "Domnus of Antioch supported his suffrage Theodoret and wrote to the emperor accusing Eutyches of embracing Apollinarianism, of teaching one nature in Christ, of mingling the divine and human and of attributing to God the sufferings of Christ."[372] This became one version of the non-orthodox position of Monophysitism. The council declared for the two natures of Christ in one person position. Those who retained the one nature position broke away from the Orthodox Church establishing the Monophysite Church. "The council resulted in the Monophysite schism, which severed Constantinople from Alexandria and Antioch."[373] This resulted in the Syrian, Coptic, and Jacobite churches in the Middle East. "But large numbers of Non-Chalcedonians, particularly in Egypt and Syria, were subjects of the Emperor, and repeated unsuccessful efforts were made to bring them back into communion with the Byzantine Church."[374] The council was called by the Emperor Marcian at the request of Leo, bishop of Rome. There were between 520-630 delegates in attendance. Both Eutyches and Nestorius were excommunicated. This council was rejected by the Monophysites.

The Council of Constantinople II was called by the Emperor Justinian in 553 C.E. It was presided over by patriarch Eutychius and reluctantly agreed to by Pope Vigilius. At that time the Monophysites were influential. Leading Monophysites were patriarchs Macedonius of Constantinople, Flavian of Antioch, Elias of Jerusalem, and Severus of Antioch. "Monophysites, after Chalcedon, generally preferred the 'first Cyril' to the 'second.' Severus, their great theologian, admitted duality in Christ's being, but for him this duality was a duality 'in imagination,' while 'in actuality' there was only one nature, or being."[375] The council repudiated the Three Chapters as Nestorian, condemned Origen, and accepted the Theopaschite Formula. The wording of the formula was an attempt to unite the Chaldeans and the Monophysites by simply declaring that one of the persons of the Trinity suffered for mankind. "Scythian monks . . . hoped to reconcile the teachings of Leo and Cyril and exclude any Nestorian interpretation of the Definition of Chalcedon. They proposed as the basis of reconciliation the Theopaschite Formula—One of the Trinity suffered for us."[376] Justinian was a Chaldean whereas his wife Theodora was a Monophysite. There were 151-168 bishops in attendance at the council. The Nestorians were Dyophysites who were opposed to and separated from the Monophysites.

The Council of Constantinople III was held in 680-681 C.E. Pope Honorius and Patriarch Sergius taught that Christ had only one will. This was an attempt by the Monophysites to re-introduce Monophysite doctrine into the church. The ideas that Christ had one will (Monothelitism) or one activity (Monoenergism) were rejected by the council. "The bishops concluded; 'wherefore we confess two wills and two operations, concurring most fitly in him for the salvation of the human race'."[377] Maximus the Confessor and Sophronius were the key defenders of the orthodox view. There were 174 bishops in attendance.

Description of the Relevant Church Councils

The first six ecumenical councils denounced the heretical views which posed a challenge within the church. The councils were: Nicaea,

325 (Arianism), Constantinople I, 381 (Apollinarianism), Ephesus, 431 (Nestorianism), Chalcedon, 451 (Eutychianism), Constantinople II, 553 (Monophysitism), and Constantinople III, 680-681 (Monothelitism and Monoenergism). The decision was made to affirm the creeds or be anathematized for refusal to do so.

These things, therefore, having been expressed by us with the greatest accuracy and attention, the holy Ecumenical Synod defines that no one shall be suffered to bring forward a different faith (ἑτέραν πίστιν), nor to write, nor to put together, nor to excogitate, nor to teach it to others. But such as dare either to put together another faith, or to bring forward or to teach or to deliver a different Creed (ἕτερον σύμβολον) to as wish to be converted to the knowledge of the truth, from the Gentiles, or Jews or any heresy whatever, if they be Bishops or clerics let them be deposed, the Bishops from the Episcopate, and the clerics from the clergy; but if they be monks or laics: let them be anathematized.[378]

By 325 C.E. there was considerable strife and disagreement in the provinces regarding the exact nature of Christ. Arius of Alexandria had been teaching that Christ was the first begotten of the Father. "Arius was accused of saying of Christ that 'before he was begotten he was not . . .'"[379] This statement was leading many people to the belief that He was only a demigod. Eusebius, bishop of Nicomedia, supported Arius' views. Opposed to them were Alexander, bishop of Alexandria, and Athanasius a deacon in Alexandria. The Emperor Constantine arrived to convene the council which he had called in order to resolve the issues. "The Emperor exerted all his influence toward securing unanimity; and at length only two bishops stood out."[380] The statements which he affirmed after listening to both parties were summarized and agreed to by the bishops attending. The atmosphere of the council was recorded later by Socrates the historian. "…for Eusebius declares, that of the ministers of God who were present at the Nicene Synod, some were eminent for the word of wisdom, others for the strictness of their life; and that the emperor himself being present, leading all into unanimity, established unity of judgment, and agreement of opinion among them."[381] The creed was drawn up and agreed to by 318 bishops who were present. Five attendees would not agree to the creed due to the insertion of the word "homoousios" meaning consubstantial and of the same essence. This became the foundational council upon which others would build.

The Council of Constantinople I was called in 381 C.E. by the Emperor Theodosius. The council was not accepted as authoritative by the Western Church until 1274 C.E. His purpose was to establish the Nicene Creed with complete unity, appoint a bishop for Constantinople, and to win support of the Macedonian party to his views. "The work of Nicaea was taken up by the second Ecumenical Council, held at Constantinople in 381. This council expanded and adapted the Nicene Creed, developing in particular the teaching upon the Holy Spirit, whom it affirmed to be God even as the Father and Son are God . . ."[382] The bishops who were of the Arian view left the council unconvinced of accepting the Nicene Creed. The bishops of the Homoousian party affirmed the Nicene Creed, elected Nectarius as bishop of Constantinople, and elevated Constantinople as second see in importance in the empire. The doctrines affirmed in the Nicene Creed were put forward by Basil of Caesarea in Cappadocia which declared the Trinity to be one "ousia" essence and three "hypostases" modes of presentation. "The *ousia* was the essence of the Godhead shared by the Holy Trinity, the *hypostasis* the identifying quality, such as 'sonship' or 'sanctification' applicable to its numbers."[383] The issue of the Holy Spirit was incorporated in the creed as the Holy Spirit is a person of the Godhead and proceeds from the Father. "The Son 'was begotten,' and the Spirit 'proceeded,' but together they made up the entire Godhead."[384] The Arians who departed stirred up trouble in the provinces. "But they paying little heed alike to admonitions and reproofs, chose rather to maintain the Arian dogma, than to assent to the 'homoousian' doctrine. Having made this declaration, they departed from Constantinople; moreover they wrote to their partisans in every city, and charged them by no means to harmonize with the creed of the Nicene Synod."[385]

The Council of Ephesus was called in 431 C.E. by Theodosius II. The bishop of Constantinople was Nestorius who taught the reality of the two natures in Christ so concretely that it appeared that he was teaching that Christ was two persons. In addition he wanted to replace the term applied to Mary which was "Theotokos" meaning God-bearer with the term "Christotokos" meaning Christ-bearer. His opponent was Cyril of Alexandria. Cyril overwhelmed the dialogue in a series of letters to Nestorius and later at the council by introducing a list of Twelve Anathemas. Nestorius was supported by the Antiochenes such as John of Antioch, Theodore of Mopsuestia, Theodoret of Cyrus, and Ibas of Edessa. Nevertheless the council voted to condemn Nestorius and his views. "The works of Nestorius were condemned by common acclamation, as was the custom at episcopal synods, and Cyril's letters were accepted as statements of orthodox doctrine."[386] The partisans of Cyril were in full attendance before the backers of Nestorius arrived at the council. Nestorius did not help his cause when he abruptly withdrew from the council without defending his views. "When many had declared that Christ was God, Nestorius said: 'I cannot term him God who was two and three months old. I am therefore clear of your blood, and shall in future come no more among you.' Having uttered these words he left the assembly, and afterwards held meetings with the other bishops who entertained similar sentiments similar to his own."[387]

The Council of Chalcedon was called in 451 C.E. by Anatolius at the request of Pope Leo I. A political change had just occurred when Emperor Theodosius died in 450 C.E and Marcian came to the throne by marriage to the Empress Pulcheria who was the sister of Theodosius. This was a contentious council meeting with 500-600 bishops and theologians attending. The council was physically divided by the seating which placed apart the Eastern bishops such as Anatolius of Constantinople and Maximus of Antioch who were opposed to the views of Eutyches. "Eutyches began to teach that before the Incarnation Christ was of two natures, but after it there was one Christ, one Son, one lord in one *hypostasis* and one *prosopon*."[388] Those on Eutyches side were Dioscurus of Alexandria, Juvenal of Jerusalem, and the bishops of Egypt. Eutyches and his views were denounced while the Tome of Leo and some of the writings of Cyril were accepted as official doctrinal interpretations of the beliefs of the bishops holding the view of the two natures of Christ and who were thereafter known as Chalcedonians. "In their Definition the bishops at last clearly distinguished between person and nature; the person of Christ being one, his natures two."[389] The unofficial council which was held at Ephesus in 449 C.E. was declared as unorthodox and its decisions reversed. "So early as the close of the first session the decisions of the Robber Synod had been annulled, the martyr Flavian declared orthodox, and Dioscurus of Alexandria, Juvenal of Jerusalem, and chiefs of Eutychianism deposed."[390] A confession of faith which embodied the creeds of Nicaea and Constantinople was agreed to and published.

The Council of Constantinople II was called in 553 C.E. The result of the council was to determine the definitions of understanding regarding Christ's natures. The findings were: (1) the three persons of the Trinity are consubstantial, (2) the two natures of Christ were not separated nor confused, (3) the Word and the flesh were hypostatically united in one person, (4) Christ was consubstantial with the Godhead and with humanity, and (5) Mary was the God-bearer. ". . . the bishops condemned first of all those refusing to confess a consubstantial Trinity . . . 'the union of God the Word is made with the flesh animated by a reasonable and living soul, and that such union is made synthetically and hypostatically, and therefore there is only one Person' . . . that Mary 'is exactly and truly the Mother of God'."[391] The Chalcedonian view was supported by patriarchs Macedonius of Constantinople, Flavian of Antioch, Elias of Jerusalem, and Emperors Justin I and Justinian. Those who opposed the Chalcedonian view were Monophysites which included: Emperors Anastasius I and Justin II, Severus of Antioch, John the Grammarian of Jerusalem, Julian of Halicarnassus, Empress Theodora, bishops Theodosius of Alexandria and Anthimus of Constantinople, patriarch Menas of Constantinople, and Bishop Jacob Baradaeus of Edessa. The council issued eleven anathemas which represented the views of the Chalcedonians. Following this council, The Monophysites and the Nestorians began to separate from the Chalcedonians. "To the end of his life, Justinian sought means to conciliate the Monophysites of Egypt and Syria, even though his Council had failed so signally to do so."[392] In Syria the Chalcedonian officials who were called Melkite's were replaced by Nestorian Jacobites. "But under Tiberius and Maurice the orthodox imperial bishops called now Melkites increasingly lost their congregations to the Jacobites."[393] Syrian and Egyptian Monophysites separated from each other. The Egyptian Monophysites became known as Copts. The Nestorians dominated for a time in Persia. Monophysites dominated in Armenia and for a time the Ghassanid Arabs in the Middle East. The decree sourcing from this council was the issuance of the Three Chapters which condemned the writings posthumously of three Antiochene theologians. "In 544 he (Justinian) published an edict, condemning three particular manifestations of the heresy known as the 'Three Chapters'. But the Monophysites were unappeased, while in the West the bishops erupted in fury. Any attack on the Nestorians, they thundered, could only be a blow in favour of the Monophysites. The Patriarch, Menas, was excommunicated on the spot."[394] "Constantinople II is a rather sad council. Its single decree, the 'Three Chapters,' which condemns various writings of three earlier supporters of Nestorius-namely, Theodore of

Mopsuestia, Theodoret of Cyrrhus, and Ibas of Edessa- resulted from the desire of Emperor Justinian to placate the Egyptian church . . ."[395]

The Council of Constantinople III was called in 680-681 C.E. Persia, as a Zoroastrian power, had conquered Syria in 611, Armenia in 613, Jerusalem in 614, and Egypt in 619 C.E. The Sassanid dynasty ruled from 226-635 C.E. until being overthrown by the Muslim Arabs. "From 226 A.D. onward, the political center of Iran swung back to Persia, under the Sassanids, who reigned until the Muslim conquest. Zoroastrianism, whose history had so far been obscure, now became the empire's official religion. It had to struggle there not only against Christianity but against a more recent religion as well, Manichaeism, preached by Mani."[396] Byzantine armies defeated the Persian army in 628 C.E. but the victory did not last a decade due to the advancing victorious Muslim armies. The issues before the members of the council were focused upon the activity and will of Christ. Pope Honorius and Patriarch Sergius of Constantinople both supported the idea that there was one activity and one will in Christ even though they both accepted the two natures of Christ. "Despite previous efforts of George of Constantinople to avoid condemnation of his predecessors, Sergius, Pyrrhus, Paul and Peter, all patriarchs of Constantinople from 610 to 666, were anathematized. The bishops evened the score by condemning Pope Honorius (d. 638)."[397] Maximus the Confessor and Sophronius defended the orthodox view that Christ had two activities, two operations, and two wills. "Sophronius insisted that activity proceeds not from the person of Christ as the sole agent but from the two natures."[398] While this debate was being settled the Byzantines had during the past half century seen their territory and influence in the eastern portion of the empire shrink due to the successes of the Muslim Arabs. "During Justinian's rule and that of his son, the Empire shrank further as Armenia in eastern Asia-Minor and all North Africa were lost to the Arabs."[399] Arab Muslims conquered Syria in 634, Palestine in 639, Egypt in 642, Mesopotamia in 641, Persia in 642; and Cyprus and Rhodes in 677 C.E. This left the Byzantine Orthodox Church in control of only Asia-Minor, Greece, and the Balkans. This freed the Nestorians and the Monophysites to control their own churches under the dominion of the Muslim occupiers. The council concluded by publishing a statement of faith supporting the two wills view of Christ.

During the four centuries from 300-700 C.E. the Christian Church had spread throughout the Roman Empire. By coupling the state government apparatus with the ecclesiastical church authority, the church had become a powerful institution. "It was a turning-point in the history of Christendom—the first time that a Churchman had had the courage to assert the rights of the spiritual power over the temporal, and the first time that a Christian prince had publicly submitted to judgement, condemnation and punishment by an authority which he recognized as higher than his own."[400] The church had defended against outside religious challenges, internal doctrinal disputes threatening the core beliefs, political interference and intrigues from within the empire, and barbarian invasions from outside the empire. "Just as religion plays a prominent role in resistance to empire, so religion is used to legitimize empire."[401] "Specifically, by the latter part of the second century, when the orthodox insisted upon 'one God.' they simultaneously validated the system of governance in which the church is ruled by 'one bishop'."[402] "But orthodox Christians, by the late second century, had begun to establish objective criteria for church membership. Whoever confessed the creed, accepted the ritual of baptism, participated in worship, and obeyed the clergy was accepted as a fellow Christian."[403] Yet the focus on the precision of the language of interpretation of the meaning of the two mysteries which clarified the definition of what would be considered orthodox divided and separated from those with a different meaning and interpretation. "The fact was, that the metaphysical terminology between the Greek and Latin Churches was hopelessly confused . . . ."[404] The mysteries of the Trinity and the Incarnation were vital to the formation of the Christian doctrine. The condemnations, anathemas, denouncements, and excommunications were many times harmful to the unity of the Christian Church.

In summary the church history during this period has been presented by description and analysis of the primary canons, creeds, and councils which were the discussion forum and battle ground for the events of the early church. The result was clarity of understanding amidst the complications and difficulties of language barriers distance between churches, different approaches to understanding the metaphysical concepts of religion by different schools of learning, and the ever present influence of secular politics intermingling in the affairs of the church.

CHAPTER 6

THE IMPACT OF THE MONOPHYSITE CONTROVERSY ON THE BYZANTINE EMPIRE AND THE SPREAD OF ISLAM

The events of the early church years between 300-700 C.E. created stresses and strains on the Byzantine Empire. With the sack of Rome in 410 and the demise of the political empire of Rome in 476 C.E., the leadership of the empire and the critical role of the church substantially transferred to Constantinople. During this period, the importance of the Greek language and culture was more dominant than the Latin culture and language. "By the year 450 there were very few in Western Europe who could read Greek, and after 600, although Byzantium still called itself the Roman Empire, it was rare for a Byzantine to speak Latin, the language of the Romans."[405] Theologians from the large centers of learning such as Alexandria, Antioch, Jerusalem, and later Constantinople shared in the leadership of the Christian Church based upon a system of provincial, metropolitan, and rural bishoprics and parishes. "A local council of this type normally met in the provincial capital, under the presidency of the bishop of the capital, who was given the title *Metropolitan.* As the third century proceeded, councils widened in scope and began to include bishops not from one but from several civil provinces. These larger gatherings tended to assemble in the chief cities of the Empire, such as Alexandria or Antioch; and so it came about that the bishops of certain great cities began to acquire an importance above the provincial Metropolitans."[406] It was inevitable that local customs of belief of long standing and ideologies in the schools of learning would influence the teachings of these theologians. Once the theologians began to think through and explain the two mysteries of the Bible i.e. the Trinity and the Incarnation, they began to use language which was not actually in Scripture. These words were all in the Greek language but carried different meanings to different audiences depending on the framework of their worldview. "Unlike the Church of Rome in the west with its insistence on Latin, the Orthodox church has never been rigid in the matter of languages; its normal policy is to hold services in the language of the people."[407] Words such as homoousian, ousia, prosopon, and Theotokos meant different concepts to the Antiochenes as compared to the Alexandrians. ". . . it marked a stage in the conflict between the two rival concepts of our Lord, that of Antioch emphasizing his humanity, redeeming mankind by his divine example, and that of Alexandria emphasizing a divinity saving man from the consequences of sin by manifesting in his life the full essence of the divine nature."[408] These differences led to debates and disputes which separated large segments of the Christian community from one another. Political intrigue, inflamed passions, and jealousies divided the formerly united and peaceful community into competing segments. The lack of coherence and unity over the internal Christian interpretation of the two mysteries concerning Christ weakened the spiritual bonds and political fabric of the empire. "One can actually see the main characteristic of Eastern Christianity, in its ethical and social attitudes, is to consider man as already redeemed and glorified in Christ, by contrast, Western Christendom has traditionally understood the present state of humanity in both a more realistic and a more pessimistic way: though redeemed and 'justified' in the eyes of God by the sacrifice of the cross, man remains a sinner."[409] This schism weakened the Byzantine Empire and contributed to the success of the Arab Muslims in overthrowing major geographical portions of the empire. "In one respect in particular, luck was on the side of the Arabs: Byzantine-Persian war had left both Empires exhausted. The Monophysite peoples of Syria and Palestine, moreover, felt no real loyalty towards Constantinople, which represented an alien Graeco-Roman culture. The Muslims, Semites and fervent monotheists like themselves, who furthermore promised toleration for all Christian beliefs, may well have seemed preferable."[410] Finally the issues of who Christ was would be incorporated in the religion of Islam as taught by Muhammad.

Division and Weakening of the Byzantine Empire

The Empire of the Byzantines was a continuation of the Roman Empire which had transferred its authority to Constantinople in 313 C.E. at the discretion of Emperor Constantine. From before this time, the worldviews of the influential schools of Alexandria and Antioch were different. "Both were equally typological. The difference between them was not, as has been said, that one was literal and the other allegorical. The exegesis of both was typological and the one was as Christological as the other; but at Antioch theologians concentrated on the catechetical tradition and laid particular stress on the part of it relating to the sacraments, while the Alexandrians concentrated on what Tradition had to say about the spiritual life and put stress on the mystical side. Both were equally rooted in Tradition."[411] Alexandrian tradition used allegorical interpretation of Scripture as influenced by Origen whereas the Antiochene tradition favored a literal interpretation. "Origen's views, then, on this side of the question are quite clear. The Bible is one vast allegory, a tremendous sacrament in which every detail is symbolic."[412]

Alexandrians were influenced by Platonic reasoning which focused on the cosmological issues of deity whereas the Antiochenes focused on the reality of Christ's humanity. "The problem of the contrast between a Christ descended from on high and displaying before man the perfection of the divine nature, and a Christ 'sprung from beneath' sharing our humanity and raising it by moral activity toward God, had been decided in favor of the former. The first round in the battle between the Alexandrian and Antiochene schools had been won by the Alexandrians."[413] The tools developed for resolution of differences of interpretation were council resolutions followed by the publication of creeds and canons to set the boundaries of interpretation on these issues. The results usually included language which denounced a theologian, barred him from office, and burned his writings. The conciliar method of resolution did not usually result in reconciliation and restoration but rather in acrimony, distrust, and division. The dividing of the Christian Church during this period was primarily based on separation of the Monophysites, Nestorians, and Orthodox from each other forming three primary groups which were influential in the Eastern portion of the Byzantine Empire. "Since all Christians were treated equally by the Muslim overlord, pressures to conform to an imperially prescribed standard of orthodoxy were lifted. Monophysites and Nestorians were free to pursue their own beliefs."[414] This split weakened the empire.

...the East found far too far-reaching the agreement with the Roman-Antiochene Christology of separation, especially in the clause "the property of both natures is preserved and comes together into a single person," which is the only sure quotation from Leo in the Chalcedonian

Definition. Thus the Council of Chalcedon did not bring the peace that had been expected from it. On the contrary, it finally caused a first great confessional split in Christianity (Heresies and Schisms). This development in turn weakened the Christian empire of Byzantium, and as a result the Christian populations of the Monophysite territories in Syria, Palestine, and Egypt eventually passed almost without a struggle under the domination of Islam."[415]

The churches in Armenia, Egypt, Ethiopia, and Syria objected to the teachings from the Creed of Chalcedon which emphasized the belief in the two natures of Christ. "Many modern scholars are inclined to think that the difference between 'Non-Chalcedonians' and 'Chalcedonians' was basically one of terminology, not of theology. The two parties understood the word 'nature' (*physis*) in different ways . . ."[416] These churches were the Monophysites in the empire. The common bond between these churches is the one nature belief of Christ.

The issues raised at the time of Chalcedon were not trivial, for the council had seemed to split the human from the divine element in the person of Christ. The emperor's part in the council was partly political but resistance to its doctrine was heartfelt and not a 'cover' for social grievances, much less for strivings for national autonomy by the eastern provinces. Centuries of Christian experience in the provinces had been flouted by the upstart capital. For the pious Greek, Copt and Syrian, Christ was the prototype of the redeemed man. To what extent, these men would ask, did God deign to take up and transform human nature, to lift it out of its frailties, in the person of Christ? If human nature was totally transformed and made one with God's nature in Christ – hence the convenient theological label 'monophysite' *monos*, single; *physis*, nature) – then the average man could eventually hope to be saved in the same way: he, also, would be transformed.[417]

These churches were not monolithic due to the differences in national identity and in cultural beliefs and practices. They preferred to be called Oriental Orthodox or Non-Chalcedonian. These churches accepted the findings of the first three ecumenical councils of Nicaea, Constantinople I, and Ephesus. They accepted the council's statements which supported the consubstantiality of Christ with the Father and the divinity of the Holy Spirit. They also supported the condemnations of Arius and Nestorius. The early Monophysites were primarily responsible for the monastic movement in Syria and Egypt beginning in the fourth century with such ascetics as Anthony of Egypt and Pachomius. "The Bible, solitary prayer and fasting took precedence over the common life, public worship and ecclesiastical control. Though salvation in Paradise was his (Antony) object, for most of his life he could never have received the Eucharist, and his monks were laymen. And yet, his friendship with Athanasius was to make his movement the most formidable weapon in the armory of the Church in Egypt."[418] "With Packom (Pachomius) (290-345) we may discern the beginnings of a more ordered community asceticism which was to extend its influence throughout the Greek world, and ultimately provide a model for the monasteries in the West."[419] The ascetics brought to the church an appreciation of the simple life of prayer and service while rejecting wealth and worldliness. However the monasteries were often in competition with the metropolitan and urban church authorities causing disputes over lifestyle in the churches. The churches which were denounced as heretical were operating as sects as late as the seventh century but died out with the advent of Islam in that century. The Ebionites, Gnostics, Manicheans, and the Arians in the east were small in numbers and no match for the invading armies of Islam. "The schism of the Monophysites remained a political nuisance to the empire and a threat to the Church, which in the east would soon be faced with the Persian Zoroastrianism and Moslem challenges."[420]

The Nestorians accepted the findings of Nicaea, Constantinople I, and Chalcedon. They rejected the findings of the Council of Ephesus. Nestorians accepted Chalcedon because their interpretation of the two natures was defined as real concrete separation of the two natures. "Nestorius held that in Christ there are two natures. By nature he meant the concrete character of being. Each of these two natures was a *prosopon*, a term expressing its external aspect as an individual; each was an *hypostasis* or concrete subsistent being."[421] The Jacobites were a branch of the Monophysites who were resident in Syria. The followers of Jacob Baradaeus took his name to distinguish their sect in the mid-sixth century. "The Monophysite church would repay its debt to Jacob Bar'adai by calling itself Jacobite . . ."[422] The Coptics were a branch of the Monophysites who resided in Egypt. The followers of Timothy Aelurus distinguished this sect from the Chalcedonians. ". . . the Monophysites at Alexandria seized the opportunity to have Timothy the Cat consecrated as patriarch."[423] This sect was influential in Nubia, Abyssinia, and Ethiopia. The Armenians separated from the Byzantine Empire in 552 C.E. They accepted the Monophysite view of Christology. "In Armenia the Monophysite church under its Catholicos remained rigidly opposed to Chalcedon and to reconciliation with the Byzantines while serving as the one unifying factor in Armenian life."[424] They have been politically dominated by Russia and Turkey since the seventh century. The Armenian Apostolic Church maintained its independence from the Orthodox Church and was considered a Monophysite sect. "The conversion of the Armenian people was achieved through the labors of St. Gregory the Enlightener, under whose influence King Tiridates III made Christianity the official religion of the kingdom, with the consequent founding in 314 of the Armenian church—called the Armenian Apostolic Church. Thus Armenia was the first country in which Christianity was made the officially established religion—one year after Constantine promulgated the Edict of Milan. A traditional conversion date of 301 is still honored officially by the church . . ."[425] The Maronites were a sect of the Monophysites founded in northern Syria which spread to Lebanon. The sect was started as a monastic movement by an ascetic known as Maron around 400 C.E. They emphasized the Monothelite belief of the one will of Christ. "The youngest sect of the Monophysites, and the solitary memorial of the Monothelite controversy, are the Maronites, so called from St. Maron, and the eminent monastery founded by him in Syria (400)."[426]

Fragmentation between the Monophysite sects was due in part to the use of differing languages and translated manuscripts. The language of Syria was Aramaic, Armenia was Syriac, Egypt was Coptic, and Abyssinia was Ethiopic. "The Monophysites are scattered upon the mountains and in the valleys and deserts of Syria, Armenia, Assyria, Egypt, and Abyssinia . . ."[427] The Orthodox Church in Asia-Minor utilized Greek while North Africa and Rome functioned in Latin. These differences led at times to confusion and mistrust in the meaning of words which heightened the differences in doctrine. "The Miaphysites, thanks to various political successes and alliances with power at crucial stages of their history, were ready to develop their culture and theology in such diverse languages as Armenian, Georgian, Coptic, Nubian and Ge'ez, and retained no common language as a point of reference."[428] Beginning in 313 C.E. there were two alliances which strengthened the Christian Church but did not always serve as a unified link sustaining the continuity of the church. The political alliance of church and state brought the backing of the political institution to the support of the church while at the same time the church supported the political institution of the empire by allegiance to the emperors. The second alliance was the cultural alliance of the Roman and Greek worlds into one unified empire sharing common leadership, government, and purposes. The political alliance was shaken with the barbarian invasions into Europe in the fifth century and the fall of political Rome. The church and state alliance was broken in the fifth century by the separation of the Monophysites and Nestorians from any spiritual authority vested in the Orthodox Church. "Thirty-three years after the Council of Chalcedon, the result of its Definition was outright schism between Eastern and Western churches."[429] Within the empire and without there were local kings, shahs, and dynasties which favored their own traditions. Some were pagan, some were based on competing religions, and some were focused on the founder of their Christian beliefs. King Abgar of Edessa accepted Christianity as early as 200 C.E. which whether fact or fiction became the revered tradition held by Christians at Edessa. ". . . individual voices were emerging in Syriac Christianity which frequently earned suspicion and condemnation from neighbors to the west."[430] In the Sassanian Empire of Persia Shah Ardashir in the third century restored Zoroastrianism which with its dualism and denial of the Trinity, came in conflict with Christianity. "A confrontation became more and more likely as Christian numbers in the Sassanian Empire grew, just as they were growing in the Roman Empire through the third century."[431] In Armenia, King Tiridates was converted to Christianity around 290 C.E. by the founding bishop Gregory the Illuminator. The king ordered mass conversions of his people. "Such wholesale conversions cannot have been as straight forward as the story implies, but it did represent the beginning of a passionate melding of Christianity and Armenian identity."[432]

The aristocracy at Rome had been stripped of its wealth and status during the incursions and occupations on the Italian peninsula by the barbarians. Most of the western territories were ruled by Arian Goths but living alongside Roman Catholics in Latin Europe. The Western Latin Church remained aloof from Arianism and from any attempt by the Eastern Orthodox Church to absorb or usurp its authority and independence. "In the case of Nicaea, the Roman world gradually accepted its Creed. Arianism lingered on largely among the German tribes, but here too slowly succumbed to Nicaea."[433] The rift between Rome and Constantinople was seen in the appointment of two ruling emperors simultaneously in Rome and in Constantinople. In addition the Acacian

Schism between 482-519 C.E. was more concerned with the relationship and status of the two ruling spiritual and political authorities than with theology. "The Pope paid all due deference to the emperor's worldly authority-unlike some of his successors in later centuries- but he asserted that the emperor ought to defer to the clergy in all matters concerning the faith."[434]

Many of the improvements in society were the result of Christianizing the empire. Paganism was finally eliminated from the public discourse by 500 C.E. The citizen's view of history became more realistic in an understanding of history as linear rather than the cyclical view of Greek mythology and philosophy. The concept of the value of man in an act of divine redemption replaced the determinism of the old culture. This supported the ideas of freedom and pacifism while condemning slavery and war as goals of society. The gladiatorial games were abolished as barbaric. The support of a rising middle class was based on the ideas of ownership of private property. The high values placed on the family unit improved the lives of women and children. The basis for morality and ethics sourced from Scripture which was determined by faith and revelation rather than on reason and philosophy. All of these changes benefited and modernized society and life within the empire.

Under the inspiring influence of the spotless purity of Christ's teaching and example, and aided here and there by the nobler instincts and tendencies of philosophy, the Christian church from the beginning asserted the individual rights of man, recognized the divine image in every rational being, taught the common creation and common redemption, the destination of all for immortality and glory, raised the humble and the lowly, comforted the prisoner captive, the stranger and the exile, proclaimed chastity as a fundamental virtue, elevated woman to dignity and equality with man, upheld the sanctity and inviolability of the marriage tie, laid the foundation of a Christian family and happy home, moderated the evils and undermined the foundations of slavery, opposed polygamy and concubinage, emancipated the children from the tyrannical control of parents, denounced the exposure of children as murder, made relentless war upon the bloody games of the arena and the circus, and the shocking indecencies of the theatre, upon cruelty and oppression and every vice infused into a heartless and loveless world the spirit of love and brotherhood, transformed sinners into saints, frail women into heroines, and lit up the darkness of the tomb by the bright ray of unending bliss in heaven.[435]

Yet the mixture of church and state brought humanizing methods to the church which converted the church into an institution rather than the body of Christ. "Constantine himself was to be looked upon by the Greek Christian world as 'the equal of the Apostles.' The union of religion and State which imperial paganism had sought in vain, was achieved by the first Christian Emperor."[436] The hierarchies of authority, the accumulation of rigid rules and traditions, and the acquisition of wealth changed the church into a legalistic bureaucracy eager to pursue power and prestige which contributed to strife and division within the church. "Yet the alliance of Church and state was by no means an unqualified advantage to the Roman imperial government. The internal dissensions of the Church threatened, as we have seen, to rend not only the Church but also the Empire. Indeed, in the next period they were to contribute to the break-up of the Empire."[437] The church pursued internal religious unity which weakened its missionary success in the Middle East and North Africa. "The attempts of the Byzantine Empire to maintain religious unity took the form either of compromises which produced a new series of heresies and schisms like that of the Monothelites, or of a policy of repression which increased the disaffection of the eastern peoples and provinces towards the Empire. Finally the whole fabric of the Orthodox Byzantine Empire in the Eastern Provinces collapsed . . ."[438] The acceptance of Christianity as the state religion by Emperor Constantine resulted in changes to Christianity. The religion became the faith of the ruling class instead of just the poor and persecuted. This became a sign of divine favor for the church. The old method of meeting in homes and in private was replaced with assembly in large public church buildings where the clergy and bureaucracy presided and church community life became regimented. "Constantine stands at a watershed in the history of the Church. With his conversion, the age of the martyrs and the persecutions drew to an end, and the Church of the Catacombs became the Church of the Empire."[439] One of the reactions to this change was the monastic movement away from urban centers toward the rural solitary lifestyle of the hermit and monk. "The spirit of the desert did not fit well with that of the hierarchical church whose bishops lived in great cities and enjoyed power and prestige."[440]

Monasticism was a movement away from the wealth and splendor of the urban churches with their rigid liturgy and regulations. "The monks by their withdrawal from society into the desert fulfilled a prophetic and eschatological ministry in the life of the Church."[441] Monastics strived to ascend above the temptations of the flesh by living a life of worldly denial. Self-denial eventually led to asceticism where hermit existence and withdrawal benefited no one. Some ascetics gathered in monasteries where a simple communal life guided the affairs of these monks. The contributions of the monastic movement included: a missionary outreach to the unconverted, the scribal functions of copying and translating religious manuscripts, and a pietistic appreciation of servant hood to Christ. ". . . the entire Eastern monastic movement remained united in its basic 'other-worldliness' and in the conviction that prayer, whatever its form, was the fundamental and permanent content of monastic life. Some monastic centers—such as the monastery of Studios—may have been relatively 'activist,' developing social work, learning, manuscript copying, and other practical concerns . . ."[442] In time the monasteries would become a power structure within the universal church which often competed with the Orthodox Christian Church for power, prestige, and wealth. "The hermit often fled, then, not so much from the world as from the world in the church. His protest of a corrupt institution led him into the dangers of a pronounced individualism."[443] Each of these forces weakened and divided loyalties within the Byzantine Empire.

Segmentation of the Byzantine Empire
The segmentation of the eastern portion of the empire had roots in the very beginning which never changed over time. "Historically, the perpetuation of the Empire in the East played a role in preventing the Byzantine Church from assuming the direct role of ruling society politically, and thus keeping more strictly to its function as a signpost of the Kingdom to come—a Kingdom fundamentally different from all political systems of this age."[444] Other causes were added progressively as the church and the empire evolved. From the very beginning of Christianity, theological emphasis differed by geographical area. "The Pastorals and Johannine letters show that there were still men of high-priestly and apostolic authority responsible for churches within a defined region . . ."[445] This was due in part by the different emphases of the apostle who evangelized the area, the tenacity of local religious beliefs

before Christianity, the influence of the schools of learning, and linguistic interpretations of the meaning of words explaining Scripture. "For example, 'the defeat of Marcionitism was mainly due not to Tertullian, but to the Alexandrian school, who took to themselves much for which Marcion had stood and presented a new Christian philosophy which in the end left no room for either Marcionitism or Gnosticism."[446] The Monophysites and the Nestorians were often favored by invading powers and bordering countries because they resisted the Orthodox Church which supported the empire. Theological controversy became the normal activity in the eastern churches. Nestorius had declared that Christ had two natures which were distinctly two persons, one divine and one human. The Orthodox Chalcedonians contended that Christ had two natures, one divine and one human, in one person. The Monophysites objected by insisting that Christ had one nature in one person. The Chalcedonians held the surviving religious view of the empire. The Monophysites were dominant in Armenia, Syria, Egypt, Ethiopia, and Lebanon. The Nestorians were dominant in Persia. These religious preferences lasted until the conversions to Islam in the seventh and eighth centuries which made the Monophysites and the Nestorians minorities in their respective countries.

Thus the late seventh and early eighth centuries, and not the age of the first Arab conquests, are the true turning-point in the history of Europe and the Near East. This happened first in a prolonged confrontation with Byzantium. In the last decades of the seventh century, the boundaries between the Christian and the Muslim worlds hardened notably. In 680/1, the sixth Oecumenical Council at Constantinople treated the patriarchates of Antioch, Jerusalem and Alexandria as no longer part of the Byzantine Christian world. In 695, the first fully Arabic coins were minted. In 699, Greek was replaced by Arabic in the chancery at Damascus. Between 706 and 714, the Great Mosque at Damascus was built, to eclipse the tantalizing magnificence of the imperial churches of Syria and Palestine. The eastern Mediterranean began to take on its Islamic face.[447]

Local Monophysite Churches

Chalcedon did not settle the differences between the competing sects of Christianity. For those who were supporters of the Council of Chalcedon, the two natures of Christ in one person was settled doctrine. The Monophysites and Nestorians however survived as groups of

Christians in segments of the empire with their own views and defended them tenaciously against the Orthodox Church. After 451 C.E., the separation of the Monophysites began to widen ". . . the Byzantine emperors tried to restore the religious unity of the empire. In the second half of the fifth century they made several unhappy attempts to heal the schism by avoiding the issue."[448] Alexandria was a stronghold of Monophysite belief and important to the Byzantine emperors as the source of grain supplies. Beginning at this juncture, the church in Egypt began to use the Coptic language while diminishing the use of the Greek language in order to distinguish their beliefs from that of the Greek Orthodox Church in Constantinople. Severus, who was deposed as bishop of Antioch, had fled to Egypt due to persecution from the Orthodox in Constantinople. "Severus fled from Antioch to Monophysite Alexandria."[449] He began to ordain bishops and priests who were Monophysites and established a competing alternative church to the Chalcedonian Church. "Since the sharp eye of the imperial police hindered the ordination of priests loyal to the Monophysite cause, Severus authorized the exiled bishop John of Tella . . . to ordain Monophysite priests and deacons."[450] Empress Theodora established Monophysite bishops in Syria and Palestine among the Ghassanid Arabs. Jacob Baradaeus established the Syriac Orthodox Church in the Ghassanid territories ordaining bishops and priests as he traveled the area. This church was distinctly Monophysite in belief despite its name. "Jacob Baradaeus ('the Ragged'), who had been consecrated bishop by the exiled Patriarch of Alexandria, had embarked on a mission to revive monophysite sentiment throughout the East, travelling the length and breadth of Syria and Palestine, Mesopotamia and Asia Minor, consecrating some thirty bishops and ordaining several thousand priests."[451] The Armenians had not been represented at the Council of Chalcedon and took an offensive view of its findings. They followed the teachings of the Cappadocian church fathers and Cyril of Alexandria who were Monophysites. "In Armenia, the church had declared itself officially Monophysite in 491. Repeatedly the Council of Chalcedon was firmly rejected."[452] Peter the Fuller was a monk from Constantinople who was influential in the spreading of Monophysitism in Armenia in the sixth century. "Peter had previously been a monk among the strongly Chalcedonian religious called Sleepless Monks (*Acoemetae*) noted for their absolute poverty and perpetual prayer."[453] The Monophysites of

Ethiopia were the result of importation of the faith from Egypt. The church did not become Coptic but used its own language known as Ethiopic. It retained a strong linkage to Jewish tradition due to historical Semitic influences. These pockets of Monophysite believers were resident in the southern and eastern portions of the empire which were the first territories adjacent to and vulnerable to Islamic invasion.

Causes of the Spread of Islam Between 610-700 CE

Islam originated in the lands of Arabia in 610 C.E. The inhabitants of Arabia were mostly Arabs who claimed descent from patriarchs of the Bible which included Cush, Shem, Abraham, Ishmael, and Esau. The geography included the mountainous areas of Petra, the sandy deserts of the peninsula, and the southern tip of Yemen. "The fatherland of Islam is Arabia, a peninsula between the Red Sea, the Indian Ocean and the Persian Gulf. It is covered with sandy deserts, barren hills, rock-bound coasts, fertile wadies, and rich pastures. It is inhabited by nomadic tribes and traders who claim descent from five patriarchal stocks, Cush, Shem, Ishmael, Keturah, and Esau. It was divided by the ancients into Arabia Deserta, Arabia Petraea (the Sinai district with Petra as the capital), and Arabia Felix (El- Yemen, i.e. the land on the right hand, or of the South)."[454] The Roman Empire did not extend southward into Arabia which was considered too distant, too worthless, and too hostile to be conquered and pacified. "Until the early seventh century, Arabia had been unknown to the West, while its inhabitants, where the Christian world was concerned, showed no interest, made no impact and certainly posed no threat."[455] The Romans traded for the products of Arabia instead of occupying the territory. The capital city of Arabia was Mecca which was the center of pagan worship for the resident merchants of the city and the traveling Bedouins who visited. Like Rome and Jerusalem, the city prospered from pilgrimages during the pagan years and thereafter during the Muslim years. The central attraction in Mecca from a religious standpoint was the Kaaba. This was first a shrine housing a sacred rock traditionally thought to have been placed there by Adam. All of the pagan gods of Arabia were represented by idols to nature, the sky, and to the elements which they represented. These numbered approximately 340 such different gods. When Islam replaced polytheism beginning in the early seventh century, the Kaaba was purged of the many idols and claimed for Islam as the spot where Abraham built the altar to God.

"Muhammad subsequently cleared the Kaaba of all relics of idolatry, and made it the place of pilgrimage for his followers. He invented or revived the legend that Abraham by divine command sent his son Ishmael with Hagar to Mecca to establish there the true worship and the pilgrim festival."[456] The sacred stone was claimed as a part of the altar. The revered Kaaba became the center of worship, was enclosed by walls and a mosque, and became the place of a required pilgrimage serving, as did the temple of Solomon to the Jews or the square of St. Peters in Rome for the Roman Catholics, as the center point for worship. The Muslim tradition also claimed that a nearby well known as Zamzam was the distant well to which Hagar and Ishmael were refreshed after their flight from Abraham's tents. A number of tribes of Jews had settled in pockets of Arabia. The largest settlement was in the town of Yathrib which would later be renamed Medina by Muhammad. Christians who had fled the Byzantine Empire during the theological disputes of the fourth and fifth centuries had settled in Arabia and other territories outside the boundaries of the empire.

The Christians belonged mostly to the various heretical sects which were expelled from the Roman Empire during the violet doctrinal controversies of the fourth and fifth centuries. We find there traces of Arians, Sabellians, Ebionites, Nestorians, Eutychians, Monophysites, Marianites, and Collyridians or worshippers of Mary. Anchorets and monks settled in large numbers in Wady Feiran around Mount Serbal, and Justinian laid the foundation of the Convent of St. Catharine at the foot of Mount Sinai, which till the year 1859 harbored the oldest and most complete uncial manuscript of the Greek Scriptures of both Testaments from the age of Constantine, But it was a very superficial and corrupt Christianity which had found a home in those desert regions, where even the apostle Paul spent three years after his conversion in silent preparation for his great mission.[457]

These did not represent Orthodox Christians but rather the heretical sects which had been expelled. The sects included: Arians, Sabellians, Ebionites, Nestorians, Eutychians, and Monophysites. Each of the three religions Judaism, Christianity, and Islam claimed Abraham as a key patriarch and some portions of the Old Testament as Scripture. Unlike the written history of missionary activity of Christians in the Middle East, North Africa, Europe, and Asia-Minor, there is no consistent record of missionary efforts by the primary Christian groups such as Orthodox, Monophysite, or Nestorian into Arabia. Just prior to the seventh century an Ethiopian backed ruler named Abraha had established Monophysite Christianity in Yemen but a natural disaster by flooding destroyed the kingdom. "The memory of the end of the Marib dam, when Sheba's gardens were replaced 'with others that yielded bitter fruit', was still traumatic enough to win a mention in Muhammad's revelations in the Qur'an, where the disaster was described as a punishment from God for Sheba's faithlessness."[458]

The spread of Islam during the seventh century either eliminated Christianity or rendered its followers as second class minorities in the Middle East and North Africa.

Viewed in its relation to the Eastern Church which it robbed of the fairest dominions, Mohammedanism was a well-deserved divine punishment for the unfruitful speculations, bitter contentions, empty ceremonialism and virtual idolatry which degraded and disgraced the Christianity of the East after the fifth century. The essence of true religion, love to God and to man, was eaten out by rancor and strife, and there was left no power of ultimate resistance to the foreign conqueror. The hatred between the orthodox Eastern church and the Eastern schismatics driven from her communion, and the jealousy between the Greek and Latin churches prevented them from aiding each other in efforts to arrest the progress of the common foe.[459]

Dyophysite Nestorian Christianity spread into Arabia through Syria. The trade routes between Mecca and Damascus were known to have been traveled by Muhammad in his early years. "He accompanied his uncle on a commercial journey to Syria, passing through the desert, ruined cities of old, and Jewish and Christian settlements, which must have made a deep impression on his youthful imagination."[460] The Ghassanid Arabs of Syria also brought Monophysitism to the northern areas of Arabia. The language of both of these Arabian Christian sects remained Syriac rather than Arabic which would later distinguish Muslims who used Arabic. "The Syriac language was the chief language spoken in regions of Syria and Mesopotamia. It is almost identical with Aramaic."[461] Chalcedonian Christianity with its use of the Greek language never penetrated Arabia partly because the Bedouins favored the Semitic languages such as Syriac over the Greek. The Monophysites were more successful in these southern lands, it will be remembered, because they were willing to use the local language of the people whereas the Nestorians clung to the Syriac thereby limiting their appeal to Semitic peoples of differing languages. The

Sassanian Empire was at war with the Byzantine Empire in the early decades of the seventh century. "Over the next four years the Persians overran much of western Mesopotamia and Syria, Armenia and Cappadocia, Paphlagonia and Galatia in a relentless tide, until in 608 their advance guard was encamped at Chalcedon . . ."[462] A peace treaty was finally signed after both sides had substantially weakened their armies. The Ghassanids were caught in the middle and destroyed as a casualty of war of nearby neighbors. ". . . the Miaphysite Ghassanids, who for more than a century had kept the Byzantine in touch with events in Arabia and had brought security to the region. The Ghassanids could have alerted the Byzantines to the early formation of a new military power which had appeared quite unexpectedly from the south: the armies of Islam. The arrival of the Muslims proved terminal for the Sassanians."[463] In Medina in 622 C.E., Muhammad established the beginnings of Islam while advancing the military conquest of the peninsula of Arabia. His successors conquered the Middle East and North Africa within one century. "The victories of the Arab armies created a political vacuum in the near East. The Byzantines were routed at the battle of Yarmuk in 636: Antioch fell in 637; Alexandria in 642; Carthage in 698. The Persian army put up a more stubborn resistance; but after the battle of Qadesiya in 637, the Sassanian state crumbled."[464] In the wake of these Islamic advances the Byzantine Empire receded to the borders of Asia-Minor. The Muslim successes in Palestine, Syria, and Egypt dramatically diminished the patriarchates of Jerusalem, Antioch, and Alexandria. "These centers of Christian learning were no longer able to debate the Christological issues with the Orthodox Church in Constantinople or the Catholic Church in Rome. Their status became that of a second class monotheistic religion tolerated in Muslim dominated lands.

Overthrow of Christian Lands by the Muslims

Muhammad died in 632 C.E. after conquering the peninsula of Arabia. His successors spread Islam to adjacent territories and beyond by invasion and settlement. After Arabia was fully converted to Islam in 632 C.E., the caliphs sought to expand the influence of Islam in other countries by wars of aggression.

The Califs, Mohammed's successors, who like him united the priestly and kingly dignity, carried on his conquests with the battle-cry: 'Before you is paradise, behind you are death and hell.' Inspired by an intense fanaticism, and aided by the weakness of the Byzantine Empire and the internal distractions of the Greek Church, the wild sons of the desert, who were content with the plainest food, and disciplined in the school of war, hardship and recklessness of life, subdued Palestine, Syria, and Egypt, embracing the classical soil of Christianity. Thousands of Christian churches in the patriarchal dioceses of Jerusalem, Antioch and Alexandria, were ruthlessly destroyed, or converted into mosques.[465]

The conquered peoples were offered conversion to Islam, death, slavery, or minority status by paying a special head tax. The opportunity to be left alone if one were to convert to Islam was a strong incentive to many people who had few good options. "Inspired by an intense fanaticism, and aided by the weakness of the Byzantine Empire and the internal distractions of the Greek Church, the wild sons of the desert, who were content with the plainest food, and disciplined in the school of war, hardship and recklessness of life, subdued Palestine, Syria, and Egypt, embracing the classical soil of primitive Christianity. Thousands of Christian churches in the patriarchal dioceses of Jerusalem, Antioch and Alexandria, were ruthlessly destroyed, or converted into mosques. Twenty-one years after the death of Mohammed the Crescent ruled over a realm as large as the Roman Empire."[466] Egypt was conquered in 641 C.E. "Byzantine attempts to impose the official imperial theology came to an end with the Arab Muslim conquest of the eastern Byzantine provinces and the separation from the Byzantine heartland of the Christian communities that were pejoratively labeled Monophysite. The Muslim rulers of Egypt for the most part permitted the free exercise of Christian faith, although Christians came to experience a variety of social, cultural, and economic pressures toward the adoption of the Arabic language and the embracing of Islamic faith."[467] The Coptics in Egypt were Monophysites and as such were not viewed by the Muslims as aligned with the Byzantines. The rivalry between patriarch Cyrus, a Dyophysite, and Benjamin, a Monophysite, was disastrous in undermining the unity and support between Egypt and the Byzantine authorities. ". . . Byzantine authority was threatened in a number of ways. The population-Aramaic in one, Coptic in the other- was alien by language and to a lesser extent by culture to the Greeks, and was resentful of Byzantine rule both because of the crushing burden of taxation which it imposed and because of official persecution of the Monophysite and other deviant churches at odds with the Orthodox creed of the Empire."[468] Syria and Palestine were under the control of the Byzantine Empire in 632 but lost to the Muslims after the battle of Yarmuk in 636 C.E. Lebanon was conquered in 644 C.E. during the reign of caliph Uthman. Iraq was part of the Persian Sassanian Empire with a majority practicing Zoroastrianism and a minority practicing Nestorian Christianity. Persia was defeated at the battle of Qadisiyya in 638 which resulted in Muslim control of both Iraq and Persia by 640 C.E. Cyprus, Rhodes, and Kos were captured by the Muslim navy at the battle of the Masts in 654 C.E. Many Christians believed that God was punishing Christians due to their acceptance of heresies such as Monophysitism and Nestorianism in Christian lands. "While the fact of the rapid Islamic conquest of so much of the historical heartland of the Christian movement posed a theological problem to the church of the seventh and eighth centuries, (it) resulting in much soul-searching and finger-pointing at sins and heresies that might have provoked God's wrath . . ."[469] The weakness and vulnerability of Christian lands were due to their own deficiencies as well as the strengths of the Muslims. "Until the reign of Heraclius, the emperors had sufficient funds to allot to substitutes for military strength, fortification and diplomacy. But money could not create soldiers. Maurice and Heraclius both revived the older, militaristic tendencies of the Roman Empire. They took the field in person. But they found they had not enough men to lead. Hence the strange combination of fragility and grandeur in the Byzantine empire after Justinian . . ."[470] The Christian population in the Middle East was decimated by an outbreak of the bubonic plague in the sixth and seventh centuries. The Byzantine emperors were weak and corrupt at times being unable to lead military armies with courage and skill. The Byzantines and the Sassanians having been at war with each other weakened their armies significantly. The divisiveness of theological disputes had weakened the bonds of friendship and unity between the different Christian sects. The citizens were not armed rendering the population defenseless against the advancing armies of Islam. From the perspective of Islam, the military forces were well trained in rapid, mobile warfare. ". . . based on the partially Islamized warrior-aristocracy of the Arab tribes. The Beduin way of life of the Arab aristocracy, though castigated by Muhammad, saved Islam. It was the chieftains of the Beduin tribes who created the Arab war-machine with their rude followers, and it was the style of life of this warrior-aristocracy—and not the sheltered piety of the core of devout Muslims—that held the empire together."[471] The armies were fighting for a religious cause that they believed was their privilege and duty. The idea of a Holy War was a clear motivation to the Muslim forces. The opportunity to win material prizes and booty from their enemies was a motivation of each individual for personal gain. "In the first years of the conquest, the Muslims did not seek to make converts. They levied a general tribute and a poll tax on the Christians . . ."[472] The Koran had given them a victory pledge. "Fight against them until idolatry is no more, and God's religion reigns supreme."(2:193) In contrast the peoples of the Byzantine Empire included Jews, Nestorians, and Monophysites who were anxious to rid themselves of Greek and Orthodox rule from Constantinople. Carthage in Tunisia fell to the Arabs in 690 C.E. which ended all Latin and Christian influence in North Africa. Spain was invaded by the Visigoths in the fifth century converting to Catholicism by 600 C.E. The Romans abandoned Spain while the Sephardic Jews of Spain aided the Muslims who invaded in 711 C.E. under Tariq the Moor. The ethnic Kurds, who were the ancient Medes, were the natural enemies of the Assyrians. These ancient rivalries prohibited a uniting of peoples in Northern Syria, Northwestern Persia, Iraq, and Armenia. The Kurds persecuted the Nestorians and Monophysites of these lands. The Kurds did not accept any form of Christianity but were converted to Islam in 641C.E. ". . . a self-designation of Iranian origin that might have been borne by successors of the Medes who had moved westward beginning in the fifth century . . . The Kurds were conquered by the Arabs in the 7th century."[473]

Analysis of Islamic Theology Concerning Christ

Islam is a monotheistic religion which claims origination from both Judaism and Christianity. It further claims Abraham as the patriarch of the faith as the key elements of the faith were based upon the blessing promised to the descendants of Ishmael. Muhammad was illiterate and hence after receiving the revelation which was recorded in the Koran did so by recitation to his followers in the Arabic language. The message of Muhammad was strong enough during his lifetime to displace all of the polytheistic idols of the people of Arabia. The core beliefs of Islam were concerned with the revelation of God, his prophets, and compliance of believers to a system of beliefs and behaviors leading to reward or punishment. The God of Islam is known as Allah. The monotheism of Islam is expressed in the well-known claim that "There is no god but Allah and Muhammad is his Prophet." The claim is similar to the proclamation in the Old Testament that "Hear, O Israel: The Lord our God is one Lord."(Deuteronomy 6:4) "Allah is a God of power and sovereignty but is not personal nor does he provide a plan of redemption for humanity. "Allah is a holy God, who Muhammad doubtless intended to be equated with the God of the Bible, but his holiness appears as a remoteness to which no human being can ever hope to attain."[474] The name Islam suggests the meaning of the relationship between man and God which is to "surrender" to his will. "Concepts of redemption common to Judaism and Christianity are replaced by the idea of submission (*islam*) to the will of God . . ."[475] Many of the prophets from the Bible are claimed as prophets in Islam. Adam, Noah, Abraham, and Jesus are named in the Koran as prophets of Allah. "In the Qur'an there are isolated references to various prophets and kings of the Old Testament, as well as to Mary and Jesus, but the understanding of the Bible which these allusions reveal is fragmentary and superficial."[476] The key prophet however is Muhammad who was claimed as the last and greatest of the prophets. He was not equated to Jesus but was held to be the best model for Muslims to imitate and follow in their own lives. He served no redemptive function nor did he have a future role in end time's events.

The understanding of Muslims through the teaching of the Koran is that Jesus was a man and a prophet but not divine. "Its (Aristotelianism) main thrust had been to emphasize the humanity of Christ and to question whether God could really become man, an approach which later commended itself to Muslims, and helps to account for the popularity of Aristotle in medieval Islam."[477] He was not the Son of God because, the argument says, God has no wife and therefore can have no son. Interestingly the Koran accepts the Virgin Birth of Jesus but places no value on this miraculous event nor places it in context with any redemptive plan. "Apparently Muhammad accepted the virgin birth of Christ but denied his crucifixion . . ."[478] "She said: 'O my Lord! How shall I have a son when no man has touched me.' He said: So (it will be), for Allah creates what He wills." (3:47). It was the teaching of the Koran that Jesus was not divine. This is because he was a created human being. "Verily, the likeness of Isa (Jesus) before Allah is the likeness of Adam. He created him from the dust . . ." (3:59). The crucifixion of Jesus is denied which rendered the redemptive plan of Christianity powerless according to the Koran. "And because of their saying (in boast), 'We killed Messiah Isa (Jesus), son of Maryam (Mary), the Messenger of

Allah,' – but they killed him not, nor crucified him, but it appeared so to them . . ." (4:157). The idea of Jesus only appearing to be crucified aligns with two heretical beliefs preceding the writing of the Koran. The Ebionites had taught that Jesus was only a human being and not divine. "They (Ebionites) regarded Him as plain and ordinary, a man esteemed as righteous through growth of character and nothing more, the child of a normal union between a man and Mary . . ."[479] The Ebionites did regard Jesus as a prophet. "Others, called Ebionites, maintained that Jesus was merely a man, a prophet, a spokesman for God, as were the great Hebrew prophets of the past."[480] The Ebionites were descendants of the Essenes who revered the law of the Old Testament, accepted the Gospel of Mathew, but rejected the writings of Paul. "The heretical Ebionites of the second century, to cite only one group out of many, continued to insist on the observance of the Jewish law and custom. For them Jesus was the elect of God and a true prophet, but they denied his virgin birth and eternal pre-existence."[481] Muslims also rejected the writings of Paul. Ebionite teachings which were deemed heretical by Christians may have influenced Islamic theology regarding the nature of Jesus. ". . . other heretical species of Judaism absorbed elements of Christian heresy; and so it came about that both Jewish and Christian heresy contributed to the origins of Islam."[482] Ebionitism regards Jesus as a person arising from within the context of Judaism. Therefore the question of his divinity was not a concern. "Jesus was thus to be understood as analogous to the great prophets of Israel- human beings who were in some way given special insight or wisdom through the Holy Spirit."[483] Docetism was a heresy which accepted the divinity of Christ but rejected his humanity as only an appearance and not a reality. "The docetic Christ (i.e. the Christ who only appeared to have a human form) has exercised his hold on religious minds from that day to this."[484] This meant that the incarnation was only an illusion and the crucifixion for redemptive purposes was not a reality. The Koran accepts the concepts of denying the crucifixion and accepting that Jesus' crucifixion was an appearance only while rejecting the divinity of Jesus. "It seems increasingly clear that the Qur'anic representation of the fundamental ideas of Christianity has been shaped by an encounter with the forms of Christianity that were prevalent in the Arabian Peninsula."[485] Finally the Koran denies any concept that the Godhead is represented as a Trinity. ". . . Say not: 'Three (trinity)!' Cease! (it is) better for you. For Allah is (the only) One 'Ilah (God), Glorified is He (Far Exalted is He) above having a son." (4:171). Since in Islam there is no Trinity with a redemptive plan for humanity, then salvation, reward, and eternity are based upon belief and behavioral merit. "And those who believe (in the Oneness of Allah-Islamic Monotheism) and do righteous good deeds, they are dwellers of Paradise, they will dwell therein forever." (2:82).

Life of Muhammad and Contacts with Christians

Muhammad was born in 570 C.E. in Mecca, Arabia. "Muhammad, born in about A.D. 570, emerged in his home town of mecca around 610 as the preacher of a divine revelation that he felt called upon to pass on to his pagan Arab tribes-people."[486] His father had died shortly before his birth. His clan was known as the Hashemite's of the tribe of the Korash. The Hashemite's claimed descent from Ishmael, the son of Abraham. His mother died when he was age six which necessitated that he be reared by his grandfather for a short time and at age eight by his uncle Abu Talib. Muhammad traveled with his uncle on caravans heading through the desert to trade in Damascus, Syria. Along the way and at the end of these journeys, Muhammad came in contact with both Jewish and Christian settlements.

It is made certain by recent research that there were at the time and before the call of Mohammed a considerable number of inquirers at Mecca and Medina, who had intercourse with Eastern Christians in Syria and Abyssinia, were dissatisfied with the idolatry around them, and inclined to monotheism, which they traced to Abraham. They called themselves Hanyfs, i.e. Converts, Puritans. One of them, Omayah of Taif, we know to have been under Christian influence; others seem to have derived their monotheistic ideas from Judaism. Some of the early converts of Mohammed as, Zayd (his favorite slave), Omayab, or Umaijah (a popular poet), and Waraka (a cousin of Chadijah and a student of the Holy Scriptures of the Jews and Christians) belonged to this sect, and even Mohammed acknowledged himself at first a Hanyf. Waraka, it is said, believed in him, as long as he was a Hanyf, but then forsook him, and died a Christian or a Jew.[487]

Historians record that he was illiterate and unlearned. "The Qur'an was recorded in written form from memory, and it remains up till today an object of pride for Muslims to be able to memorize and cite the text of the Qur'an."[488] The clearest evidence is that the Koran states that he should "recite" what he has heard rather than he should "write" what he has heard. "We have sent among you a Messenger of your own, reciting to you Our Verses (the Qur'an) and purifying you, and teaching you the Book. . ." (2:151). Also, "Those who follow the Messenger, the Prophet who can neither read nor write (i.e. Muhammad). . ."(7:157) In addition his closest followers testified that Muhammad recited to them the verses which they afterward wrote down and collected as the Koran. "The process of compiling the Qur'an is reported by Muslim historians. According to Islamic tradition different fragments of the Qur'an were revealed to Muhammad verbatim by the angel Gabriel over a period of twenty-three years (25:32, 17:106). After each such occasion the prophet would recite the words of revelation to those present (thus the word 'Qur'an,' which means reading or reciting)."[489] At age twenty-five he married a widow known as Khadija who was age forty and herself a prosperous caravan trader. He was contemplative and frequently engaged in prayer and fasting. From childhood, he was subject to convulsions which were thought at times to be demonic possessions and later as divine visitations. His revelation began at age forty when he claimed the angel Gabriel had visited him and given him directions to warn others of the dangers of hell, to give up polytheistic idolatry, and to worship the one true monotheistic god Allah. "But as often as he approached the precipice, he beheld Gabriel at the end of the horizon saying to him: 'I am Gabriel, and thou art Mohammad, the prophet of God."[490] His wife was the first to believe in him as a prophet of God. Several associates and family members were converted to accepting Muhammad as the prophet of the true god Allah. These included his father-in-law Abu Bakr, Omar, his daughter Fatima, his adopted son Ali, and his slave Zayd. These loyal followers would become his faithful companions in battle, in leadership, and in recording the recitations collected in the Koran and the Hadith (the sayings of the prophet).

In 622 C.E. Muhammad and his companions fled to Yathrib (later Medina) where he was recognized as a prophet and administrative leader. "Then he publicly announced his determination to assume by command of God the office of prophet and lawgiver, preached to the pilgrims flocking to Meccan idolatry, reasoned with his opponents, answered their demand for miracles by producing the Koran 'leaf by leaf,' as occasion demanded, and provoked persecution and civil commotion. He was forced in the year 622 to flee for his life with his followers from mecca to Medina (El-Medina an-Nabi, the City of the Prophet), a distance of two hundred and fifty miles North, or ten days' journey over the sands and rocks of the desert."[491] He returned to Mecca with an army to convert the Meccans by force to the new religion of Islam. Muhammad died of an illness in Medina in 632 C.E. after having converted the peninsula of Arabia to Islam. He had founded a universal monotheistic religion which would conflict and contend with Judaism and Christianity.

It is apparent from examination of the Koran that Muhammad came in contact with Jews and Christians. "At a time when the emperor Justinian was laying down which version of the Scriptures the Jews should be allowed to read in the synagogues of his empire, the rabbis of Ctesiphon were free to conduct a vigorous polemic against the Christian doctrines of the Trinity and the Virgin Birth. Searching criticisms aired in the cities of Persian Mesopotamia soon filtered along the caravan routes into Arabia, where they had a decisive influence on the epoch-making monotheism of Muhammad."[492] The Koran has borrowed accounts from the Old Testament of Judaism but in doing so has changed the historical record to either a mistaken view or a view more favorable to Islamic claims. The most significant claim in the Old Testament was concerned with Abraham's sacrifice of his son from the Genesis 22:1-14 account regarding Isaac at Mt. Moriah. Muhammad's recital of this account substitutes Ishmael for Isaac at Mecca.(37:102-109) Other similar Old Testament accounts included: creation, the flood, and the lives of Abraham, Joseph, Moses, Saul, and Haman. The Koran includes accounts of the New Testament events concerning Mary, Zechariah, and Jesus. This suggests an awareness of the history recorded in the Gospel with the notable absence of any recording that parallels the epistles of Paul. The claims concerning Jesus found in the Koran are primarily disclaimers as to Jesus' actions, beliefs, or relationships. "The crucifixion of Jesus is denied. He was delivered by a miracle from the death intended for him, and taken up by God into Paradise with His mother. The Jews slew one like Him, by mistake."[493] Surah 5:111 claims that Jesus taught to believe in Allah and his prophet Muhammad. Surah 5:116-117 says Jesus denied worship to himself and Mary. Surah 5:72 denies worship to a plural Godhead which suggests denial of the Trinity. The outright denial of the Trinity was expressed in Surah 4:171. This verse also claimed Jesus was a created being. One example of a direct reference to Jesus which was not in the form of a denial of His deity was stated in Surah 19:22-23 which suggested restating the historical event to a desert setting and culture.

"According to the Koran Jesus was conceived by the Virgin Mary at the appearance of Gabriel and born under a palm tree beneath which a fountain opened. This story is of Ebionite origin."[494] "So she conceived him, and she withdrew with him to a far place (i.e. Bethlehem valley about 4-6 miles from Jerusalem). And the pains of childbirth drove her to the trunk of a date palm." The Bible during the lifetime of Muhammad was not known to have been available in Arabic. If Muhammad was literate, he would have been unable to read the Bible in Hebrew, Greek, or Aramaic which did exist at the time. "It is quite probable that portions of the Bible were read to Mohammed; but it is very improbable that he read it himself; for according to the prevailing Moslem tradition he could not read at all, and there were no Arabic translations before the Mohammedan conquests, which spread the Arabic language in the conquered countries. Besides, if he had read the Bible with any degree of care, he could not have made such egregious blunders. The few allusions to Scripture phraseology-- as giving alms to be seen of men, none forgiveth sins but God only—may be derived from personal intercourse and popular tradition."[495]

Muhammad's contacts with Jews and Christians are limited to a few testimonies, analysis of words and concepts from Scripture which would have been received orally, and the impact of discussions with a few of his Christian relatives. "We know that he had esoteric conversations with the monks Bahira and Nestur. His view of Christ seems to have been influenced by Nestorian Christianity."[496] Muhammad's contacts with Christians would have occurred in his early years during travel to Syria which may have included the three Christian sects (Nestorian, Monophysite, and Chalcedonian Orthodox) at the time. Later Muhammad dealt with leaders from two Jewish tribes in Medina and Christian communities north of Arabia. "Concerning the Qur'an, we would like to point out that, based on the findings of reputable scholars of Islam, much of the content of the Qur'an can be traced to either Jewish or Christian works (often from Jewish or Christian apocrypha) or pagan sources."[497] During Muhammad's time at Medina, he came in contact with three Jewish tribes with which he had administrative dealings and thereafter military battles. These were the Banu Qainuqa, Banu Nadir, and the Banu Quraizah tribes. Since these Jews rejected him as prophet, he turned against them in battle and denounced his former affection for these People of the Book. "From the beginning there was opposition from the Jews and the Jewish community toward Muhammad and his claim of being a prophet. They knew he could not be their Messiah since he was not an offspring of the family of David."[498] A relative of Muhammad and at least two of his wives were Christians which undoubtedly resulted in some knowledge of Christianity to enter Muhammad's thinking. "Waraqa ibn Nofal, considered to be Muhammad's uncle, was also a Nestorian and is alleged to have translated portions of the Gospels into Arabic. He was very influential to Muhammad."[499] It should be recalled that following the anathemas of Nestorius in 431 C.E. at the Council of Ephesus, many Nestorians fled from the reach of the Byzantine Empire into foreign lands which included Arabia. "The materials of the Koran, as far as they are not productions of the author's own imagination, were derived from the floating traditions of Arabia and Syria, from rabbinical Judaism, and a corrupt Christianity, and adjusted to his purposes."[500] Muhammad's seventh wife, Raihana, was a Jewess from the Banu Quraizah tribe. Maryam was Muhammad's eighth wife who was an Egyptian Christian slave before her marriage. Saffiyya was Muhammad's ninth wife who was a Jewess from the Khaibar tribe in Syria. Presumably these inter-religious marriages contributed to Muhammad's understanding of Christianity and Judaism. "His wife Chadijah and her cousin Waraka (a reputed convert to Christianity, or more probably a Jew) are said to have been well acquainted with the sacred books of the Jews and the Christians."[501]

Many of the themes and words from Scripture have a similar recital in the Koran. This suggests that Muhammad had learned of these Biblical accounts and incorporated them later in his recitations. The accounts differ from the Biblical accounts but the core events of the account are clearly present. In Genesis 4:1-16 the Bible records the account of Cain and Abel regarding the sacrifices offered by each. The nature of the acceptability of the blood sacrifice of Abel as opposed to the human effort sacrifice of Cain is emphasized. The Koran puts forward a similar account in Surah 5:27-32. The Genesis account supports the theme of redemption for a fallen humanity. The Koranic account, however, introduces the legal theme of punishment for wrongdoing.

The Koran especially in the earlier Suras, speaks often and highly of the Scriptures; calls them 'the Book of God,' 'Word of God,' 'the Tourat' (Thora, the Pentateuch), 'the Gospel' (Ynyil), and describes the Jews and Christians as 'the people of the Book,' or 'of the Scripture,' or 'of the Gospel.' It finds in the Scriptures prophecies of Mohammed and his success, and contains narratives of the fall of Adam and Eve, Noah and the Deluge, Abraham and Lot, the destruction of Sodom and Gomorrah, Moses and Joseph, John the Baptist, the Virgin Mary and Jesus, sometimes in the words of the Bible, but mostly distorted and interspersed with rabbinical and apocryphal fables.[502]

Again in the Old Testament in Psalms 37:29 the theme is introduced that "the righteous shall inherit the earth". The Koran has a similar account in Surah 21:105 that "my righteous slaves shall inherit the land (i.e. the land of Paradise". The Surah even acknowledges that the concept of righteous inheritance is recorded in the Psalms and the Gospels. Themes from the New Testament are also present in the Koran. In John 14:24-26 Jesus declares that He speaks the words of the Father and that after Him another (the Comforter) will also teach the words that Jesus has spoken. The Comforter is revealed as the Holy Spirit. The Koran in Surah 61:6 claims that Jesus was a messenger of Allah, rather than Jehovah and that the messenger who follows Jesus will be the Praised One. The name of Muhammad is translated as the Praised One and so the Koran has claimed that the Holy Spirit (which is not accepted by Muslims) is actually Muhammad instead. "Jesus predicted the coming of Mohammed, when he said: 'O children of Israel! Of a truth I am God's apostle to you to conform the law which was given before me, and to announce an apostle that shall come after me whose name shall be Ahmed!' Thus the promise of the Holy Ghost, 'the other Paraclete,' (John xiv. 16) was applied by Mohammed to himself by a singular confusion of Paracletos . . ."[503] These are but a few of the examples where the writings in the Koran were taken from the Bible and altered by Muhammad when he recited the Koran

Muhammad was a busy fellow. He conducted twenty-seven battles and planned thirty-nine others.

Jesus was busy about His Father's business of teaching, healing, and serving:

> At first he proclaimed toleration: "Let there be no compulsion in religion;" but afterwards he revealed the opposite principle that all unbelievers must be summoned to Islam, tribute, or the sword. With an increasing army of his enthusiastic followers, he took the field against his enemies, gained in 624 his first victory over the Koreish with an army of 305 (mostly citizens of Medina) against a

force twice as large, conquered several Jewish and Christian tribes, ordered and watched in person the massacre of six hundred Jews in one day, while their wives and children were sold into slavery (627), triumphantly entered Mecca (630), demolished the three hundred and sixty idols of the Kaaba, and became master of Arabia.[504]

The Koran mentions the name of Jesus (Isa) a total of ninety-seven times which reflects the awareness of Muhammad to the life and teachings of Jesus.

Influences of People on the Beliefs of Muhammad

Several civilizations were influential in creating the culture and beliefs of the people of the Arabian Peninsula. The Sabaeans were early inhabitants who counted the Queen of Sheba as monarch during the years of Solomon's reign. ". . . the Sabean kingdom flourished in the late 2 ND and early 1 ST millennium BC, and discovered there the Temple of the Moon in the city of Marib . . . remains of the large dams which diverted into the fields the flood waters streaming down the dry river beds, thus providing the basis for the prosperity of the ancient kingdoms of southern Arabia."[505] By the sixth century C.E. the Sabaeans constructed a dam in the Marib section which caused the area to flourish with fertility. In 542 C.E. the dam burst wiping out the crops and soil. The people abandoned the Sabean culture fearing that the gods had punished them. Later Muhammad would recall this historical event as punishment for disobedience to Allah. Surah 34:16 records the flood within the context of the history of Sheba. The northern borders of Arabia were once home to the Nabateans civilization. This territory encompassed the north-south caravan trade routes between Mecca and Jerusalem and Damascus to the north. ". . . the Nabateans established a spice trade with southern Arabia and India and for this purpose they founded a network of caravanserais (inns) along the routes in the Negev."[506] Muhammad would have traveled along this desert road which by his time was an abandoned civilization. "Gradually, trade activity dwindled. Palmyra surpassed Nabataea as an overland trading center and seaborne trade around the peninsula increasingly diminished the importance of the overland routes. Petra was slowly abandoned, becoming uninhabited probably in the fourth century A.D."[507] The Byzantine civilization had little impact on the people of

Arabia. They spoke Greek rather than Arabic and favored an urban lifestyle. The Bedouin's were desert wanderers favoring a nomadic lifestyle. They tended to resist domination, control, and taxation by outside powers such as the Byzantine authorities. "In A.D. 500 Bedouin invaded Syria and Palestine and raided Jerusalem. The warring dynasties whose lands bordered Bedouin territory (Byzantium, Sassanid, and southern Arabia) tried to enlist them as allies against the dynasties' enemies. Byzantium formed alliances with tribes on the Syrian border, the Salih and Bani Ghassan, at the beginning of the sixth century. This marked the establishment of the Ghassanid confederation, which supported the Byzantines." [508]

The decision of Muhammad to accept other monotheistic religions as compatible with Islam was unique. Religions which successfully overcome other previously existing religions usually try to either obliterate from memory any references or to allow the religion by syncretism to survive. Instead Muhammad accepted and incorporated Judaism and Christianity into the history of Islam. "These three races and religions, though deadly hostile to each other, alike revered Abraham, the father of the faithful, as their common ancestor. This fact might suggest to a great mind the idea to unite them by a national religion monotheistic in principle and eclectic in its character. This seems to have been the original project of the founder of Islam."[509] He claimed the same authenticity for Islam as was the norm of authenticity for Jewish and Christian beliefs but then claimed their accounts had become corrupted and replaced by the later and final revelations of the prophet. "Rather than deny the validity of other monotheistic religions of the time (Christianity and Judaism), Islam built upon them. Muhammad accepted Abraham and Moses as prophets of God, and he placed Jesus in the same position: a chosen messenger rather than a divine being."[510] Muhammad ultimately rejected the People of the Book because they would not accept him as a prophet. "Never will the Jews nor the Christians be pleased with you (O Muhammad) till you follow their religion."(2:120) He then further disavowed them by re-orienting the direction of prayer from Jerusalem to Mecca.(2:142-144)

In neighboring Iran, the Sassanid dynasty came to power in the mid-sixth century C.E under the reign of Khosrow who favored the religion of Zoroaster. The peoples of the Byzantine Empire were divided in their support for Nestorianism, Monophysitism, and Orthodox beliefs where political and religious headship was vested in Constantinople. The

Byzantines under Emperor Heraclius and the Sassanids under Khosrow exhausted themselves fighting each other by 622 C.E. The Sassanids fell to the armies of Islam under Caliph Umar in 636 C.E. "Just six years before. In September 622—the year Heraclius had launched his Persia expedition—the Prophet Mohammed had fled from hostile Mecca to friendly Medina, thereby initiating the Muslim era; and just five years afterwards, in 633, the armies of Islam would begin the advance . . ."[511] Palestine and Syria were conquered between 632-640 C.E. In 634 C.E. the patriarch of Jerusalem, Sophronius, declared an end to pilgrimages due to the dangers associated with the occupation of the Muslim armies. In Syria, the Ghassanids and Monophysite Arabs sided with the Muslim forces. The Arab Muslims invaded Egypt in 639 C.E. "It seems that the devastation caused by the Muslim invasion and the departure of the Byzantine troops took place amidst the confusion of an Egyptian civil war, with old scores being settled by Christian renegades and among Monophysite Copts and Orthodox Greeks."[512] The Muslim generals offered terms of peace to populations who surrendered. They had only to pay a poll tax that Muslims did not have to pay as a condition of their surrender and occupation. The defeated peoples could choose death, conversion to Islam, or to remain as subjects of the Muslim overlords with payment of the jizya (head tax). The political capital of Islam was established in Damascus, Syria by the Caliph Mu'awiya thereby inaugurating the first Muslim dynasty known as the Umayyads. "In 661 the Caliph Ali had been assassinated; since then Muawiya had reigned supreme, establishing his capital at Damascus and founding the Omayyad dynasty that was to endure for the next eighty years."[513] This occurred in 661 C.E. which transferred control of Syria from Constantinople and effectively shut down the patriarchate of Antioch. "With the departure of the emperor, the remaining Byzantine cities were left to their own devices. Antioch, the ancient capital of Syria, put up little resistance . . ."[514]

Theology of the Koran Pertaining to Jesus Christ

The Koran was the source for discovery of the Islamic belief regarding the nature of Jesus. Abu-Bakr and Zayd collected the fragments of the recitations of Muhammad and published the entire book of the Koran by 650 C.E. "About a year after his death, at the direction of Abu-Bakr, his father-in-law and immediate successor, Zayd, the chief ansar or amanuensis of the Prophet, collected the scattered fragments of the Koran 'from palm-leaves, and tablets of white stone, and from breasts of men' but without any regard to chronological order or continuity of subjects."[515] The Koran was written in a combination of poetry and prose and was ordered thematically rather than chronologically. The Koran contained history, moral and religious code, civil and political code, and doctrine and belief statements encompassed in the context of oriental style and imagery. The theology of the Koran was devoid of the redemption of mankind because there was no belief in original sin or in a fallen humanity. ". . . the Koran, like the Old Testament, is also a civil and political code. Both are oriental in style and imagery. Both have the fresh character of occasional composition growing out of a definite historical situation and specific wants. But the Bible is the genuine revelation of the only true God in Christ, reconciling the world to himself; the Koran is a mock-revelation without Christ and without atonement."[516] Muslims believed that Adam disobeyed out of ignorance and that God forgave him. "Allah wishes to lighten (the burden) for you; and man was created weak." (4:28). Therefore humans were on their own to work out their own salvation based upon good works and obedience to the legal codes of Islam. Because humanity was assumed not to be fallen, there was no need for a Savior. Thus the role of any mediator between humanity and God was only as a prophet and messenger of Allah. The two primary doctrines which pertained to Jesus Christ were in relationship to the Koranic interpretation of the Trinity and the role of Jesus Christ as it related to divinity and humanity. This latter concept was revealed in the concepts of his birth, death, and resurrection.

Islam was a monotheistic religion and hence had a straight forward statement of belief regarding the Godhead. "Monotheism is the corner-stone of the system.

It is expressed in the ever-repeated sentence:

'There is no god but god (Allah, i.e., the true, the only God), and Mohammed is his prophet (or apostle)'."[517] God in Islam is known by the name Allah. The belief in his absolute oneness was known in Arabic as "tawhid". Allah was not knowable personally by any human being. Allah did not reflect any human gender. He was the first cause and first mover that the ancient Greeks defined as God. The primary witness of Muslims was the "shahadah" which claimed "There is no God but Allah". The Koran states ". . . none has the right to be worshipped but I, so worship me Alone and none else."(21:25) To Muslims God was known by ninety-nine names which declared his attributes. "And the Most Beautiful Names belong to Allah, so call on Him by them. . ."(7:180) Allah was omnipresent according to the Koran. "And to Allah belong the east and the west, so wherever you turn, there is the Face of Allah.(2:115). Humanity was neither fallen nor sinful in the essence of one's nature. Rather humans were born with knowledge of God and had simply forgotten about Him. It was a forgetting of the truth by the intellect rather than a disobedience of the will. In Islam the greatest sin was to forget the oneness of God by accepting the plurality of God such as in polytheism or in the Trinity concept in Christianity. This was known in Arabic as "shirk" which was unforgivable. Islam viewed the dispensing of blessing through the written words of the Koran rather than in the person of an incarnated Christ. ". . . in Christianity, because of the emphasis on the Triune God, God the One is seen more in terms of the relationality of the three Hypostases, what one might call 'Divine Relativity'; the vision of the manifestation of the Divine then became confined to the unique Son and Incarnation, in whom all the previous prophets were absorbed."[518] The Koran taught several concepts regarding the person of Jesus. The Koran accepted the basic premise that Jesus experienced a miraculous birth which was from a virgin. "And Maryam (Mary), the daughter of Imran who guarded her chastity. And we breathed into (the sleeve of her shirt or her garment) through our Ruh [i.e. Jibrail (Gabriel)], and she testified to the truth of the Words of her Lord [i.e. believed in the Words of Allah: 'Be! - and he was; that is Isa (Jesus) . . ." (66:12). Thus Muslims accepted the Virgin Birth of Jesus as the son of a very human Mary and of the spirit of Allah. The Koran also accepted the concept that Jesus was sinless. "(The angel) said: 'I am only a messenger from your Lord, (to announce) to you the gift of a righteous son."(19:19)

As regards the crucifixion of Jesus, the Koran denies this event.(4:157-158) There is no recognition of the event other than to claim someone else died in the place of Jesus on the cross that resembled him. Yet the Koran in Surah 19:33 attests that "And Salaam (peace) be upon me the day I was born, and the day I die, and the day I shall be raised alive!" The Koran declares a partial truth regarding the resurrection to life in Surah 3:55 while at the same time denying the divinity of Christ. "And (remember) when Allah said: 'O Isa (Jesus)! I will take you and raise you to Myself...."

The New Testament declares clearly the doctrine of the Trinity. I John 5: 7 says, "For there are three that bear record in heaven, the Father, the Word, and the Holy Spirit; and these three are one." Muslims understand the term "Son of God" to mean that God had relations which produced a physical union with Mary and a resultant offspring in Jesus. Surah 19:35 declares that "It befits not (the Majesty of) Allah that He should beget a son [this refers to the slander of Christians against Allah, by saying that Isa (Jesus) is the son of Allah]." This obviously misses the point of Scripture in declaring the nature of the incarnation as the miraculous union of the Holy Spirit with the Virgin Mary (Matthew 1:18-24). Another misconception in the Koran is in regard to the messianic role of Jesus. The Koran accepts Jesus as Messiah but places no importance of divinity associated with the title. Isaiah 9: 6 says, "... a child is born ... a son is given ... his name shall be called ... The Mighty God ...." The Koran declares Jesus as Messiah but the definition expresses only the role of a messenger. "The Messiah [Isa (Jesus)], son of Maryam (Mary), was no more than a Messenger..."(5:75) The Bible says that Jesus Christ is the only begotten Son of God (John 3:16). Muslims understand this claim in an anthropomorphic sense which the Bible does not claim in this sense. Muslims also believe that the term "beget" means to be created. Christians understand the term to mean a relationship between two members of the Godhead which implies a proceeding from Father to Son. "The Son, on the other hand, owed his beginning to the Father, who had begotten him in eternity ... The process of begetting in eternity was a mysterious one, but it had happened, and it determined the eternal relationship of the Son to the Father."[519] The mistaken Koranic interpretation may be seen in Surah

5:116 which says, ". . . O Isa (Jesus), son of Maryam (Mary)! Did you say unto men: 'Worship me and my mother as two gods besides Allah? " "In summation, the Muslim rejection of the eternal sonship of Christ is based on a serious misunderstanding of the Christian concept of what it means for Christ to be God's Son. 'Son' should be understood in a figurative sense (like the word, ibn), not in a physical sense (as in the Arabic word, walad)."[520] Christianity declares that the Godhead is one in essence or substance and this is not a point of argument with Islam. The difference resides in the plurality in the Godhead and the nature of Christ. Muslims argue that Christianity is tritheistic because the Trinity implies three gods. Christianity however believes in one God in three persons. "Therefore we understand that there is no difference whatever in the incomprehensibility of the three persons [according to the essence], for none of them is more incomprehensible, or less, than the other two. . ."[521] This misunderstanding is enough to separate the two religions over these differences. The ability to conceptualize plurality in unity should have been easy if one compares the nature of a human being as one person with three parts that represent the one which are body, soul, and spirit. Muslims would have to defend their position that the existence of a triune god would be impossibly difficult for god to relate to his own creation as three in one because creation is unable to conceptualize further than a singular god. This means either god is not all powerful to present himself in any form other than the singular or humanity is powerful enough to insist that god be limited to singularity for their sake due to our comprehension being based on mathematical understanding alone. "The Trinity is not the belief that God is three persons and only one person at the same time and in the same sense. That would be a contradiction. Rather, it is the belief that there are three persons in one nature. This may be a mystery, but it is not a contradiction."[522]

The issue of the natures of Christ was probably not seriously considered by Muhammad since he uniformly only recognized the human nature of Jesus. Because of the strict interpretation of the unity of God and the stated desire to become the universal religion replacing polytheism, Judaism, and Christianity; Muhammad was not open to what he considered a competing prophet (Jesus) being considered as deity which would have placed Muhammad in a lesser role as only another messenger of god. The Monophysite and Nestorian versions of Christianity were unlikely to have been the source of Muhammad's views concerning the

Trinity and the natures of Christ. As will be recalled, Monophysitism combined the two natures of Christ, both divine and human, into one person. Islam did not accept the deity of Jesus from the beginning. Nestorianism separates the two natures of Christ into two persons, one divine and one human. "Nestorius, brought up in the school of Antioch, upheld the integrity of Christ's humanity, but distinguished so emphatically between the humanity and the Godhead that he seemed in danger of ending, not with one person, but with two persons coexisting in the same body."[523] Islam neither accepted the deity of Christ nor the plurality of persons in the Godhead. Thus it is unlikely that either sect had any influence on Muhammad's understanding of who Jesus was in history. It is far more likely that Muhammad understood these concepts from the point of view of his nephew Waraqa who was an Ebionite Christian with whom Muhammad associated. ". . . The prophet returned to Khadija while his heart was beating rapidly. She took him to Waraqa bin Naufal who was a Christian convert and used to read the Gospel in Arabic. Waraqa asked (the Prophet), 'What do you see?' When he told him, Waraqa said, 'That is the same angel whom Allah sent to the Prophet Moses. Should I live till you receive the Divine message, I will strongly support you."[524] Ebionites denied the divinity of Christ and rejected the Pauline epistles as does Islam. This appears to be the most likely influence on Muhammad's thinking as it came from Waraqa, a close family member, at the encouragement of his wife Khadija. "His wife Chadijah and her cousin Waraka (a reputed convert to Christianity, or more probably a Jew) are said to have been well acquainted with the sacred books of the Jews and the Christians."[525]

    In summary, the divisiveness incurred from the theological disputes between Monophysites, Nestorians, and orthodox contributed to the weakening of the Byzantine Empire. The successful spread of Islam into the Byzantine Empire was due to many factors which tend to focus on the many military successes. However the segmentation within the empire of peoples with loyalties to their own form of Christianity and their hatred for the political and religious authorities in Constantinople facilitated the spread of Islam. Muhammad as the founder of the religion of Islam and the one, who recited the words of the Koran, came in contact with Christian heresies which served as his understanding of Jesus which were described in the Koran

CONCLUSIONS

The purpose of this study has been to determine the impact of the Monophysite Controversy on the growth and spread of Christianity during the critical period when the orthodox position was being formulated and as Christianity came in contact with the new religion of Islam. The Byzantine Empire was the dominant civilization during the period 300-700 C.E. The political authority and Christian religion ruled the empire. Within this monolithic empire were differences in language, culture, worldview, and religion. The controversies over the Trinity and natures of Christ came to symbolize these differences which weakened the bonds of loyalty and unity. When the new religion of Islam emerged in 610 C.E., a military and theological clash began in 632 C.E. which divided and reduced the Byzantine Empire, replaced Christianity as the majority religion in many parts of the empire, and facilitated the spread of Islam.

The implications of this research have traced the development of the Christian religion in the East during the period 300-700.C.E. After the apostles had passed from the scene, church fathers defended the faith against paganism, Judaizing, and Gnostic errors which would have, if accepted, destroyed Christianity. "These skirmishes with the philosophers on points central to the Christian faith led to the creation of an extensive early Christian literature of 'apologetic', or defence of the faith."[526] Following this early period the Christian leaders attempted to describe and understand the mysteries of the Trinity and the Incarnation. Various theologians wrote about their understanding of these issues. Three key positions were debated which were Monophysitism, Nestorianism, and Orthodox. Positions held by various theologians and emperors established different historical events, theological beliefs, and political power. The debates resulted in the establishment of standards of the faith which would be deemed to be orthodox while any belief outside these boundaries would be deemed to be heretical. Once the understanding of the Trinity was resolved in 325 C.E., the nature(s) of Christ would be discussed and debated for four centuries. In doing so an orthodox form of Christianity was protected and preserved but only at the expense of disunity within both the empire and the church. There were several outcomes to these events. The church established a conciliar method to resolve issues of belief and practice. The church councils and the resulting published creeds gave a forum for discussion and a written record of the findings. The creeds embodied the theological beliefs of the majority of theologians at a given counsel. "The focus on the creeds encouraged increasingly systematic teaching by way of catechesis, or instruction, of the adults who were converted to the faith."[527] The canons provided a record of the acceptable and unacceptable practices regarding church organization and discipline. These documents serve to explain a historical narrative provided in chronological sequence of the history of the church, the role of the emperors, the political intrigues of the leaders, the political and geographical history of the empire, and the biblical and philosophical arguments of the theologians of the early church. The issues of the Trinity and the nature(s) of Christ have never been resolved to everyone's satisfaction such that the explanations of these church theologians remain pertinent in explaining and defending Christianity today. "The discussion of the creeds goes on in a modern ecumenical context."[528]

It has been shown how the Byzantine Empire was weakened in the face of Islam. Segments of the empire such as Syria, Palestine, Egypt, and Armenia were somewhat receptive to the forces of Islam and neutral or disloyal to the defense of the authority in Constantinople. Translation of more of the Syriac manuscripts into Western languages is needed to fill in the gaps of understanding of this period. In addition since it was the policy of the church to anathematize a heretic and his writings, the finding and reconstructing of material thought to be burned would be beneficial in understanding the thinking of the heretics because we often know them only through the writings of their orthodox critics. "The efforts of the majority to destroy every trace of heretical 'blasphemy' proved so successful that, until the discoveries at Nag Hammadi, nearly all our information concerning alternative forms of early Christianity came from the massive orthodox attacks upon them."[529] Finally more research needs to be done in determining the origin of Muhammad's theology. Too much of the Christian literature is speculative and thinly researched. The Muslim literature alternately appears to be biased against accepting much Christian influence on Muhammad and the contacts with Christians are briefly referenced in the Hadiths which are very close to being legends rather than authentic history.

CHAPTER REFERENCES

CHAPTER TWO ORIGIN AND BASIS FOR THE MONOPHYSITE BELIEF

[1] W. G. T. Shedd and A.W. Gomes, *Dogmatic Theology* (Phillipsburg, NJ: P &R Publishing, 2003), 957.

[2] C. Soanes and A. Stevenson, *Concise Oxford English Dictionary,* 11th ed., (Oxford: Oxford University Press, 2004) s.v. "Monophysite".

[3] E. Fahlbusch and G.W. Bromiley, *The Encyclopedia of Christianity,* Vol. 4 (Grand Rapids, Mich.: Wm. B. Eerdmans, 1999-2003), s.v. "The Doctrine of the Two Wills in Christ."

[4] Origen, "On First Principles: Book 4," in *Biblical Interpretation in the Early Church,* ed. Karlfried Froehlich (Philadelphia: Fortress Press, 1984), 67.

[5] H. M. Gwatkin, *The Arian Controversy*, ed. M. Creighton (New York: Anson D. F. Randolph, 1889), 139.

[6] P. Schaff and D. S Schaff, *History of the Christian Church* (Oak Harbor, WA: Logos Research Systems, Inc., 1997), 1549.

[7] Charles E. Raven, *Apollinarianism: An Essay on the Christology of the Early Church* (Eugene, OR: Wipf & Stock Publishers, 2004), 184.

[8] Schaff and Schaff, 1550.

[9] Ibid, 1552.

[10] Ibid, 1550.

[11] Ibid, 1552.

[12] Ibid, 1550.

[13] Raven, 204.

[14] Sozomenus, "The Ecclesiastical History of Sozomenus: History of the Church," in *Nicene and Post-Nicene Fathers*, ed. Phillip Schaff and Henry Wace (Grand Rapids: Wm. B. Eerdmans, 1952), 364.

[15] Schaff and Schaff, s.v. "Nestorians."

[16] Ibid.

[17] F.L. Cross and E.A. Livingstone, *The Oxford Dictionary of the Christian Church*, 3rd ed. rev. (Oxford; New York: Oxford University Press, 2005), s.v. "Nestorius."

[18] Socrates, *"The Ecclesiastical History of Socrates Scholasticus,"* in *Nicene and Post-Nicene Fathers,"* ed. Philip Schaff and Henry Wace (Grand Rapids: Wm. B. Eerdmans, 1952), 171.

[19] Schaff and Schaff, 1598.

[20] Friedrich Loofs, *Nestorius and His Place in the History of Christian Doctrine* (Memphis, TN: General Books, 2010), 3.

[19] Ibid, 13.

[22] Socrates, 170-71.

[23] Loofs, 9.

[24] Ibid, 29.

[25] Ibid, 32.

[26] Ibid, 37.

[27] Ibid, 43.

[28] Ibid, 45.

[29] Ibid, 49.

[30] J.D. Douglas, P.W. Comfort and D. Mitchell, *Who's Who in Christian History* (Wheaton, Ill.: Tyndale House, 1997) s.v. "Eutyches".

[31] Charles Hodge, *Systematic Theology* Vol. 2 (Oak Harbor, WA: Logos Research Systems, Inc, 1997), 402.

[32] Douglas, Comfort, and Mitchell s.v. "Eutyches".

[33] Ibid, s.v. "Eutyches."

[34] A. H. Strong, *Systematic Theology* (Bellingham, WA. Logos Research Systems, Inc., 2004), 672.

[35] Ibid, s.v. "Eutyches."

[36] Hodge, 404.

[37] Ibid, 405.

[38] Richard A. Norris, trans. and ed., *The Christological Controversy* (Philadelphia,: Fortress Press, 1980), 154.

[39] Hodge, 402.

[40] Norris, 142.

[41] Cross and Livingstone, s.v. "The Doctrine of the Two Wills in Christ."

[42] Iain R. Torrance, Christology and Chalcedon: Severus of Antioch and Sergius the Monophysite (Eugene, OR: Wipf and Stock, 1998), 85.

[43] Leo Donald Davis, *The First Seven Ecumenical Councils (325-787): Their History and Theology* (Collegeville, MN: The Liturgical Press, 1990), 223.

[44] J.N.D. Kelly, *Early Christian Doctrines* (San Francisco: Harper & Row, 1978), 334.

[45] Davis, 221.

[46] Cross and Livingstone, s.v. "The Doctrine of the Two Wills in Christ."

[47] Kelly, 333.

[48] Cross and Livingstone, s.v. "Alexandrian and Antiochian Schools."

[49] Davis, 212.

[50] Davis, 260-61.

[51] Schaff and Schaff, 1545.

[52] Fahlbusch and Bromiley, s.v. "Alexandrian and Antiochian Schools."

[53] Diarmaid MacCulloch, *Christianity: The First Three Thousand Years* (New York: Viking, 2009), 147.

[54] Cross and Livingstone, s.v. "Alexandrian and Antiochian Schools."

[55] Ibid, s.v. "Alexandrian and Antiochian Schools."

[56] Ibid, s.v. "Alexandrian and Antiochian Schools."

[57] Ibid, s.v. "Alexandrian and Antiochian Schools."

[58] Ibid, s.v. "Alexandrian and Antiochian Schools.".

[59] Davis, 172.

[60] Kelly, 305.

[61] Ibid, 319.

[62] Ibid, 320.

[63] Schaff and Schaff, 2053.

[64] Harold O.J. Brown, *Heresies: Heresy and Orthodoxy in the History of the Church* (Peabody, MA: Hendrickson, 2007), 176.

[65] Kelly, 342.

[66] Ibid, 331.

[67] Schaff and Schaff, 2035.

[68] Phillip R. Amidon, trans., John J. O'Keefe, ed., *The Fathers of the Church: St. Cyril of Alexandria Festal Letters 1-12* (Washington, D.C.: Catholic University of America Press, 2009), 5.

[69] Ibid, 146.

[70] Ibid, 8.

[71] Ibid, 75.

[72] Ibid, 213.

[73] Ibid, 30.

[74] Davis, 89.

[75] Gwatkin, 54.

[76] Socrates, 10.

[77] Hans Lietzmann, *The Era of the Church Fathers* (New York: Charles Scribner's Sons, 1952), 177.

[78] Socrates, 29.

[79] F. A. Forbes, *Saint Athanasius-The Father of Orthodoxy* (Lexington, KY: Filiquarian Publishing, 2010), 46.

[80] Kelly, 302.

[81] Ibid, 288-289.

CHAPTER 3 AN ANALYSIS OF THE DEBATE REGARDING THE NATURE (S) OF CHRIST

[82] C. F. H. Henry, *God, Revelation, and Authority* (Wheaton, Ill.: Crossway Books, 1999), 290-302.

[83] Alister McGrath, *Heresy: A History of Defending the Truth* (New York: HarperCollins, 2009), 80.

[84] McGrath, 198.

[85] Brown, 184-185.

[86] Torrance, 27.

[87] Ibid, 28.

[88] Torrance, 90.

[89] Ibid, 101.

[90] Ibid, 93.

[91] Douglas, Comfort, and Mitchell, s.v. "Justinian I".

[92] Cross and Livingstone, s.v. "Peter The Fuller."

[93] Ibid, s.v. "Julian of Halicarnassus."

[94] M. Anders *Galatians-Colossians Holman New Testament Commentary* (Nashville, TN: Broadman & Holman Publishers, 1999), 315-319.

[95] Ibid, 315-319.

[96] Kelly, 339-40.

[97] Anders, 315–19.

[98] Charles Ryrie, *Basic Theology* (Chicago: Moody Press, 1986), 250.

[99] Schaff and Schaff, 1647.

[100] Ibid, 1642.

[101] W.A. Elwell and B.J. Beitzel, *Baker Encyclopedia of the Bible* (Grand Rapids, Mich.: Baker Book House, 1988), 1027-28.

[102] Ibid, 1027-1028.

[103] J.I. Packer, *Concise Theology: A Guide to Historic Christian Beliefs* (Wheaton, Ill.: Tyndale House, 1995) s.v. "Two Natures".

[104] Douglas, Comfort, and Mitchell s.v. "Justinian I".

[105] Ibid, s.v. "Justinian I."

[106] M. Galli and T. Olsen, *131 Christians Everyone Should Know* (Nashville, TN: Broadman & Holman Publishers, 2000), 316.

[107] Fahlbusch and Bromiley, s.v. "Leo The Great."

[108] MacCulloch, 226.

CHAPTER 4 HISTORICAL TIMELINE OF THE MONOPHYSITE CONTROVERSY

[109] Justo Gonzalez, *Christian Thought Revisited: Three Types of Theology* (Maryknoll, NY: Orbis Books, 2002), 18.

[110] W.H.C. Frend, *The Rise of Christianity* (Philadelphia, PA: Fortress Press, 1984), 206.

[111] Gonzalez, 19.

[112] Ibid, 45.

[113] Ibid, 34.

[114] Jean Danielou, Translated by Walter Mitchell (New York: Sheed and Ward, 1955), 182.

[115] Ibid, 254.

[116] Gonzalez, 39.

[117] Danielou, 209.

[118] Ibid, 216.

[119] W.H.C. Frend, *The Early Church* (Minneapolis, MN: Fortress Press, 1991), 9.

[120] Frend, *The Rise of Christianity*, 109-110.

[121] Ibid, 148.

[122] Ibid, 177.

[123] Ibid, 420.

[124] Davis, 17.

[125] Gerald Bray, *The Doctrine of God* (Downers Grove, IL: InterVarsity Press, 1993), 134-135.

[126] Frend, *The Rise of Christianity*, 322.

[127] MacCulloch, 212.

[128] Frances Young, *The Making of the Creeds* (London: SCM Press, 2002), 47.

[129] Ibid, 213.

[130] Frend, 206.

[131] Gonzalez, 88.

[132] Gonzalez, 89.

[133] Timothy Ware, *The Orthodox Church* (New York: Penguin Putnam Inc., 1997), 47.

[134] Davis, 74.

[135] Ibid, 124.

[136] Ibid, 142.

[137] Ibid, 186.

[138] Ibid, 244.

[139] Elaine Pagels, *The Gnostic Gospels* (New York: Vintage Books, 1979), 37.

[140] Gonzalez, 19.

[141] E.C. Blackman, *Marcion and His Influence* (Eugene, OR: Wipf and Stock Publishers, 2004), 55.

[142] Gonzalez, 42.

[143] Davis, 46.

[144] Ibid, 47.

[145] Ibid, 47.

[146] Ibid, 49.

[147] Ibid, 52.

[148] Ibid, 52.

[149] Ibid, 60.

[150] Ibid, 60-61.

[151] Ibid, 83.

[152] Ibid, 89.

[153] Ibid, 104-105.

[154] Ibid, 112.

[155] Ibid, 119.

[156] Ibid, 119.

[157] Ibid, 125.

[158] Ibid, 117.

[159] Ibid, 135-136.

[160] Ibid, 140.

[161] Ibid, 142.

[162] Young, 74.

[163] Davis, 143.

[164] Ibid, 143.

[165] Ibid, 144-145.

[166] Ibid, 146-147.

[167] Ibid, 149-153.

[168] Ibid, 166.

[169] Ibid, 171.

[170] Ibid, 175.

[171] Ibid, 176.

[172] Ibid, 177.

[173] Ibid, 185.

[174] Ibid, 186.

[175] Ibid, 188.

[176] Ibid, 190.

[177] Ibid, 195-196.

[178] Ibid, 213.

[179] Ibid, 213.

[180] Ibid, 215.

[181] Ibid, 217.

[182] Ibid, 229.

[183] Ibid, 223-224.

[184] M. Galli and T. Olsen, 314.

[185] Davis, 235.

[186] Ibid, 238.

[187] Ibid, 244-245.

[188] Ibid, 250.

[189] Ibid, 261.

[190] Cross and Livingstone, s.v. "Monoenergism."

[191] Davis, 264.

[192] Ibid, 268.

[193] Ibid, 273.

[194] Ibid, 283.

[195] Cross and Livingstone, s.v. "Monothelitism."

[196] Davis, 287.

[197] Young, 19.

[198] Frend, 38.

[199] Ibid, 41.

[200] Ware, 11-12.

[201] Henry Chadwick, *The Early Church* (New York: Penguin, 1967), 77.

[202] Frend, 66.

[203] Ibid, 82.

[204] Ibid, 83.

[205] Ibid, 93.

[206] Ibid, 91.

[207] Ibid, 87.

[208] Ibid, 113.

[209] Ibid, 113.

[210] Ibid, 102.

[211] Ibid, 147.

[212] Ibid, 213.

[213] Ibid, 212.

[214] Ibid, 215.

[215] Chadwick, 199.

[216] Chadwick, 205-206.

[217] John Meyendorff, *Byzantine Theology; Historical Trends and Doctrinal Themes* (New York: Fordham University Press, 1983), 157.

[218] Ibid, 37.

[219] Frend, 128.

[220] Chadwick, 223.

[221] Gonzalez, 89-90.

[222] Ware, 211.

[223] Frend, 220.

[224] Ibid, 68.

[225] Davis, 40.

[226] Gonzalez, 21.

[227] Davis, 46.

[228] Frend, 83.

[229] Danielou, 254-255.

[230] William G. Rusch, ed., *The Trinitarian Controversy* (Philadelphia: Fortress Press, 1980), 30.

[231] Frend, 137.

[232] Gonzalez, 79.

[233] Davis, 72.

[234] Cross and Livingstone, s.v. "John the Grammarian."

[235] Davis, 202.

[236] Douglas, Comfort, and Mitchell s.v. "Gelasius I".

[237] Cross and Livingstone, s.v. "Henoticon."

[238] Davis, 179.

[239] Ibid, 236.

[240] Ibid, 192.

[241] Ibid, 235.

[242] Douglas, Comfort, and Mitchell, s.v. "Honorius I".

[243] Schaff and Schaff, s.v. "Gregory I".

[244] G.R. Evans, *A Brief History of Heresy* (Malden, MA: Blackwell Publishing, 2003), 8-9.

[245] Frend, 146.

[246] Ibid, 136.

[247] Christopher A.Hall, *Reading Scripture with the Church Fathers* (Downers Grove: InterVarsity Press, 1998), 57.

[248] Davis, 117.

[249] Hall, 76.

[250] Davis, 112.

[251] Hall, 91.

[252] Ware, 36.

[253] Ibid, 96.

[254] Evans, 10.

[255] Ibid, 151.

CHAPTER 5 ANALYSIS OF THE CANONS, CREEDS, AND COUNCILS DURING THE MONOPHYSITE CONTROVERSY

[256] Ware, 20.

[257] Ibid, 15.

[258] Meyendorff, 79.

[259] Ibid, 80.

[260] Frend, 74.

[261] Ibid, 26-27.

[262] Ware, 202.

[263] Davis, 72.

[264] Ibid, 71.

[265] Ibid, 122.

[266] Ibid, 162.

[267] Ibid, 187.

[268] Ibid, 244.

[269] Ibid, 283.

[270] Ibid, 310.

[271] Ibid, 323.

[272] Ware, 205.

[273] Davis, 63.

[274] Norman P. Tanner, *The Councils of the Church; A Short History* (New York: Crossroad Publishing, 2001), 41.

[275] Davis, 126.

[276] Socrates, 122.

[277] Davis, 189.

[278] Ibid, 190.

[279] Ibid, 190.

[280] Ibid, 190.

[281] Chadwick, 204.

[282] Davis, 285.

[283] Ibid, 286.

[284] Meyendorff, 35.

[285] Ibid, 79.

[286] Davis, 175.

[287] Henry Bettenson and Chris Maunder, ed., *Documents of the Christian Church* (New York: Oxford University Press, 1999), 54.

[288] Meyendorff, 23.

[289] Bettenson and Maunder, 100.

[290] Davis, 203.

[291] Phillip Schaff, *The Nicene and Post-Nicene Fathers Second Series Vol. XIV* (Oak Harbor: Logos Research Systems, 1997), 400-401.

[292] Phillip Schaff, *The Nicene and Post-Nicene Fathers Second Series Vol. XIII* (Oak Harbor: Logos Research Systems, 1997), 91.

[293] D.R.W. Wood and I.H. Marshall, *New Bible Dictionary* (3rd ed.), (Downers Grove: InterVarsity Press, 1996), s.v. "Syriac Canon.".

[294] Ware, 29.

[295] Phillip Schaff, 82-84.

[296] Davis, 207-208.

[297] Bettenson and Maunder, 98.

[298] Davis, 203.

[299] Cross and Livingstone, s.v. "Acacian Schism."

[300] Davis, 187.

[301] EWTN Online Services, "Tome of Leo" Eternal Word Television Network, http://www.ewtn.com/faith/teachings/incac1.htm (accessed January 10, 2011).

[302] Catholic Encyclopedia, "Three Chapters," New Advent, http://www.newadvent.org/cathen/14707b.htm (accessed January 10, 2011).

[303] Schaff, *The Nicene and Post-Nicene Fathers Second Series Vol. XIV*, 400-401.

[304] Schaff, The Nicene and Post-Nicene Fathers Second Series Vol. XIII, 91.

[305] Wood and Marshall, s.v. "Syriac Canon."

[306] Schaff, *The Nicene and Post-Nicene Fathers Second Series Vol. XIII*, 82-84.

[307] Original Catholic Encyclopedia, "Henoticon," Catholic Answers, http://oce.catholic.com/index.php?title=Henoticon (accessed January 10, 2011).

[308] Davis, 221.

[309] Ware, 51.

[310] Henry Bettenson, Editor and Translator, *The Early Christian Fathers* (New York; Oxford University Press, 1969), 50.

[311] Evans, 23.

[312] J.N.D. Kelly, *Early Christian Creeds* (New York: Longman Inc., 1972), 204.

[313] Evans, 30.

[314] Bettenson, 26.

[315] Bray, 83.

[316] Ibid, 128.

[317] Ibid, 127.

[318] Bettenson, 26.

[319] Davis, 89.

[320] Ibid, 90.

[321] Ibid, 91.

[322] Kelly, 243-244.

[323] Davis, 123.

[324] Ibid, 105.

[325] Young, 53.

[326] Ibid, 69.

[327] Kelly, 340.

[328] Davis, 140.

[329] Young, 74.

[330] Davis, 142.

[331] Loofs, 35.

[332] Amidon and O'Keefe, 213.

[333] St Cyril of Alexandria, *On the Unity of Christ,* Translated and Introduced by John Anthony McGuckin (Crestwood, NY: St Vladimir's Seminary Press, 1995), 35.

[334] Chadwick, 199.

[335] Bettenson and Maunder, 50-51.

[336] Davis, 187.

[337] Ibid, 196.

[338] Ibid, 186.

[339] Ibid, 245.

[340] John Julius Norwich, *A Short History of Byzantium* (New York: Vintage Books, 1999), 48.

[341] Ibid, 95.

[342] Meyendorff, 153.

[343] Ware, 22.

[344] Jaroslav Pelikan, *The Christian Tradition: A History of the Development of Doctrine* (Chicago: University of Chicago Press, 1971), 191.

[345] Bray, 158.

[346] Early Church.org.uk, "First Council of Nicaea-325 AD (St. Michael's Depot)," http://www.piar.hu/councils/ecum01.htm (accessed January 13, 2011).

[347] Frend, 172.

[348] Norris, 105.

[349] McGuckin, 40.

[350] Justo L. Gonzalez, *The Story of Christianity: The Early Church to the Present Day* (Peabody, MA: Prince Press, 2006), 188.

[351] The Catholic Encyclopedia, "The Nicene Creed", New Advent, http://www.newadvent.org/cathen/11049a.htm (accessed January 13, 2011).

[352] Davis, 141.

[353] Ibid, 146-147.

[354] McGuckin, 40.

[355] The Daily Catholic, "The Council of Ephesus", http://www.dailycatholic.org/history/3ecumen1.htm (accessed January 13, 2011).

[356] The Daily Catholic, "Declaration of Mary as Theotokos", http://www.dailycatholic.org/3ecumen2.htm#Declaration%20of%20Theotokos (accessed January 13, 2011).

[357] Bruce L. Shelley, *Church History in Plain Language* (Nashville: Thomas Nelson Publishers, 1995), 113-114.

[358] Definition of Chalcedon, "Definition of Chalcedon", http://www.creeds.net/ancient/chalcedon.htm (accessed January 13, 2011).

[359] Meyendorff, 32.

[360] Ibid, 34.

[361] Davis, 163.

[362] Ibid, 243.

[363] Chadwick, 209.

[364] Davis, 261.

[365] Davis, 273.

[366] Christia File Archives, "Later Creeds" http://www.creeds.net/ancient/later.htm (accessed January 14, 2011).

[367] Frend, 139.

[368] Ware, 22.

[369] Davis, 91.

[370] Young, 70.

[371] Norwich, 45.

[372] Davis, 172.

[373] Meyendorff, 3.

[374] Ware, 29.

[375] Meyendorff, 36.

[376] Davis, 222.

[377] Ibid, 284.

[378] Schaff, *The Nicene and Post-Nicene Fathers Second Series Vol. XIV*, 264-265.

[379] Evans, 81.

[380] Frend, 141.

[381] Socrates, *The Nicene and Post-Nicene Fathers Second Series Vol. II*, 9-10.

[382] Ware, 22.

[383] Frend, 173.

[384] Ibid, 173.

[385] Socrates, 121.

[386] McGuckin, 25.

[387] Socrates, 172.

[388] Davis, 171.

[389] Ibid, 187.

[390] Schaff and Schaff, 1627.

[391] Davis, 244.

[392] Ibid, 249.

[393] Ibid, 251.

[394] Norwich, 79.

[395] Tanner, 33.

[396] Jacques Duchesne-Guillemin, *Symbols and Values in Zoroastrianism: Their Survival and Renewal* (New York: Harper & Row, 1966), 9.

[397] Davis, 282.

[398] Ibid, 264.

[399] Ibid, 287.

[400] Norwich, 34.

[401] Richard A. Horsley, *Religion and Empire; People, Power, and Life of the Spirit* (Minneapolis, MN: Fortress Press, 2003), 93..

[402] Pagels, 34.

[403] Ibid, 104.

[404] Frend, 113.

CHAPTER 6 THE IMPACT OF THE MONOPHYSITE CONTROVERSY ON THE BYZANTINE EMPIRE AND THE SPREAD OF ISLAM

[405] Ware, 46.

[406] Ibid, 16.

[407] Ibid, 74.

[408] Frend, 209.

[409] Meyendorff, 215.

[410] Norwich, 95.

[411] Danielou, 164.

[412] Ibid, 184.

[413] Frend, 114.

[414] Davis, 269.

[415] Fahlbusch and Bromiley, s.v. "Heresies and Schisms."

[416] Ware, 29.

[417] Peter Brown, *The World of Late Antiquity* (New York: Sheed and Ward, 1989), 144-145.

[418] Frend, 191.

[419] Ibid, 192.

[420] Meyendorff, 36.

[421] Davis, 146.

[422] Ibid, 231.

[423] Ibid, 197.

[424] Ibid, 270.

[425] Fahlbusch and Bromiley, s.v. "The Monophysite Sects ".

[426] Schaff and Schaff, 1710.

[427] Ibid, 1691.

[428] MacCulloch, 251.

[429] Davis, 204.

[430] MacCulloch, 181.

[431] Ibid, 185.

[432] Ibid, 187.

[433] Davis, 207.

[434] MacCulloch, 323.

[435] Schaff and Schaff, 698.

[436] Frend, 150.

[437] Kenneth Scott Latourette, *A History of Christianity Volume I: to A.D. 1500* (Peabody, MA: Hendrickson Publishers, 2000), 253.

[438] Christopher Dawson, *The Formation of Christendom* (San Francisco: Ignatius Press, 2008), 164.

[439] Ware, 18.

[440] Gonzalez, 143.

[441] Ware, 37.

[442] Meyendorff, 66.

[443] Shelley, 118.

[444] Meyendorff, 178.

[445] Frend, 41.

[446] Blackman, 127.

[447] Brown, 200.

[448] Meyendorff, 33.

[449] Davis, 221.

[450] Ibid, 223.

[451] Norwich, 79.

[452] Davis, 252.

[453] Ibid, 199.

[454] Schaff and Schaff, 141.

[455] Norwich, 94.

[456] Schaff, 147.

[457] Ibid, 148.

[458] MacCulloch, 245.

[459] Schaff and Schaff, 139.

[460] Schaff, 154.

[461] G.P. Duffield and N.M. Van Cleave, *Foundations of Pentecostal Theology* (Los Angeles, CA: L.I.F.E. Bible College, 1983), 37.

[462] Norwich, 89.

[463] MacCulloch, 253.

[464] Brown, 194.

[465] Schaff and Schaff, 162.

[466] Schaff and Schaff, s.v. "The Conquests of Islam".

[467] Fahlbusch and Bromiley, 72-74.

[468] Bernard Lewis, *The Arabs in History* (Oxford: Oxford University Press, 1992), 47.

[469] Fahlbusch and Bromiley, 759.

[470] Brown, 157.

[471] Ibid, 194.

[472] Davis, 269.

[473] Fahlbusch and Bromiley, 140.

[474] Bray, 121.

[475] Ibid, 121.

[476] Ibid, 120-121.

[477] Ibid, 42.

[478] Ibid, 121.

[479] Eusebius, *The History of the Church from Christ to Constantine,* ed. and trans. by G.A. Williamson (New York: Penguin Group, 1989), 90.

[480] Latourette, 121.

[481] Davis, 34.

[482] Pelikan, 25.

[483] McGrath, 109.

[484] Frend, 54.

[485] McGrath, 228.

[486] Fahlbusch and Bromiley, 749.

[487] Schaff and Schaff, 148-149,

[488] Fahlbusch and Bromiley, 469.

[489] Norman L. Geisler and Abdul Saleeb, *Answering Islam: The Crescent in the Light of the Cross* (Grand Rapids, MI: Baker Books, 1993), 90.

[490] Schaff and Schaff, 156.

[491] Ibid, 156.

[492] Brown, 165.

[493] Schaff and Schaff, 192.

[494] Ibid, 191.

[495] Schaff and Schaff, 174.

[496] Bruce A. McDowell and Anees Zaka, *Muslims and Christians at the Table* (Phillipsburg, NJ: P&R Publishing, 1999), 37.

[497] Geisler and Saleeb, 308.

[498] Reza F. Safa, *Inside Islam: Exposing and Reaching the World of Islam* (Lake Mary, FL: Charisma House, 1996), 27.

[499] Anis A. Shorrosh, *Islam Revealed: A Christian Arab's View of Islam* (Nashville, TN: Thomas Nelson, 1988), 155.

[500] Schaff and Schaff, 171.

[501] Ibid, 173.

[502] Ibid, 173.

[503] Ibid, 194.

[504] Ibid, 156-157.

[505] Abraham Negev, *The Archaeological Encyclopedia of the Holy Land* (New York: Prentice Hall Press, 1996), s.v. "Arabia".

[506] Abraham Negev, *The Archaeological Encyclopedia of the Holy Land* (New York: Prentice Hall Press, 1996), s.v. "Negev".

[507] James Wynbrandt, *A Brief History of Saudi Arabia* (New York: Checkmark Books, 2004), 14-15.

[508] Wynbrandt, 19.

[509] Schaff and Schaff, 148.

[510] Wynbrandt, 33.

[511] Norwich, 94.

[512] Bat Ye'or, *The Decline of Eastern Christianity: From Jihad to Dhimmitude,* trans. Miriam Kochan and David Littman (Cranbury, NJ: Associated University Press, 1996), 47.

[513] Norwich, 101.

[514] Hugh Kennedy, *The Great Arab Conquests: How the Spread of Islam changed the World We live In* (Philadelphia, PA: Da Capo Press, 2007), 88.

[515] Schaff and Schaff, 169.

[516] Ibid, 178.

[517] Ibid, 185.

[518] Seyyed Hossein Nasr, *The Heart of Islam: Enduring Values for Humanity* (New York: HarperCollins Publishers, 2002), 21.

[519] Bray, 160.

[520] Geisler and Saleeb, 258.

[521] Georges A. Barrois, Editor and Translator, *The Fathers Speak: St Basil the Great St Gregory Nazianzus St Gregory of Nyssa* (Crestwood, NY: St Vladimir's Seminary Press, 1986), 126.

[522] Geisler and Saleeb, 265

[523] Ware, 24.

[524] Islamic Awareness, "Did Waraqa Ibn Nawfal Teach the Prophet?" Hadith Volume 4, Book 55, Number 605, http://www.islamic-awareness.org/Quran/Sources/BBwaraqa.html (accessed February 1, 2011).

[525] Schaff and Schaff, 173.

CONCLUSIONS

[526] Evans, 28.

[527] Ibid, 34.

[528] Ibid, 34.

[529] Pagels, xxiv.

BIBLIOGRAPHY

Amidon, Phillip R., trans., O'Keefe, John J. ed., *The Fathers of the Church: St. Cyril of Alexandria Festal Letters 1-12.* Washington, D.C.: Catholic University of America Press, 2009.

Anders, Max, Vol. 8, Galatians-Colossians. Holman New Testament Commentary; Holman Reference. Nashville, TN: Broadman & Holman Publishers, 1999.

Barrois, Georges A., *The Fathers Speak: St Basil the Great St Gregory Nazianzus St Gregory of Nyssa.* Crestwood, NY: St Vladimir's Press, 1986.

Bettenson, Henry and Maunder, Chris. ed., *Documents of the Christian Church.* New York: Oxford University Press, 1999._____Editor and Translator, *The Early Christian Fathers.* New York: Oxford University Press, 1969.

Blackman, E.C., *Marcion and his Influence.* Eugene, OR: Wipf and Stock Publishers, 2004.

Boer, Harry R., *A Short History of the Early Church.* Grand Rapids, MI: Wm. B. Eerdmans Publishing, 1976.

Bray, Gerald, *The Doctrine of God.* Downers Grove, IL: InterVarsity Press, 1993.

Brown, Harold O.J., *Heresies: Heresy and Orthodoxy in the History of the Church.* Peabody, MA: Hendrickson, 2007.

Brown, Peter, *The World of Late Antiquity.* New York: W.W. Norton and Company, 1989.

Catholic Encyclopedia, "Three Chapters." New Advent. http://www.newadvent.org/cathen/14707b.htm (accessed January 10, 2011)._____ "The Nicene Creed." New Advent. http://www.newadvent.org/cathen/11049a.htm (accessed January 13, 2011).

Chadwick, Henry, *The Early Church.* New York: Penguin, 1967.

Christia File Archives, "Later Creeds." http://www.creeds.net/ancient/later.htm (accessed January 14, 2011).

Comfort, Philip Wesley and David P. Barrett, *The Text of the Earliest New Testament Greek Manuscripts.* A corrected, enlarged ed. of the complete text of the earliest New Testament manuscripts. Wheaton, Ill.: Tyndale House, 2001.

Cross, F. L. and Elizabeth A. Livingstone, *The Oxford Dictionary of the Christian Church.* 3rd ed. rev. Oxford; New York: Oxford University Press, 2005.

Danielou, Jean, *Origen.* Translated by Walter Mitchell. New York: Sheed and Ward, 1955.

Davis, Leo Donald, *The First Seven Ecumenical Councils (325-787): Their History and Theology.* Collegeville, MN: The Liturgical Press, 1990.

Dawson, Christopher, *The Formation of Christendom.* San Francisco: Ignatius Press, 2008. Definition of Chalcedon "Definition of Chalcedon." http://www.creeds.net/ancient/chalcedon.htm (accessed January 13, 2011).

Douglas, J. D., Philip Wesley Comfort and Donald Mitchell, *Who's Who in Christian History.* Wheaton, Ill.: Tyndale House, 1997.

Duchesne-Guillemin, Jacques, *Symbols and Values in Zoroastrianism: Their Survival and Renewal.* New York: Harper & Row, 1966.

Duffield, G.P. and N.M. Van Cleave, *Foundations of Pentecostal Theology*. Los Angeles, CA: L.I.F.E. Bible College, 1983.

Early Church.org.uk, "First Council of Nicaea-325 AD (St. Michael's Depot)." http://www.piar.hu/councils/ecum01.htm (accessed January 13, 2011).

Elwell, Walter A. and Barry J. Beitzel, *Baker Encyclopedia of the Bible*. Grand Rapids, Mich.: Baker Book House, 1988.

Eusebius, *The History of the Church from Christ to Constantine*. Edited and Translated by G.A. Williamson. New York: Penguin Group, 1989.

Evans, G.R., *A Brief History of Heresy*. Malden, MA: Blackwell Publishing, 2003.

EWTN Online Services, "Tome of Leo." Eternal Word Television Network. http://www.ewtn.com/faith/teachings/incac1.htm (accessed January 10, 2011).

Fahlbusch, Erwin and Geoffrey William Bromiley, *The Encyclopedia of Christianity, V 3*. Grand Rapids, Mich.; Leiden, Netherlands: Wm. B. Eerdmans; Brill, 1999-2003. _____*The Encyclopedia of Christianity, V 4*. Grand Rapids, Mich.; Leiden, Netherlands: Wm. B. Eerdmans; Brill, 2005.

Forbes, F.A., *Saint Athanasius-The Father of Orthodoxy*. Lexington, KY: Filiquarian Publishing, 2010.

Frend, W.H.C., *The Early Church*. Minneapolis, MN: Fortress Press, 1991. _____*The Rise of Christianity*. Philadelphia, PA: Fortress Press, 1984.

Galli, Mark and Ted Olsen, *131 Christians Everyone Should Know*. Nashville, TN: Broadman & Holman Publishers, 2000.
Geisler, Norman L. and Abdul Saleeb, *Answering Islam: The Crescent in the Light of the Cross*. Grand Rapids, MI: Baker Books, 1993.

Gonzalez, Justo L., *The Story of Christianity: The Early Church to the Present Day*. Peabody, MA: Prince Press, 2006._____*Christian Thought Revisited: Three Types of Theology*. Maryknoll, NY: Orbis Books, 2002.

Gwatkin, H.M., *The Arian Controversy*. Edited by M. Creighton. New York: Anson D. F. Randolph, 1889.

Hall, Christopher A., *Reading Scripture with the Church Fathers*. Downers Grove: InterVarsity Press, 1998.

Henry, Carl Ferdinand Howard, *God, Revelation, and Authority, V 6*. Wheaton, IL: Crossway Books, 1999.

Hodge, Charles, *Systematic Theology Vol. 2*. Oak Harbor, WA: Logos Research Systems, Inc., 1997.

Horsley, Richard A., *Religion and Empire: People, Power, and the Life of the Spirit*. Minneapolis, MN: Fortress Press, 2003.

Islamic Awareness, "Did Waraqa Ibn Nawfal Teach the Prophet?" Hadith Volume 4, Book 55, Number 605. http://www.islamic-awareness.org/Quran/Sources/BBwaraqa.html (accessed February 1, 2011).

Kelly, J.N.D., *Early Christian Doctrines*. San Francisco: Harper & Row, 1978._____*Early Christian Creeds*. New York: Longman Inc., 1972.

Kennedy, Hugh, *The Great Arab Conquests: How the Spread of Islam changed the World We live In*. Philadelphia, PA: Da Capo Press, 2007.

Latourette, Kenneth Scott, *A History of Christianity Volume I: to A.D. 1500*. Peabody, MA: Hendrickson Publishers, 2000.
Lewis, Bernard, *The Arabs in History*. Oxford: Oxford University Press, 1992.

Lietzmann, Hans, *The Era of the Church Fathers.* New York: Charles Scribner's Sons, 1952.

Loofs, Friedrich, *Nestorius and His Place in the History of Christian Doctrine.* Memphis, TN: General Books, 2010.

MacCulloch, Diarmaid, *Christianity: The First Three Thousand Years.* New York: Viking, 2009.

McDowell, Bruce A. and Anees Zaka, *Muslims and Christians at the Table.* Phillipsburg, NJ: P&R Publishing, 1999.

McGrath, Alister, *Heresy: A History of Defending the Truth.* New York: HarperCollins, 2009.

Meyendorff, John, *Byzantine Theology: Historical Trends and Doctrinal Themes.* New York: Fordham University Press, 1983.

Nasr, Seyyed Hossein, *The Heart of Islam: Enduring Values for Humanity.* New York: HarperCollins Publishers, 2002.

Negev, Avraham, *The Archaeological Encyclopedia of the Holy Land.* New York: Prentice Hall Press, 1996.

Norris, Richard A., trans. and ed., *The Christological Controversy.* Philadelphia: Fortress Press, 1980.

Norwich, John Julius, *A Short History of Byzantium.* New York: Vintage Books, 1999.

Original Catholic Encyclopedia, "Henoticon." Catholic Answers. http://oce.catholic.com/index.php?title=Henoticon (accessed January 10, 2011).

Origen, "On First Principles: Book 4." in *Biblical Interpretation in the Early Church,* edited by Karlfried Froehlich, 48-78. Philadelphia: Fortress Press, 1984.

Packer, J. I., *Concise Theology: A Guide to Historic Christian Beliefs*. Wheaton, Ill.: Tyndale House, 1995.

Pagels, Elaine, *The Gnostic Gospels*. New York: Vintage Books, 1979.

Pelikan, Jaroslav, *The Christian Tradition: A History of the Development of Doctrine*. Chicago: University of Chicago Press, 1971.

Raven, Charles E., Apollinarianism: *An Essay on the Christology of the Early Church*. Eugene, OR: Wipf & Stock Publishers, 2004.

Ryrie, Charles Caldwell, *Basic Theology*. Chicago: Moody Press, 1986.

Rusch, William G., ed., *The Trinitarian Controversy*. Philadelphia: Fortress Press, 1980.

Safa, Reza F., *Inside Islam: Exposing and Reaching the World of Islam*. Lake Mary, FL: Charisma House, 1996.

Schaff, Phillip and Henry Wace, *The Nicene and Post-Nicene Fathers Second Series* 14 vols. Oak Harbor: Logos Research Systems, 1997.

Schaff, Philip and David Schley Schaff, *History of the Christian Church*. 8 vols. Oak Harbor, WA: Logos Research Systems, Inc., 1997.

Shedd, William Greenough Thayer and Alan W. Gomes, *Dogmatic Theology*. 3rd ed. Phillipsburg, N.J.: P & R Publishing, 2003.

Shelley, Bruce L., *Church History in Plain Language*. Nashville: Thomas Nelson Publishers, 1995.

Shorrosh, Anis A., *Islam Revealed: A Christian Arab's View of Islam*. Nashville, TN: Thomas Nelson, 1988.

Soanes, Catherine and Angus Stevenson, *Concise Oxford English Dictionary*. 11th ed. Oxford: Oxford University Press, 2004.

Socrates, *"The Ecclesiastical History of Socrates Scholasticus."* in *Nicene and Post-Nicene Fathers."* Edited by Philip Schaff and Henry Wace. Grand Rapids: Wm. B. Eerdmans, 1952.

Sozomenus, "The Ecclesiastical History of Sozomenus: History of the Church." in *Nicene and Post-Nicene Fathers*, Edited by Phillip Schaff and Henry Wace. Grand Rapids: Wm. B. Eerdmans, 1952.

St Cyril of Alexandria, *On the Unity of Christ*. Translated and Introduced by John Anthony McGuckin. Crestwood, NY: St Vladimir's Seminary Press, 1955.

Strong, Augustus Hopkins, *Systematic Theology*. Bellingham, WA: Logos Research Systems, Inc., 2004.

Tanner, Norman P, *The Councils of the Church: A Short History*. New York: Crossroad Publishing, 2001.

The Daily Catholic, "The Council of Ephesus." http://www.dailycatholic.org/history/3ecumen1.htm (accessed January 13, 2011)._____ "Declaration of Mary as Theotokos."http://www.dailycatholic.org/3ecumen2.htm#Declaration%20of%20Theotokos (accessed January 13, 2011).

Torrance, Iain R, *Christology and Chalcedon: Severus of Antioch and Sergius the Monophysite*. Eugene, OR: Wipf and Stock, 1998.

Ware, Timothy, *The Orthodox Church*. New York: Penguin Putnam Inc., 1997.

Wood, D.R.W. and Marshall, I.H, *New Bible Dictionary* (3rd ed.) Downers Grove: InterVarsity Press, 1996.

Wynbrandt, James, *A Brief History of Saudi Arabia*. New York: Checkmark Books, 2004.

Ye'or, Bat, *The Decline of Eastern Christianity: From Jihad to Dhimmitude*. Translated by Miriam Kochan and David Littman. Cranbury, NJ: Associated University Press, 1996.

Young, Frances, *The Making of the Creeds*. London: SCM Press, 2002.

CPSIA information can be obtained at www.ICGtesting.com
Printed in the USA
LVOW121822020413

327121LV00002B/5/P

9 781937 064457